In Little Need of Divine Intervention

In Little Need of Divine Intervention

Takezaki Suenaga's
Scrolls of the Mongol Invasions
of Japan

TRANSLATION
WITH AN INTERPRETIVE ESSAY

Thomas D. Conlan

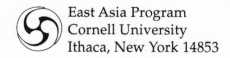

East Asia Program
Cornell University
Ithaca, New York 14853

The Cornell East Asia Series is published by the Cornell University East Asia Program (distinct from Cornell University Press). We publish reasonably-priced books on a variety of scholarly topics relating to East Asia as a service to the academic community and the general public. Standing orders, which provide for automatic billing and shipping of each title in the series upon publication, are accepted.

If after review by internal and external readers a manuscript is accepted for publication, it is published on the basis of camera-ready copy provided by the volume author. Each author is thus responsible for any necessary copy-editing and for manuscript formatting. Address submission inquiries to CEAS Editorial Board, East Asia Program, Cornell University, Ithaca, New York 14853-7601.

Number 113 in the Cornell East Asia Series.
Copyright © 2001 by Thomas Conlan. All rights reserved
ISSN 1050-2955
ISBN 1-885445-44-X hc
ISBN 1-885445-13-X pb
Library of Congress Control Number: 2001093358
Printed in the United States of America
15 14 13 12 11 10 09 08 07 06 05 04 03   9 8 7 6 5 4 3 2

COVER DESIGN BY KAREN K. SMITH

⊗ The paper in this book meets the requirements for permanence of ISO 9706:1994.

For Jeffrey Mass
My teacher, mentor, and friend

Contents

Preface

This interpretation of the attempted Mongol invasions of Japan is coupled with a translation of surviving Japanese sources, including documents and, most notably, Takezaki Suenaga's narrative of the battles of 1274 and 1281. I hope to provide a new perspective on the invasions, and to disseminate widely Japanese sources pertaining to this conflict. This translation of the *Scrolls of the Mongol Invasions* (*Mōko shūrai ekotoba* 蒙古襲来絵詞) is based upon the *Tankaku sōsho* (丹鶴叢書) copy of the original, which was published as an appendix to the *Fukutekihen* (伏敵編), compiled by Yamada An'ei in 1891, and is reproduced here courtesy of the Harvard–Yenching Institute. In order to reproduce these images, this book unfolds in Japanese order, from right to left.

The *Tankaku* version of the *Scrolls of the Mongol Invasions* is identical to the one annotated by Ishii Susumu in *Chūsei seiji shakai shisō 1* (中世政治社会思想上), pp. 415–28, save for the captions–which Ishii omits–that I reproduce in italics where they appear in each scene. I transcribed these captions from the *Tankaku* illustrations of the *Fukutekihen*, although I compared those passages I found particularly difficult to decipher with photos of the original scrolls reproduced in Komatsu Shigemi, *Mōko shūrai ekotoba Nihon no emaki 13* (蒙古襲来絵詞・日本の絵巻 13), and with copies located at Kyūshū University and Kumamoto University. The calligraphy that appears next to the illustrations, such as those reproduced immediately after Passage 7 of the first scroll (p. 91), are only excerpts from the full *Tankaku* text and should not be considered to be definitive representations of its content. I included them simply to convey the flavor of the original.

I numbered the scenes and passages of text for reference purposes, using the schemata devised by Miya Tsugio in his *Kassen no emaki* (合戦絵巻). Numbers in bold next to each text passage correspond to those found in Ishii Susumu's annotated version of the Mongol scrolls. I provided character transcriptions of some crucial terms, following generally the interpretations of Ishii Susumu. Nevertheless, the original is written phonetically, so some of these transcriptions remain debatable.

Most of the reference works I consulted are readily available in major collections in the United States and Japan. Documents were drawn from the fifty-one volumes of the *Kamakura ibun* (鎌倉遺文), compiled by

Takeuchi Rizō during 1971–97, which constitutes the essential reference work for the Kamakura era (1185–1333). Most documents pertaining to the invasions can be found in volumes 14 through 16. Nevertheless, this compendium must be used with care, for errors in transcription exist, and in addition some important documents are missing. Furthermore, the dating of documents without era names is problematic. At times, the same document appears more than once and is attributed to different individuals. When possible, each document dated only by the month and day must be analyzed in tandem with Seno Sei'ichirō's *Kamakura ibun munengō monjo mokuroku* (鎌倉遺文無年号文書目録). Ideally, printed documents should be compared with the photographs of originals, or the originals themselves, as I had the opportunity to accomplish with Documents 48, 52, and all of Takezaki Suenaga's surviving documents.

In cases where a comparison with original sources or photographs is impossible, documents should be checked with more reliable transcriptions, such as those appearing in Kawazoe Shōji's 1971 compilation, the *Chūkai, Genkō bōrui hennen shiryō–Ikokuhen keigo ban'yaku shiryō no kenkyū* (注解元寇防塁編年史料). The only drawback of Kawazoe's highly reliable sourcebook is that its coverage is confined to administrative issues, the construction of the wall, and guard duty. It omits documents that describe the nature of military encounters. Although compiled in 1891, Yamada An'ei's *Fukutekihen* remains valuable, for it comprehensively reproduces chronicles, diaries, religious texts, and administrative documents. Nevertheless, the format is unwieldy, and some documentary lacunae are evident. Furthermore, not all transcriptions or dates for particular documents are accurate. Finally, *Takezakijō–Jōseki chōsa to Takezaki Suenaga* (竹崎城–城跡調査と竹崎季長), volume 17 of Kumamoto prefecture's cultural properties report (*Kumamoto ken bunkazai chōsa hōkoku* 熊本県文化財調査報告), remains indispensable for its insightful analysis of Takezaki Suenaga, his lands, scrolls, and documents.

Acknowledgements

A confluence of fortuitous circumstances allowed me to formulate and publish this monograph. A desire to provide Japanese narratives of the Mongol Invasions for my courses at Bowdoin College caused me to initially embark on my translation of Takezaki Suenaga's scrolls. My discovery of the illustrations, found in the *Fukutekihen*, located at the Harvard–Yenching Institute, allowed me to conceive of this project as something larger than a textual translation. After talking with Joan Piggott I had the epiphany of publishing this as a book. Both Christopher Lupke and Kidder Smith aided and encouraged me in innumerable ways with valuable comments and advice for my draft manuscript. In addition, I deeply appreciate the meticulous care with which the anonymous readers of the Cornell East Asia Series scrutinized my manuscript.

I would also like to thank Peter Schilling, Deborah Gibson, and everyone at the Education and Technology Task Force for their professional scanning of the images. Arnie Olds and Joan Piggott have done a wonderful job of designing this book, for which I am exceedingly grateful. I owe special thanks to Andrew Lewis for his generous help in editing the manuscript, and his valuable suggestions regarding the structure of this book. Thanks, too, to Karen Smith for her help in the publication process.

I managed to visit the fortifications in Northern Kyūshū, tour Takezaki Suenaga's homelands, and engage in research that would otherwise have been impossible thanks to the generous financial support of the Freeman Foundation. In Japan, I would like to thank Professor Ōyama Kyōhei for his advice and support. Both he and Satō Yasuhiro helped me arrange a stimulating trip to Kyūshū, as did Professor Katsuyama Seiji. I remain indebted to Professor Seno Sei'ichirō as well for his boundless generosity and support in so many ways over the years.

In Fukuoka, Professor Saeki Kōji proved most hospitable, helpful, and unstinting with his time. I found my perusal of the Kurishima documents, and Kyūshū University's copy of Takezaki Suenaga's scrolls to have been most informative. Thanks too to the staff at Kyūshū University's main library for allowing me to view their copy of these scrolls at my leisure. I am also grateful to Professor Kawazoe Shōji for his generosity in both time and materials. Horimoto Kazushige, of the Fukuoka

City Museum, proved to be an excellent guide to recent monographs regarding the scrolls, the intricacies of Fukuoka geography, and the best ramen in Hakata. Thanks, too, to Sujaku Shinjō, for providing copies of his informative articles.

In Kumamoto, I owe a profound debt to Haruta Naoki. Without his kindness, support, and help in so many ways, I would not have been able to have such a stimulating, productive, and enjoyable trip. I also cannot adequately thank Professor Kudō Kei'ichi for his informative tour and explanation of Kaitō village and Takezaki castle. Thanks, too, to the proprietors of Tōfukuji for allowing me to view their copy of Suenaga's scrolls, and also to Akioka Takao for allowing me to view the documents of Takezaki Suenaga. I would also like to thank Takahama Sugako, and everyone at the Kumamoto Prefectural Museum of Art, for allowing me to view their copies of Takezaki Suenaga's precepts. Finally, last but not least, I would like to express my gratitude to the staff at the main library at Kumamoto University, and to Professors Kudō, Haruta, Inaba, and for enabling me to view and to better understand both the magnificent documents of Aso shrine and Kumamoto University's copy of Suenaga's scrolls.

Words cannot adequately describe my debt to Jeffrey Mass for his inspiration and guidance as a translator of Kamakura documents. And I thank my wife Yūko for putting up with the long hours that this project kept me away from her. Thanks too to my parents, Gary and Jean, for their love and advice. My love, respect, and gratitude to them transcends words. Recognition is likewise due to International Thomson Publishing Services Ltd. for granting me permission to use the map of the Mongol Invasions, located between pages 508-9 of James Murdoch's *A History of Japan*, Vol. 1, published by "The Chronicle" in Kobe, Japan, 1910, and recently reprinted by Routledge in 1996. I owe a debt to many for their advice and encouragement. Responsibility for all errors is solely my own.

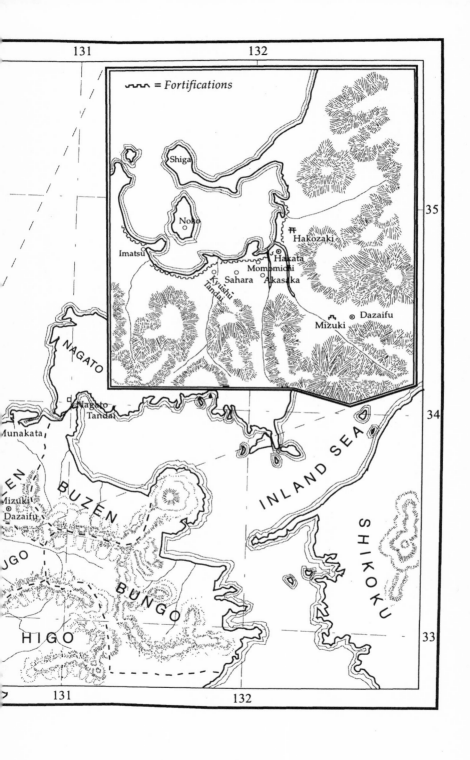

= *Fortifications*

Shiga

Noko

Imatsu

Hakozaki

Hakata
Momochi
Sahara Akasaka
Kyushu
Tandai

Mizuki   Dazaifu

NAGATO

Nagato
Tandai

Munakata

Mizuki
Dazaifu

BUZEN

INLAND SEA

SHIKOKU

BUNGO

HIGO

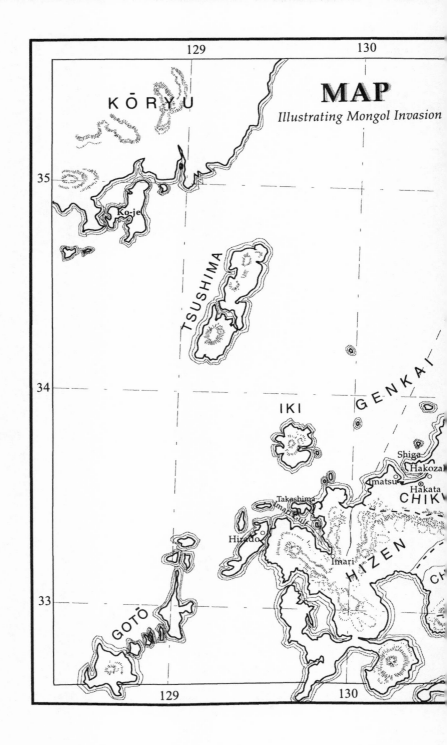

MAP

Illustrating Mongol Invasion

KŌRYU

TSUSHIMA

Ko-je

GENKAI

IKI

Shiga
Hakoza
Imatsu
Hakata
CHIKU

Takeshima

Imari

Hirado

Imari

HIZEN

GOTŌ

CH

Introduction

A Brief History of Takezaki Suenaga and His Scrolls

Even though the Mongols forged the largest land empire that the world has ever known, twice in 1274 and 1281 their armies met with unexpected defeat on the beaches of Japan. The Mongol debacle generated the myth that the chance passing of a typhoon, referred to as "divine winds" (*kamikaze* 神風), spared the Japanese defenders from a devastating defeat. Relegated to the realm of legend, these invasions have attracted little scholarly attention outside of Japan. This study provides a revision of these campaigns, and reveals that the Japanese repulsed the Mongols with little need of divine intervention.

Primary sources, translated here in English for the first time, indicate that the invasions have been profoundly misunderstood. This monograph first introduces Takezaki Suenaga (竹崎季長), a warrior who fought against the Mongols in both encounters and reproduces his illustrated account, the Scrolls of the Mongol Invasions (*Mōko shūrai ekotoba* 蒙古襲来絵詞).[1] Suenaga's record is supplemented by sixty-nine documents pertaining either to the invasions or to Suenaga himself, which recount the military sophistication of the Japanese defenders and reveal their contemporary beliefs. These sources provide context for the analysis of part three that explains how military parity existed between the Mongol invaders and the Japanese defenders. As we shall see, the notion of the "divine winds" represented a function of the medieval mindset, which emphasized otherwordly causality, rather than as a caustic commentary on the ineptitude of the Japanese defenders, as has been commonly assumed.

Among the letters, prayers, edicts, and battle reports that recount the Mongol invasions of Japan, the two picture scrolls that portray the exploits of Takezaki Suenaga are perhaps the most remarkable. Suenaga, a resident of Kyūshū's Higo (肥後) province, fought in both encounters with considerable élan, recorded his experiences, and employed skilled artists to embellish his narrative.

Little is known about Takezaki Suenaga, save that he was a *gokenin* (御家人), or "houseman," who possessed a surname and family lands and

---

[1]Japanese names are in Japanese word order except when listed as authors of works printed in English.

1

performed guard duty on behalf of the Kamakura *bakufu* (幕府), the judicial and administrative authority located in eastern Japan.[2] He was capable of leading five men into battle in 1274, which was perhaps the norm for warriors drawn from Kyūshū, but above average when compared to the gokenin of central Japan.

Four artists collaborated in creating Suenaga's scrolls, and careful analysis also reveals that the text contains five distinct calligraphic styles.[3] Hence Suenaga commissioned the scrolls but did not personally write more than a section of the text at most.[4] Although some sections of the scrolls survive only in fragments, the work as a whole maintains narrative coherence. In all probability the scribes reproduced the story as presented by Suenaga.

A close reading of the scrolls provides valuable insight regarding Takezaki Suenaga's life after the Mongol invasions. Two men are singled out for particular praise: Shōni Kagesuke, who witnessed Suenaga's deeds, and Adachi Yasumori, the *bakufu* official who granted him rewards for his battle service.[5] Of the two men, Yasumori occupies a central position in

---

[2]Japan in the thirteenth century can be characterized as having a "dual polity," with powers of administration and judicial authority divided between the Kyōto court and the Kamakura *bakufu*. Kamakura placed *shugo*, or constables, in each province. These men were responsible for keeping order, apprehending criminals and making lists of *gokenin*, or "housemen," who were eligible to perform guard duty on behalf of Kamakura. Likewise, some of these *gokenin* were appointed as *jitō*, or "land stewards." For the best introduction to the Kamakura period, see Jeffrey P. Mass, "The Kamakura Bakufu," in *The Cambridge History of Japan*, vol. 3 (Cambridge: Cambridge University Press, 1990), pp. 46–88.

[3]For Miya Tsugio's determination that the scrolls were drawn by at least four artists, see Miya Tsugio, *Kassen no emaki* pp. 122–27. For Ohta Aya's analysis of the calligraphic styles, see her "Mongol Invasion," in *Twelve Centuries of Japanese Art*, ed. Lynne Shaner (Washington, D.C., Smithsonian Institution, 1997), 90–93. Ohta mirrors Matsumoto Aya's opinion, found in "Mōko shūrai ekotoba no seiritsu to denrai ni tsuite–sono saikō," *Sannomaru Shōzōkan nenpō kiyō*, vol. 1 (1996), 61–76. Recently Satō Tetsutarō has claimed, to the contrary, that only two distinct styles are evident. See his *Mōko shūrai to Takezaki Suenaga* (Fukuoka, Tōkashobō, 1994), pp. 115–32.

[4]Matsumoto Aya claims that none of the scrolls' passages were written by Suenaga but she mistakenly bases this comparison on Suenaga's precepts, which are all in fact later copies. See her "Mōko shūrai ekotoba no seiritsu to denrai ni tsuite–sono saikō," p. 70. A comparison with Suenaga's only surviving handwritten document, a 1324 commendation currently in the possession of the Akioka family, suggests that the final two passages of the scrolls and those describing Suenaga's audience with Adachi Yasumori may be of Suenaga's hand. Nevertheless, the match is far from conclusive.

[5]Shōni Kagesuke can be documented as investigating the claims of other warriors as well. See Document 24.

the narrative. His audience with Suenaga is portrayed in greater detail than any other episode, and a tribute to Yasumori's generosity appears near the end of the second scroll.

Such praise of Adachi Yasumori reveals Takezaki Suenaga's political allegiances. Yasumori attempted to carve out a power base within the bakufu that was autonomous from both the figurehead *shōgun* (将軍) and the regent (*shikken* 執権), who had dominated the bakufu throughout much of the thirteenth century.[6] Prior to the Mongol invasions, Yasumori had served in the *hikitsuke*, one of the consultive organs within the bakufu, and as head of the bakufu's court of appeals.[7] Yasumori took advantage of the death of his brother-in-law, the *shikken* Hōjō Tokimune, to embark on a bold series of legal reforms,[8] but he fell victim to the factional infighting that periodically convulsed Kamakura. Shortly after his nephew Sadatoki had become the new regent, Yasumori was killed by Taira Yoritsuna during the depths of winter in 1285, in what became known as the "frosty moon incident." The rationale for this incident is not clear, but Yoritsuna's close ties with Sadatoki–he was the husband of Sadatoki's wet nurse–coupled with his later prominence suggests that he was acting in collusion with the young Hōjō leader (*tokusō* 得宗).

Unlike most previous bloodlettings, Yasumori's assassination generated unprecedented turmoil and spawned a war in the provinces. Yasumori's son Morimune fought at Iwato castle in northern Kyūshū with several warriors, including Shōni Kagesuke.[9] All were defeated and killed in 1285.

[6]For a fine summary of these events, see Murai Shōsuke, "Jūsan yon seiki no Nihon," in *Iwanami kōza Nihon tsūshi 8 chūsei 2* (Iwanami shoten, 1994), pp. 26–30.

[7]For these appointments, which occurred in 1264, see the *Kamakura nendaiki*, found in *Kamakura nendaiki, Buke nendaiki, Kamakura dai nikki* in *Zōho zoku shiryō taisei 51*, comp. Takeuchi Rizō (Rinsen shoten, 1979), p. 19. Likewise, in 1269, Adachi Yasumori was appointed one of the few heads of the *hikitsuke* who had not been born into the Hōjō family. He held this post continuously until his death in 1285. See *Kamakura nendaiki*, pp. 20–23.

[8]Hōjō Tokimune, Kamakura's *shikken* during the Mongol invasions, died suddenly on 4.4.1284, shortly after the second invasion. Yasumori's new laws were promulgated on 8.17.1284. See *Chūsei hōsei shiryōshū*, vol. 1 (Iwanami shoten, 1955), pp. 359–61. For more on the far-reaching impact of the 1284 legal reforms, see Thomas Conlan, "State of War: The Violent Order of Fourteenth Century Japan" (Ph.D. diss., Stanford University, 1998), pp. 210–15. Yasumori's sister became the wife of Tokimune. See the Hōjō genealogy, found in *Gunsho ruijū keizubushū*, comp. Hanawa Hokinoichi (Zoku gunsho ruijū kanseikai, 1985), vol. 4, p. 84. To confuse matters further, Yasumori may also have adopted his younger sister as well. For this insight, I am indebted to Robert Morrell.

[9]Kagesuke's genealogical references are most conveniently found in

Suenaga, however, survived–either he was unwilling or unable to take up arms in spite of his affection for Kagesuke and Yasumori. Perhaps Suenaga commissioned his laudatory scrolls to atone for his inaction and to pray for their souls.[10]

Of Suenaga, little else is known, save for what can be gleaned from his scrolls and his surviving documents–two illuminating and highly unusual precepts (*okibumi* 置文) and two commendations. The first precept, written on 1.23.1293, describes how Suenaga, in his forty-eighth year, established regulations for the Kaitō (海頭) shrine to pray for him, the court in Kyōto, and Kamakura.[11] The second, written on 1.17.1314, constitutes a revision of the first. Suenaga signed this latter precept with the name Hōki, indicating that he had taken Buddhist vows by the age of sixty-nine.[12] It was at this time that he restored the Kaitō shrine on his lands. Finally, Suenaga commended further lands for the upkeep of the Kaitō in 1324.[13]

Suenaga's precepts reveal how he relied on control over the shrine to expand his powers of lordship. Ritually and symbolically, Suenaga established his presence in the Kaitō, whose lands had originally belonged to the Kōsa shrine.[14] He appropriated shrines and temples and took it upon

---

Fukutekihen, comp. Yamada An'ei (Yoshikawa kōbunkan, 1891), volume (hereafter maki) 4, p. 19. For references to Morimune's downfall, see Document 56. Finally, for more on the scale of the fighting, see the writings (*uragaki* 裏書) found on the back of the *Kamakura nendaiki*, p. 55.

[10]The face and accoutrements of Shōni Kagesuke are drawn in a particularly realistic manner, and the drawings themselves are referred to as "close likenesses" or *nise-e,* which designates respect. For more on portraits providing a memorial in the afterlife, see Yonekura Michio, *Minamoto Yoritomo zō chinmoku no shōzōga* (Heibonsha, 1995), pp. 14–22, and Miyajima Shinichi, *Shōzōga* (Yoshikawa kōbunkan, 1994).

[11]*Kamakura ibun,* 51 vols., comp. Takeuchi Rizō (Tōkyōdō shuppan, 1971–1997), vol. 23, doc. 18098.

[12]*Kamakura ibun,* vol. 23, doc. 18097. Both of Suenaga's precepts have been translated in appendix 1. These documents, designated as originals in the *Kamakura ibun,* are in fact later copies (*utsushi* 写). See *Takezakijō –Jōseki chōsa to Takezaki Suenaga,* comp. Kumamoto ken kyōiku iinkai (Kumamoto, 1975), pp. 151–52. A comparison of the Tōfukuji copies with those in the possession of the Akioka family reveals that the date of 1.16.1314 represents a copyist's error. The second precept and Suenaga's oldest surviving commendation were both written on 1.17.1314. Suenaga's only original document dates from 1324. See below.

[13]See Ibid., vol. 37, doc. 28691, 3.4.1324 (Genkō 4) Shami Hōki Takezaki Suenaga kishinjō.

[14]See *Dai Nihon komonjo iewake 13 Aso monjo 1* (Tōkyō daigaku shiryōhen sanjō, 1932), doc. 8, 2.8.1195 (Kenkyū 6) Kōsa sharyō monjo an, pp. 24–29, particularly p. 27. According to a 1334 shrine complaint, Kamakura "abused its authority and confiscated some shrine lands in the Hōji era (1247–49)." See *Nanbokuchō ibun*

himself to keep them in good order. In exchange he had both religious institutions pray for the court, the Kamakura bakufu, and his own salvation, thereby linking his authority with the prestige of central authority and the bakufu.

Takezaki intensified his powers of lordship by requesting both his retainers and commoners (*hyakushō* 百姓) of the region to donate funds to the shrines, even though he officially possessed no authority over the latter. Usurious interest rates (fifty percent) when lending seeds for planting also proved to be another effective stratagem for amassing revenue and authority. Cultivators who could not repay the loans had their lands confiscated at a rate of one *tan* of land per *koku* of debt and reallocated to kinsmen or followers more appreciative of Suenaga's rule.[15] Suenaga's financial acumen also explains how he was able to commission such impressive scrolls.

After Takezaki Suenaga received rewards from Adachi Yasumori, neighboring warriors chose to serve with him. Three are depicted in Scene 13 as fighting in the same boat as Suenaga during the second invasion of 1281. Yaigome no Gorō came from the same Toyofuku estate as did the Takezaki, while Miyahara Saburō lived to the south of Suenaga's Kaitō lands.[16] The third, Ono no Daishin Raijō, resided in Ono estate, which was located to the northwest of Suenaga's Kaitō holdings, and immediately to the south of the Takezaki homelands in Toyofuku estate.[17] Raijō appears to have been particularly close to Suenaga, for he alone is also mentioned in Passage 13. Furthermore, this camaraderie between the Ono and the Takezaki continued among their descendants, for Ono Shinsaemon and Takezaki Shingorō fought and died together shortly after the 1336 onset of civil war.[18]

One cannot precisely date when Suenaga had his scrolls created. Suenaga or his scribes dated the scrolls to 1293, but in doing so, they

---

Kyūshū hen, 7 vols., comp. Seno Sei'ichirō (Tōkyōdō shuppan, 1985–1992), vol. 1, doc. 86, 7.19.1334 (Kenmu gannen) Uji Korehira keijō.

[15]One *tan* equals .294 acres. One *koku* constitutes approximately 4.5 bushels of rice, the amount one person could eat in one year.

[16]Yaigome no Gorō resided in Toyofuku estate, which bordered the original Takezaki homelands. See *Takezakijō*, p. 156 and *Kamakura ibun*, vol. 7, doc. 4945, 3.17.1236 (Kaitei 2) Ōtomo Chikahide yuzurijō for documentary reference to Yaigome being located inside Toyofuku. For more on the Yaigome and the Miyahara, see *Takezakijō*, p. 164.

[17]For the geographic proximity of the Ono and the Takezaki, see *Takezakijō*, pp. 88–92.

[18]Both were killed early in 1337 while fighting at Ono and Toyofuku estates. See *Nanbokuchō ibun*, vol. 3, doc. 2536, 9.1348 (Shōhei 3) Era Koresumi gunchūjō.

erred. According to the Japanese calendar, the first eight months of 1293 were known as the sixth year of the Shō-ō era, but on the twenty-fifth day of the eighth month, the court adopted the new era name of "Einin." Nevertheless, the anachronistic date of the ninth day of the second month of the first year of Einin appears at the end of the Mongol scrolls.

The old warrior probably had his scrolls dated to 1293 for a combination of reasons. The first was to portray the scrolls' creation as coinciding with the establishment of Tōfukuji (塔福寺), a temple in the Kaitō lands, as his clan temple (ujidera 氏寺).[19] The second is that Yasumori's murderer, Taira Yoritsuna, was killed during the fourth month of 1293 and so, by dating these scrolls to prior to Yoritsuna's death, this memorial to Yasumori and Shōni Kagesuke appears to be a braver act than in fact it was. The third is that Kamakura established a network of shrines in each province to pray for the "subjugation of the enemy country" (*tekikoku kōfuku* 敵国降伏) in 1293, which accordingly became a year of unusual religious fervor, with reports of divine intervention commonplace.[20]

As no evidence exists of materials or artistic styles postdating the Kamakura era, one can ascertain that the scrolls were created prior to Suenaga's death, sometime between 1293 and 1324.[21] For long it has been argued that textual evidence suggests that the second of the Mongol scrolls was completed shortly after Suenaga copied his shrine regulations in 1314, for one warrior referred to as Shimazu Hisanaga did not adopt this name until 1316. Although this theory has recently fallen from favor,[22]

[19]See *Kamakura ibun*, vol. 23, doc. 18097; Kuroda Toshio, *Nihon no rekishi 8: Mōko shūrai* (Chuō kōronsha, 1974), pp. 184–85; and *Takezakijō*, p. 150–51. According to the latter, 1293 also represents the year that Suenaga took religious vows, and adopted the name Hōki.

[20]This was first mentioned by Aida, *Mōko shūrai no kenkyū*, pp. 111–14. See also Documents 60–64 herein. References to the gods of shrines "fighting" the Mongols during 1293 appear in *Kamakura ibun*, vol. 23, doc. 18134, 3.28.1293 (Shō-ō 6) Dajōkan chō, and Document 64. Likewise, as Hanazono's diary attests, 1314, the year that Suenaga revised his precepts, represented another peak of otherworldly activity. See Document 65.

[21]This consensus of scholarly opinion has been most recently expressed by Matsumoto Aya, "Mōko shūrai ekotoba," *Emaki–Mōko shūrai ekotoba, Eshi no sōshi, Kitano Tenjin engi*, comp. Sannomaru Shōzōkan (Sannomaru Shōzōkan, 1994), p. 9.

[22]Both Kuroda, *Nihon no rekishi 8*, p. 184, and Ryō, *Mōko shūrai*, pp. 90–94 have emphasized this discrepancy regarding Hisanaga's name. Nevertheless, Ishii Susumu has claimed that Nagahisa was the same person as Hisanaga. See his "Takezaki Suenaga ekotoba no seiritsu," *Nihon rekishi* no. 273 (1971): 12–32, and Ishii Susumu, ed., *Chūsei seiji shakai shisō 1* (Iwanami shoten, 1972), pp. 562–63. Miya attempts to rebut Ishii in his *Kassen no emaki*, pp. 115–16 by noting

Introduction

both 1293 and 1314 constituted years when fears of a third Mongol invasion were rife, and times when reports of divine intervention were commonplace. As artistic styles reveal that the scrolls were commissioned over a period of years, a precise dating of the scrolls remains impossible.[23] Furthermore, the drawings and the text were originally stored seperately, so evidence drawn from any scene or passage can not be used to date the entire work.[24]

Perhaps the first scrolls, written as an eulogy to Adachi Yasumori, were created during or shortly after 1293, while the later scrolls, extolling the virtue of Kōsa shrine, were penned sometime during the years of 1314–16.[25] Of Suenaga, little else is known, save that by 1324 he lived in retirement at Hirabaro, perched high in the eastern hills of the Kaitō. Suenaga's final commendation reveals that he continued his avid interest in shrine affairs and the levying of revenue from his lands.

Of all the Takezaki documents, only Suenaga's commendations and precepts remain. Ensconced in the Kaitō shrine, they survived the destruction of the Kamakura bakufu in 1333. With the renewed outbreak of civil war in 1336 between partisans of competing "Northern" and "Southern" Courts, the Aso, a fractious family of shrine attendants that dominated Higo province and supported the Southern Court, attacked and killed a certain Takezaki Shingorō in 1337.[26] A decade after Shingorō's death, Takezaki Nagaaki surrendered to Southern Court forces. Shortly thereafter, during the ninth month 1346, Takezaki Saemon Tarō, possibly the same

that Shimazu Nagahisa and Hisanaga were distinct individuals, but the weight of scholarly opinion now suppports Ishii. See Kawazoe's "Kaisetsu," in *Gyobutsuhon Mōko shūrai ekotoba (fukusei) honbun, sakuin, kaisetsu, kenkyū mokuroku* (Fukuoka kyōiku iinkai, 1975), particularly pp. 38–42. Sujaku Shinjō also provides an excellent survey of recent research and current debates concerning the scrolls in his "Mōko shūrai ekotoba kenkyu no genjō to kadai" *Hōgōdachi* no. 5 (Hakata, 1997), pp. 7–18.

[23]See Matsumoto Aya, "Mōko shūrai ekotoba ni tsuite no ichikōsatsu–arata na mondaiten o kuwaete," *Emaki–Mōko shūrai ekotoba, Eshi no sōshi, Kitano Tenjin engi,* pp. 62–63.

[24]For more information on the fragmentary nature of the scrolls when they were first "discovered" in the eighteenth century, see Sujaku Shinjō, "Mōko shūrai ekotoba denzon katei no fukugen ni tsuite," *Hakata kenkyūkaishi* no. 7 (Fukuoka, 1999), pp. 100–5 and "The Transmission of the Scrolls," below.

[25]For more on the difficulty of dating the scrolls, and problems concerning their transmission, see ""The Transmission of the Scrolls," below. Matsumoto Aya claims that stylistically, Takezaki Suenaga's scrolls were created over a period of several decades. See her "Mōko shūrai ekotoba no seiritsu to denrai ni tsuite–sono saikō," p. 69.

[26]*Nanbokuchō ibun*, vol. 3, doc. 2536, 9.1348 (Shōhei 3) Era Koresumi gunchūjō.

7

person as Nagaaki, fought with the Aso.[27] Ono estate became the focus of battles during the ninth month of 1347, and once again the Aso were victorious,[28] which resulted in their increasing control over this region. Tellingly, the Kōsa shrine was forced to surrender its administrative records to the Aso in 1349.[29]

The Kaitō shrine endured a fate similar to that of the Kōsa, for the Aso successfully laid claim to the "legacy" of the Kaitō in 1393,[30] and even managed to gain control of the Takezaki clan temple of Tōfukuji in the fifteenth century.[31] The Kaitō shrine survived, however, and remarkably, the Fujii, a family of shrine attendants mentioned in Suenaga's precepts, still reside in the Hirabaro region of the Kaitō to this day.

In contrast to the Fujii, the Takezaki lost control of the Kaitō, and suffered the indignity of losing Suenaga's magnificent scrolls. How they did so remains a mystery. The internecine warfare that plagued Higo Province during the latter half of the fourteenth century, coupled with the totality of the Takezaki's eclipse, mitigates against constructing a detailed narrative of their descent into obscurity. The sources only reveal that the Takezaki continued their allegiance to the Southern Court. In 1357, Takezaki Suruga Gon no kami Nagaari acted as a representative (*onshisetsu* 御使節) on behalf of Kikuchi Takemitsu in an attempt to restore order to Kōsa shrine lands.[32] He was unsuccessful, and in 1361 Nawa Akioki wracked these lands with bloodshed.[33] Akioki, a Southern Court stalwart, had occupied lands in the nearby Yatsushiro region after arriving in Higo province.[34] Thereupon he constructed fortifications on Kōsa lands in order to

---

[27]Ibid., vol. 2, doc. 2226, 8.8.[1346 (Shōhei 2)] Shijō Takasuke shojō utsushi, and vol. 3, doc. 2536, 9.1348 (Shōhei 3) Era Koresumi gunchūjō.

[28]Ibid., vol. 2, doc. 2366, 9.20.1347 (Shōhei 2) Era Koresumi moshijō an utsushi, and vol. 3, doc. 2536, 9.1348 (Shōhei 3) Era Koresumi gunchūjō.

[29] Ibid., vol. 3, doc. 2584, 3.28.1349 (Jōwa 5) Uji Koretsuna Tanji Moritoki rensho uketorijō. For a 1351 report of mysterious events in the shrine, see Ibid., vol. 3, doc. 3243, 11.2.1351 (Shōhei 6) Asosha shikan rensho chūshinjō.

[30]The grant of the Kaitō "legacy" (*ato* 跡) appears in *Nanbokuchō ibun*, vol. 6, doc. 6257, 2.9.1393 (Genchū 10) Seisei shōgun no miya ryōji utsushi.

[31]See *Dai Nihon komonjo iewake 13 Aso monjo 1*, docs. 247–49, 11.20.1426 (Ōei 33) Higo Kaitō no gō Kōsa sannomiya kuji nikki, 4.15.1425 Higo Kaitō no gō Kōsasha menden shayaku shidai, and 12.2.1425 Higo Kaitō no gō Tashirochō. For *Tōfukuji* (塔福寺) being under Aso control, see p. 648.

[32]*Nanbokuchō ibun*, vol. 4, doc. 3951, 2.1357 (Shōhei 12) Kōsasha zasshō Sō Tsugishige moshijō an, and doc. 4093, 2.1359 (Shōhei 14) Era Koresumi moshijō an.

[33]Ibid., docs. 4298–99, 8.1361 (Shōhei 16) Kōsasha chō no utsushi.

[34]The Nawa were descended from Nawa Nagatoshi, who helped Go Daigo escape from his exile in Oki island in 1333. Nagatoshi and many of his progeny

further solidify his local control,[35] which made conflict with Suenaga's descendants inevitable. The Nawa apparently seized Suenaga's scrolls because of "turmoil" within the Takezaki family.[36] Presumably, it was Akioki who stole Suenaga's scrolls.

Forces allied with the Northern Court pacified this region in the final decades of the fourteenth century. Although the Nawa maintained their regional influence, the Takezaki did not. As we have seen, the Aso shrine ultimately gained possession of the Kaitō "legacy" in 1393, and even solidified its control over the Takezaki clan temple of Tōfukuji early in the fifteenth century. The Takezaki maintained a tenuous existence near Toyofuku, where they constructed Takezaki castle on a small hill, but archeological evidence reveals that even this structure was consigned to the flames sometime during the fifteenth century.[37] From then on, the Takezaki would languish in obscurity until Suenaga's scrolls were rediscovered late in the eighteenth century.

The Transmission of the Scrolls

Although Suenaga's Scrolls of the Mongol Invasions survived the downfall of the Takezaki, they did not do so unscathed. The scrolls remained in the possession of the Nawa until late in the sixteenth century, when Nawa Akinori married his daughter to Amakusa Ōyano Tanemoto.[38] Tanemoto belonged to a long-standing Higo family, whose ancestors were mentioned in the scrolls.[39] Accordingly, Akinori gave the scrolls to Tanemoto as part of his daughter's dowry. Nevertheless, Tanemoto and his son died during the 1592 invasion of Korea, and the Ōyano fell onto hard times.

Suenaga's scrolls appear to have deteriorated under the Ōyano's

died while fighting for Go Daigo's Southern Court in 1336. According to the Nawa genealogy, Nagatoki's grandson Akioki travelled to Higo with Prince Kaneyoshi during the Shōhei era (1346–69). See *Gunsho ruijū keizubushū*, vol. 3, p. 401 and Kawazoe, "Kaisetsu," p. 35.

[35]For references to Akioki's violent attempts to gain control over the Kōsa lands, see *Nanbokuchō ibun*, vol. 4, doc. 4282, 6.1361 (Shōhei 16) Era Koresumi kasane moshijō an, docs. 4298–99, 8.1361 (Shōhei 16) Kōsasha chō no utsushi. See also docs. 4300, 4309, 4314, and 4322–23.

[36]Ōyano Jurō claimed so when he commended his scrolls in 1890. This narrative is reproduced in the *Fukutekihen* and also appears in Matsumoto Aya, "Mōko shūrai ekotoba no seiritsu to denrai ni tsuite–sono saikō," p. 67.

[37]*Takezakijō*, pp. 21–82.

[38]This narrative comes from Ōyano Jurō's explanation of how the scrolls were transmitted. See the *Fukutekihen* and Matsumoto Aya, "Mōko shūrai ekotoba no seiritsu to denrai ni tsuite–sono saikō," p. 67.

[39]The Ōyano are depicted in Scenes 14 and 16.

stewardship. According to lore, they were once dropped into the ocean and suffered extensive water damage—even the glue that held the pages together dissolved. The oldest copies of Suenaga's work, created late in the eighteenth century, reveal how the images and passages were preserved loosely and in no clear order.[40] Late eighteenth-century inventories also explain how the "sixteen records" that constitute the passages of this work were stored separately from the scenes.[41] To confuse matters further, the Ōyano possessed two old copies of the scrolls.[42] Ōyano house precepts prohibited anyone from looking at these images, or reading the passages, which hindered their dissemination. Although one copy of the scrolls was loaned to ranking officials of the Tokugawa *bakufu* (1603–1867) twice during the eighteenth century, fragments of the other copy remained stored in secret until 1823.[43]

Arai Hakuseki, the noted scholar and *bakufu* official borrowed the scrolls early in the eighteenth century, for he mentioned viewing them, but not their written passages, in a treatise written in 1709.[44] In 1793, the bakufu offical Matsudaira Sadanobu once again requested the scrolls, and they were dispatched to Edo. The earliest surviving copies of the scrolls were created at this time. Suenaga's work was not, however, "restored" into two scrolls, as they exist today, until 1797. Thenceforth, the "original" has changed little, except that Scene 2 and Passage 2 were added upon their discovery some twenty-six years later.[45]

Fearing that they might lose their scrolls or cause them to suffer further damage, the impoverished Ōyano entrusted them with the records

---

[40]These earliest copies vary greatly in the ordering of the images and the placement of textual passages. For more on the scrolls' scattered state of preservation, see Sujaku Shinjō, "Mōko shūrai ekotoba denzon katei no fukugen ni tsuite," *Hakata kenkyūkaishi* no. 7 (Fukuoka, 1999), p. 105.

[41]Sujaku, Ibid., pp. 100–5.

[42]For this path-breaking research, see Horimoto Kazushige, "Mōko shūrai ekotoba no genjō seiritsu katei ni tsuite–Aoyanagi Tanenobu hon no kentō to shōkai," *Fukuokashi hakubutsukan kenkyū kiyō* no. 8 (Fukuoka, 1998), pp. 15–57, particularly p. 39, which reproduces an 1832 account of the discovery of Scene 2 and Passage 2.

[43]Horimoto, Ibid.

[44]Horimoto has reconstructed the transmission of the scrolls in Ibid., p. 15. According to Horimoto, in 1708 all the visual images were preserved in one scroll, but without any written narrative. Horimoto also asserts that they were first preserved as *two* separate scrolls in 1797. See Ibid., p. 16. See also Kawazoe, "Kaisetsu," pp. 36–42.

[45]See Horimoto, Ibid., pp. 15–22, 39, particularly pp. 21–22 and 39. For other informative explanations of the restoration of the scrolls, see Sujaku,"Mōko shūrai ekotoba denzon katei no fukugen ni tsuite," pp. 102–5 and Matsumoto Aya, "Mōko shūrai ekotoba no seiritsu to denrai ni tsuite–sono saikō," pp. 75–76.

of Hosokawa Tadatoshi, the lord of Kumamoto domain (*han* 藩) and Higo province, in 1825. There they remained until 1869, when the Meiji government abolished all domains. The Hosokawa returned these scrolls to Ōyano Jurō, who presented them to the Meiji sovereign in 1890. In 1989 the scrolls were bestowed to the nation, and now they are housed in the Museum of the Imperial Collections (*Sannomaru Shōzōkan*).[46]

The fact that nearly fifty copies of the scrolls were created from the late eighteenth-century onward attests to the immediate and continuing interest that they generated.[47] Takezaki Suenaga became glorified as a hero, and his popularity peaked during the Sino-Japanese war of 1894–95. A small shrine commemorating this later conflict was built on the grounds of the Kaitō, as were two torpedo-shaped monuments advocating "worship of the gods and the ancestors," and "loyalty to lord and love of country," which survive to this day. Interest in Suenaga receded in the aftermath of Japan's defeat in the Second World War. Suenaga's Kaitō shrine remains a lonely backwater, little changed except for a series of placards that the descendants of Fujii Suenari have recently erected, extolling their ancestor's virtue as being a "trusted retainer" of Takezaki Suenaga.

A Note on the Illustrations

Takezaki Suenaga's scrolls have been altered through repeated restorations, so that even the "original" varies significantly from how it must have appeared in the late thirteenth or early fourteenth century. Most of the changes serve to emphasize the role of Takezaki Suenaga.[48] Not only has Suenaga's face and armor been redrawn repeatedly, but his name has often been added to particular figures at a much later date.[49] One exception to this trend appears in Scene 16 where Takezaki Suenaga's name has been erased in order to emphasize the valor of three Ōyano brothers.[50]

---

[46]Matsumoto Aya, Mōko shūrai ekotoba," p. 9.

[47]For more analysis of research regarding the scrolls during the Tokugawa period, see Kawazoe Shōji, *Mōko shūrai kenkyū shiron* (Tōkyō: Yūzankaku, 1977).

[48]For significant monographs that reveal how images were added to the scrolls, see Satō Tetsutarō, *Mōko shūrai to Takezaki Suenaga* and Matsumoto Aya, "Mōko shūrai ekotoba ni tsuite no ichikōsatsu–arata na mondaiten o kuwaete."

[49]A perusal of the copies of the scrolls located at Kyūshū and Kumamoto Universities reveals that a later observer sometimes added Suenaga's name in the scrolls. For example, the name of "Suenaga" that appears in Scene 12 of the second scroll is missing from the Kyūshū copy, and was accordingly added at a later time. For the best recent analysis of writing styles in the scrolls appears in Matsumoto Aya, "Mōko shūrai ekotoba no seiritsu to denrai ni tsuite–sono saikō."

[50]Close observation of the Scene 16 in the original reveals that Suenaga's

A Note on the Illustrations

More significantly, some Mongol warriors have been added to the scrolls sometime after their original creation, but prior to their "discovery" in 1793.[51] For example, the Mongol general, drawn out of proportion in Scene 20, constitutes a later addition. Recognizing this, one astute copyist, Fukuda Taka, even omitted this figure, in order to better convey the original state of the scrolls.[52]

The most significant revision appears in what constitutes Scene 6 of this monograph. Here, Suenaga is dramatically depicted as being thrown from his wounded horse. A projectile (teppō 鉄砲) explodes above him and three large Mongol soldiers, expertly drawn, stand firm in front of their already fleeing compatriots. Recently, however, it has been shown that this scene represents an almagamation of what should be considered two scenes. Close observation of the original reveals that the page depicting Suenaga had been pasted onto a scene of fleeing Mongols, and that the three Mongol soldiers, and perhaps the exploding projectile as well, were drawn on the seam of both pages at a later time.[53] Likewise, the pine tree appearing behind Suenaga's bucking horse represents a later addition, as does the amount of blood flowing from his wounded mount.[54] Hence, the falling Suenaga and his mount belong to Scene 5, but the rest of Scene 6 (minus the three Mongol warriors), and all of Scene 7, should be attached to the end of Scene 8.

Fukuda Taka, a noted Higo artist, has attracted considerable attention

name has been scraped from the page. Suenaga's identity can be ascertained from Passage 11, because his helmet made from shin-guards is shown falling off his head. By contrast, the Ōyano names remain legible. Nevertheless, in the version reproduced in this monograph, Suenaga's name has been restored.

[51]This can be ascertained because all copies of the scrolls, created from 1795 onward, depict these figures.

[52]For more on this general, see Takezakijō, pp. 134–36.

[53]Matsumoto, "Mōko shūrai ekotoba ni tsuite no ichikōsatsu–arata na mondaiten o kuwaete," pp. 66–67. Matsumoto maintains that the projectile is probably an original part of the scrolls (see pp. 65–66) but admits that the phrase teppō probably represents a later addition. I believe, however, that this image is suspicious as well. Numerous projectiles were discovered in the wreckage of the Mongol fleet, but most represent large rocks that had been rounded into balls, rather than explosive devices. See Takashima kaitei iseki, 3 vols., comp. Nagasaki ken Takashima chō kyōiku iinkai (Takashima chō bunkazai chōsa hōkokusho, 1992–96), particularly vol. 1, pp. 75–79, 88, 93. For another illustration of the stone projectiles, see David Nicole, The Mongol Warlords (London: Firebrand books, 1990), p. 87.

[54]For this observation, see Satō Tetsutarō, Mōko shūrai to Takezaki Suenaga and Matsumoto Aya, "Mōko shūrai ekotoba ni tsuite no ichikōsatsu–arata na mondaiten o kuwaete."

12

because he has been long believed to be the one who restored Suenaga's images and texts. An 1832 memorial describes how Taka, lamenting the poor state of the "original version," collected the scattered images and pasted them in two scrolls.[55] Recently, however, interest in Fukuda Taka has waned because an examination of the original reveals that they were reconstructed in 1797, when Taka was only one year old! Fukuda Taka's mentor, Nagase Saneyuki, was primarily responsible for restoring the scrolls.[56]

Fukuda Taka is believed to have created six copies of the Mongol scrolls. Takashima Chiharu copied one of Fukuda's six reproductions and Mizuno Tadanaka, the daimyo of Kii province, included this copy in his compilation, the *Tankaku sōsho* (丹鶴叢書). This version, published as an appendix to Yamada An'ei's *Fukutekihen*, is reproduced here in its entirety.[57]

The most significant variation of the *Tankaku* scrolls is that they contain scenes of two warriors carrying the heads of Mongol captives coupled with images of a group of warriors (see the final six pages of Scene 3). These scenes no longer survive in the original, although they are mentioned in the text. Takashima Chiharu claimed that they were created by Fukuda Taka, who attempted to reconstruct the scrolls as they must have originally existed.[58]

These scenes found in Fukuda Taka's "reconstructions" should not be so simply dismissed, for they fit in seamlessly with a fragmentary portion of the scrolls. This, coupled with the fact that none of the scrolls' other obvious lacunae were "restored" by Fukuda Taka leaves open the possibility that he managed to copy scenes that have since been lost. As implausible as this may seem, Horimoto Kazushige has shown that one

---

[55]For reference to this passage, which comes from the *Takeda sōshi yūgaroku* (竹田荘師友画録), see Matsumoto Aya, "Mōko shūrai ekotoba no seiritsu to denrai ni tsuite–sono saikō," p. 75 and Kawazoe, "Kaisetsu," p. 36.

[56]This theory was first proposed by Kawazoe Shōji in his "Kaisetsu," p. 36. Examinations of the scrolls conducted during 1975–78 confirm Kawazoe's thesis. See Matsumoto Aya, "Mōko shūrai ekotoba no seiritsu to denrai ni tsuite–sono saikō," pp. 75–76.

[57]See "Takezaki Suenaga Mōko shurai ekotoba," in the appendix of Yamada An'ei, *Fukutekihen*, pp. 1–157. The best summary of the transmission of these scrolls appears in Miya, *Kassen no emaki*, pp. 105–17; Kawazoe, "Kaisetsu," p. 35; and *Takezakijō*, pp. 134–36.

[58]*Takezakijō*, pp. 133–36 and Miya Tsugio, *Kassen no emaki*, p. 111. For the most recent summary of differences between the *Tankaku* text and other versions, see Horimoto, "Mōko shūrai ekotoba no genjō seiritsu katei ni tsuite–Aoyanagi Tanenobu hon no kentō to shōkai," p. 21.

scene and one passage were discovered by the Ōyano as late as 1823.[59] Fukuda Taka is thought to have pasted scattered "original" images belonging to the Ōyano into scrolls a mere two years later.[60] Perhaps the images that Taka restored came from the Ōyano's *second* copy, which has since been lost. Further research is needed to determine whether the *Tankaku* version depicts otherwise lost scenes, or merely represents an excellent reconstruction of the scrolls by an early nineteenth-century artist.

The textual and visual progression of the *Tankaku sōsho* narrative unfolds more logically than does the current reconstruction of the original. Takezaki Suenaga's brother-in-law, Mii Saburō, is depicted as attacking retreating Mongols after Suenaga's horse had been shot in the *Tankaku* version, but not so in the original, which juxtaposes events by showing Mii Saburō to be chasing Mongols, in full flight, before Suenaga was unhorsed.[61] Nevertheless, the Mongols did not flee from the battlefield until after Suenaga's horse had been shot. Hence, the flow of the *Tankaku* scenes corresponds better to the written narrative than does the original.

Furthermore, the copyist of the *Tankaku* version restored some scenes as they had originally appeared. For example, in Scene 12, two foot soldiers are depicted as sprinting in front of the walls. One of these warriors was transformed in the original to a man standing awkwardly behind his nimble compatriot, but Fukuda portrays both as running. Another variation is that the first fourteen lines that constitute Passage 7 of the text appear again at the end of the first scroll, but are absent from the *Tankaku* version. This "missing" passage is, however, a remnant of the second copy of the scroll that has been added to the images twice and hence is omitted.[62]

A close reading of the *Tankaku* copy also reveals that it provides a snapshot of the scrolls when they were better preserved than the present.

---

[59]See Horimoto, Ibid.

[60]See Ōyano Jurō's explanation of how the scrolls were transmitted in the *Fukutekihen,* and also Kawazoe, "Kaisetsu," pp. 35–36.

[61]The six pages of Scene 8 are now pasted immediately between Scenes 5 and 6 in the current version of the original scrolls.

[62]For the definitive study of the different textual variations, see Miya, *Kassen no emaki,* pp. 124–31, particularly the chart on pp. 124–25. Review of photographs of the original reveals that the "missing" passage constitutes a repetition of the first fourteen lines of Passage 7. See Komatsu Shigemi's *Mōko shūrai ekotoba*, in *Nihon no emaki 13* (Chuō kōransha, 1988), pp. 64–65 (hereafter *Mōko shūrai ekotoba*). Although these fourteen lines of Passage 7 are classified as Section 9 of the text by Miya Tsugio, they do not appear in the *Tankaku* version or, for that matter, Ishii's annotated text.

14

For example the name Takefusa is clearly visible in Scene 4 of this reproduction but is no longer legible in the original.[63]

Evaluating the Scrolls

That Takezaki Suenaga secured enough funds to even create such scrolls is perhaps as remarkable an accomplishment as their later survival. Originally, picture scrolls had been created to illustrate various sutras or to describe the lives of priests. Nevertheless, from the eleventh and twelfth centuries onward, scrolls became based on literary works. Some, strongly influenced by Buddhist beliefs, were devoted to illustrating the pleasures of paradise or the tribulations of hell; others portrayed the lives of famous priests, miracles associated with temples and shrines, scenes of courtly life, or visual narratives of battle.[64]

Masterworks of this genre represent unsurpassed sources for recreating life in medieval Japan because they depict many aspects of society and culture that do not otherwise survive in the historical record.[65] Painted by skilled artists using lavish color, these scrolls increased in popularity as the thirteenth century progressed. Even today, ten scrolls survive that were created between 1288, the year that marks the creation of the *Sannō reigenki*, and 1309, when the ranking courtier Saionji Kinhira presented the *Kasuga gongen kenki-e* scrolls to the Kasuga shrine.[66]

Battles were depicted in some scenes of these scrolls, such as the *Kasuga gongen kenki-e*, while other works were devoted to recreating a particular military encounter. The earliest references to such battle scrolls indicate that they were created by artisans from the capital of Kyōto early in the thirteenth century, and that they were patronized by the highest echelons of society, such as the third *shōgun*, Minamoto Sanetomo.[67]

---

[63]Compare Scene 4 with the illustrations of *Mōko shūrai ekotoba*, p. 23.

[64]For a good introduction to the genre, see "emaki" in the *Kokushi daijiten,* vol. 2 (Yoshikawa kōbunkan, 1979–97). Other informative sources include *Emaki*, a catalog published by the Kyōto National Museum in 1987, and for scrolls pertaining to military events, Miya, *Kassen no emaki*.

[65]Recently, dictionaries of images have been published that are based on these scrolls, which vividly reveal much about the nature of life in medieval Japan. See, for example, *Shinpan Emakimono ni yoru Nihon jōmin seikatsu ebiki*, comp. Shibuzawa Keizō (Heibonsha, 1994). Another such valuable source is *Yūsoku kojitsu daijiten*, comp. Suzuki Keizō (Yoshikawa kōbunkan 1995).

[66]In addition, five more surviving scrolls were created between 1311 and 1323. See Miya, *Kassen no emaki*, p. 101. For more on the Kasuga scrolls, see Royall Tyler, *The Miracles of the Kasuga Deity* (New York: Columbia University Press, 1990).

[67]For the retired sovereign Go Shirakawa viewing such scrolls, see Miya,

Takezaki Suenaga was unusual, for he possessed both the ambition and the financial resources to commission his own scrolls. Most contemporary scrolls were the product of patronage by central elites rather than by provincial warriors. For example, it was the Minister of the Left and *Kantō mōshitsugi*, or mouthpiece for the Kamakura *bakufu* at the Kyōto court, Saionji Kinhira, who commissioned the *Kasuga gongen kenki-e*. Kinhira had Takashina Takakage, head of the court's office of painters (*edokoro* 絵所), create this masterpiece, which is admittedly a much longer work than the Mongol scrolls.[68] By contrast, Suenaga's scrolls represent an amalgamation of courtly and provincial painting styles. Some sections, such as the earliest surviving scenes, are of the highest quality, while others were drawn with a weaker line.[69] In contrast to works commissioned by capital nobility, which emphasized portraiture, the artists who created Suenaga's scrolls possessed varied perspectives: some attempted to recreate the appearance of warriors, such as Shōni Kagesuke, as had been typical for courtly inspired work, while others lavished more attention on horses and their gear than on the likenesses of warriors per se.[70] In short, Suenaga's scrolls represent an amalgamation of central and regional artistic styles, which reflect the value system of thirteenth-century warriors.[71]

Although written decades after the event, Takezaki Suenaga's scrolls are particularly valuable because they provide an eye-witness account of the invasions. Other sources were either not composed by participants or became littered with the garbled inaccuracies of careless copyists. For example, some Japanese texts, such as the *Hachiman gudōki*, portray the

---

Kassen no emaki, pp. 36–39. For references to Minamoto Sanetomo enjoying battle scrolls, see *Azuma kagami*, ed. Kuroita Katsumi, in *Kokushi taikei*, 1932–33, vol. 2, 11.26.1204, p. 622, and 11.23.1210, pp. 653–55.

[68]See Tyler, *Miracles of the Kasuga Deity*, pp. 9–13.

[69]For stylistic distinctions among the artists who drew Suenaga's scrolls, see Miya, *Kassen no emaki*, pp. 122–27.

[70]The identity of the artists who created this work continues to generate debate. Both Matsumoto Aya in her "Mōko shūrai ekotoba no seiritsu to denrai ni tsuite–sono saikō," and Satō Tetsutarō in his *Mōko shūrai to Takezaki Suenaga* have argued that court artists composed the scrolls. According to Ōyano Jūro's history of the scrolls, they were created by Tosa Nagataka and his son Nagaaki. See Matsumoto, Ibid., p. 67-69. Recently, however, Fujimoto Masayuki has advanced the possibility that Scene 2 of the scrolls was penned by an artist from the Dazaifu, familiar with the styles of the capital and yet immersed in the mentalities of the provinces. See his *Yoroi o matō hitobito* (Yoshikawa kōbunkan, 2000), pp. 33–36.

[71]See Miya, *Kassen no emaki*, pp. 122–27 and Fujimoto, Ibid. Like Suenaga's scrolls, later military documents depicted horses, and if need be, the causes of their deaths in greater detail than they provided for men. See Conlan, "State of War," pp. 66–68.

area of Mizuki, near Dazaifu, as if it were a single castle, based on a misreading of this region's name.[72] Likewise, the *Yosōki* (予章記), a chronicle of the Kawano family, was not compiled until the late sixteenth century, and contains some anachronisms and inaccuracies.[73] By contrast, knowledgeable figures–perhaps Suenaga himself–reviewed the artists' renditions of the invasion and noted inaccuracies in red ink.[74]

The veracity of Suenaga's scrolls continues to generate debate. While some art historians dismiss the scrolls as being subjective monuments to self-aggrandizement,[75] the historian Murai Shōsuke reflects the majority opinion by proclaiming that "in general authenticity and artistic excellence, such a valuable source is found nowhere else in the world."[76] As we shall see, this divergence in opinion stems from whether the scrolls are simply viewed or "read" in conjunction with their appended text. Suenaga's text shall be supplemented here by as many contemporary sources as possible.

[72]Ryō, *Mōko Shūrai*, pp. 41–42. A comparison of the *bunmei* (1469–87) copy of the *Hachiman gudōki* (*Fukutekihen*, maki 2, page 19) with another version, the *Hachiman gudō kun*, pp. 469–70, is illustrative. The former refers to "allies" (*mikata* 味方) while the latter contains the error of Mizuki castle. The latter version, now consisting of two maki, has been published together in volume one of *Gunsho ruijū*, compiled by Haniwa Hokinoichi. The first maki recounts the deeds of Hachiman, from Jingū's mythical conquest of Korea in the fifth century and ending with the attempted Mongol invasions of Japan. It can also be found in *Jisha engi*, pp. 169–205.

[73]As an individual record of battle, this source is perhaps only surpassed by Takezaki Suenaga's scrolls, but nevertheless, it contains forged documents pertaining to the twelfth and thirteenth centuries. As Kageura Tsutomu has revealed in his introduction to the *Kawano ke monjo* and *Zennōji ke monjo*, some *Yosōki* documents dating from the late thirteenth century can be independently verified with other surviving original sources. Nevertheless, Tanaka Minoru has shown that many documents reproduced in this chronicle are untrustworthy. See his "Kamakura jidai ni okeru Iyo no kuni no jitō gokenin ni tsuite," in *Shōensei to buke shakai* (Yoshikawa kōbunkan, 1969), pp. 245–92. Frequently the Kawano's name has been romanized as Kōno, but phonetic (*kana*) passages in Suenaga's picture scrolls reveal that in fact Kawano is the correct pronunciation. See the references to the Kawano in Scene 11. For a photograph of the original, see *Mōko shūrai ekotoba*, p. 67.

[74]See Scene 11, immediately before Passage 9 of the scrolls. Not only was the artist criticized for improperly drawing a door, but the house customs of the Kawano family were explained as well. For analysis of these passages, see Matsumoto Aya in her "Mōko shūrai ekotoba no seiritsu to denrai ni tsuite–sono saikō," particularly p. 70, and Fujimoto Masayuki, *Yoroi o matō hitobito*, pp. 54–56.

[75]Ohta, "Mongol Invasion," pp. 90–93.

[76]Murai Shōsuke, "Takezaki Suenaga ekotoba," *Shūkan Asahi hyakka Nihon no rekishi 9 chūsei I Mōko shūrai* (Asahi Shinbun, June 8, 1986), pp. 276–77.

A Note on the Translation

As any student of classical Japanese knows, the subject of a sentence is often implied but rarely stated. Suenaga's account is no exception. One passage of his narrative can be translated quite literally as: "have messenger take a mere hundred coppers, saying pray well, pass by, arrive barrier" but such a telegraphic construct must be embellished to form a coherent sentence. I transformed this passage as follows: "Giving a mere hundred coppers to my retainer, I had him ask the pilgrim to pray deeply for me. Passing by, I made my way to the barrier." I translated this account into the first person singular because one can detect interior dialogue—Suenaga often reveals his own thoughts, dreams, and prayers. Nevertheless, classical Japanese prose draws little distinction between first person and third. His scrolls could be translated in the third person, an approach which in some ways more closely reflects the tone of the narrative, given that Suenaga never uses the personal pronoun "I."

Dialogue is recorded in Suenaga's narrative as if spoken. I tried to retain the spirit of the original by reproducing most as direct quotations. For the sake of readability, I added the subject and clearly implied objects and have only provided brackets in cases where the language remains unusually telegraphic or difficult to interpret. In addition, I have translated passages where Suenaga refers to himself in the third person somewhat prosaically as "I Suenaga." Regarding supplementary materials, I chose a more literal approach, suitable to the terseness of the language, for nearly all were written in kanbun (漢文), a Japanese writing style that closely resembles classical Chinese, and bracketed all that was not explicitly elucidated.

Cast of Characters
(in general order of appearance)

I. Suenaga's family and retainers

TAKEZAKI SUENAGA	The protagonist, a *gokenin* from Higo province.
SABURŌ JIRŌ SUKEYASU	Suenaga's bannerman.
TŌGENDA SUKEMITSU	One of Suenaga's retainers.
MII SABURŌ SUKENAGA	Suenaga's younger brother-in-law.
MOROZANE	A retainer of Suenaga.
NONAKA TARŌ NAGASUE	A relative who fought with Suenaga in 1281.
YASABURŌ	The two lowly followers of
MATAJIRŌ	Suenaga who accompanied him on his 1275 trip to Kamakura.

II. Members of the Takezaki clan

EDA MATATARŌ HIDEIE	A relative of Suenaga who agreed to witness his actions in 1274.
THE JUEI PRIEST	A powerful member of Suenaga's clan who advised him not to travel to Kamakura in 1275.

III. Suenaga's battle comrades (non-relatives)

KIKUCHI JIRŌ TAKEFUSA	*Gokenin* from Higo province who witnessed Suenaga's deeds during the first invasion of 1274.
SHIROISHI ROKURŌ MICHIYASU	*Gokenin* from Hizen province who stood as a witness for Suenaga in 1274.
MITSUMOTO MATAJIRŌ	*Gokenin* from Chikugo province whom Suenaga witnessed being shot in the neck.

KAWANO MICHIARI	Iyo gokenin who fought notably in the Mongol invasions, and also had holdings in Chikuzen province prior to the second invasions.
ONO KOJIRŌ KUNITAKA TAKUMA BETTŌ JIRŌ TOKIHIDE	Warriors who attempted to attack the enemy in boats in 1281 with Suenaga.
KOTABE NO HYŌBU NO BŌ	Follower of Adachi Morimune who threw Suenaga off his boat in 1281.
HIDA NO JIRŌ HIDETADA	Neighbors of Suenaga who boarded the same boat as he did at Iki Island in 1281.
YAIGOME NO GORŌ MIYAHARA SABURŌ ONO NO DAISHIN RAIJŌ	Raijō, at least, was a retainer of Adachi Morimune (the Echizen lord).
KUSA NO JIRŌ TSUNENAGA	Otherwise unknown warrior who fought against the Mongols in 1281.
AMAKUSA ŌYANO NO JURŌ TANEYASU	See Ōyano no Jurō Taneyasu below.
AKITSUKI KURŌ TANEMURA TAKAMASA	A gokenin from Chikuzen. An otherwise unknown man who allowed Takezaki Suenaga to board his boat.
ŌYANO NO JURŌ TANEYASU	Higo gokenin who fought with Suenaga. The Ōyano gained possession of Suenaga's scrolls in the sixteenth century.
SABURŌ TANEMURA ŌYANO SHIGEMORI	Ōyano Taneyasu's son and heir. Higo gokenin. Taneyasu's brother, who fought with Suenaga on the high seas in 1281.
ARISAKA YOSHINAGA HATAKEYAMA KAKU AMIDABUTSU, IWAYA SHIRŌ HISACHIKA, AND HONDA SHIRŌ SAEMON KANEFUSA	A gokenin from Shinano province. Satsuma warriors who fought under the Shimazu.
HASHIZUME HYŌGO JIRŌ	A Bungo province gokenin, and witness for Suenaga in 1281.

TAMAMURA SABURŌ MORIKIYO	A retainer of the Adachi, related to Tamamura Yasukiyo (see minor characters):
TOSA NO BŌ DŌKAI	Warrior killed in 1281.

IV. *Regional (Kyūshū and Nagato province) officials*

SHŌNI KAGESUKE	Younger brother to Tsunesuke, the shugo of Chikuzen province, and a commander of Japanese forces in 1274. Killed in the political disturbances of 1285.
SHŌNI TSUNESUKE	*Shugo* of Chikuzen province. Also commands troops in 1281.
ŌTOMO YORIYASU	*Shugo* of Bungo province.
MII SHINSAEMON SUESHIGE	Acting *shugo* of Nagato province. Aided Suenaga on his journey to Kamakura in 1275.
ADACHI MORIMUNE	Younger brother of Adachi Yasumori and acting *shugo* of Higo province who perished with Shōni Kagesuke in 1285.
SHIMAZU HISACHIKA	*Shugo* of Satsuma province.

V. *Kamakura bakufu officials*

ADACHI YASUMORI	High-ranking Kamakura official, head of the board of appeals. Shugo of Higo province. Killed in 1285.
HŌJŌ TOKIMUNE	The regent (*shikken*) to the Kamakura *shōgun*. Also known as the Yamanouchi lord. Dies suddenly in 1284.
GŌTA GORŌ TŌTOSHI AND ANDŌ JIRŌ SHIGETSUNA	Commanders dispatched from Kamakura during the second invasions of 1281.

VI. Minor characters

NODA SABURŌJIRŌ SUKESHIGE	A retainer of Shōni Kagesuke.
ŌTA SAEMON	A retainer of Shōni Kagesuke (?).
ASHINA NO HANGAN	A retainer of Adachi Yasumori.
NOTO JIRŌ	A Hizen *gokenin* who met Suenaga in Kamakura.
TAMAMURA UMA NO TARŌ YASUKIYO	A retainer of Adachi Yasumori who handed documents and a horse to Suenaga when he was in Kamakura.
SAEDA GORŌ	Stable master in Kamakura.
JŌ NO KURŌ HANGAN	One of Adachi Yasumori's younger brothers.
KAWANO HACHIRŌ	Kawano Michiari's heir.
TOKICHI TARŌ AND HIDAKA SABURŌ	Men depicted on walled defenses waiting for the Mongols in 1281.
SHIMAZU HISANAGA	Brother of the *shugo* of Satsuma.
SHIMAZU SHIKIBU NO SABURŌ	Nephew to Shimazu Hisanaga.

PART ONE

The Scrolls of the Mongol Invasions of Japan

The First Scroll: The Invasion of 1274

[1] I set off to attack before knowing how many warriors had assembled at Okinohama.[1] Of all the members of my clan (*ichimon* 一門), Eda Matatarō Hideie begged me to stand as his witness. We traded helmets so that we could recognize each other.[2] Just at that time, we heard that the foreign pirates (*izoku* 異賊) had set up camp at Akasaka. As the warriors of our clan set off for battle, we saw the commander (*taishōgun* 大将軍), Dazai no Shōni Saburō Saemon Kagesuke. He dispatched Noda Saburō Jirō Sukeshige, who came up to Eda Matatarō Hideie and said: "In order to be seen [we] should fight together. As Akasaka has poor terrain, you should pull back here. When the enemy attacks, as they most certainly will, bear down on them, firing at once."[3] Determined to keep our word [to fight with Kagesuke we all] pulled back. Nevertheless, I Suenaga said: "Waiting for the general will cause us to be late to battle. Of all the warriors of the clan, I Suenaga will be first to fight from Higo," and set off to attack.

---

[1]Suenaga's scrolls were meant to be read and viewed in tandem. The alternation of text and image may seem disjointed, but this style accurately reflects the staccato nature of the narrative. Perhaps Suenaga began his scrolls with an introduction, but these passages have been lost. One can only surmise that the Mongols had already landed in northern Kyūshū and established camp in the marshy, wooded lands of Akasaka and Torikai. Meanwhile, Japanese defenders had arrived in the east, near Hakozaki, and attacked westward toward Sumiyoshi and Akasaka. For more on the lay of the land, see Irumada Nobuo, *Nihon no rekishi 7 Musha no yo ni* (Shūeisha, 1991), p. 319.

[2]The *ichimon* consisted of autonomous families of a common lineage, who possessed no obligation to fight together. For a good example of this term, see Conlan, "State of War," p. 164.

[3]*Omonoi ni irubeki* 追物射に射るべき, a reference to the practice of shooting dogs and other animals from galloping horses.

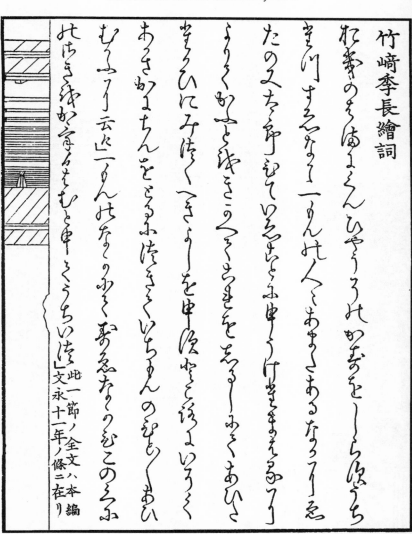

Followers of Bungo province's shugo, Ōtomo Hyōgo no kami Yoriyasu.[1]

---

[1]Written in red above the warriors. Phrases appearing in the illustrations are translated in italics.

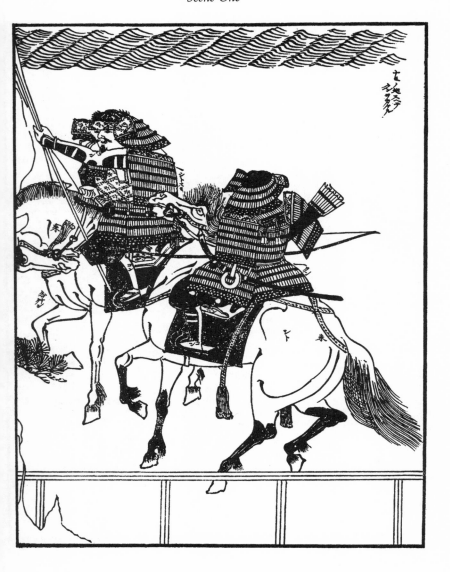

The gate (torii) of Hakozaki shrine.

肥後國竹崎
五郎兵衛尉
季長

Takezaki Gorō Hyōe no jō Suenaga of Higo province.

36

[2] I passed by the hills where Shōni Kagesuke, the commander (*taishō*) of the day, had fortified his encampment. [Kagesuke's] retainer Ōta Saemon told me to dismount, but because I intended to attack [text missing] . . . . I said: "We five horsemen are going to fight before you. We won't limit ourselves to merely shooting down the enemy! I have no purpose in my life but to advance and be known[1] [text missing]. I want [my deeds] to be known by his lordship."[2] Kagesuke said: "I don't expect to survive tomorrow's battle but if I do I will stand as a witness for you [text missing]." "I am ashamed to speak to you on horseback," I said but Kagesuke merely replied: "As you were." I followed his command and set off to attack Akasaka [text missing], first of all the warriors in my clan. From the Hakozaki (筥崎) encampment I made my way to Hakata.

---

[1]*Susunde kenzan ni iru yori hoka ha go suru tokoro nakimono nete sōrō* 進むで見参に入るよりほかは期するところなきものにて候.

[2]*Kimi no kenzan* 君の見参. The "lord" here refers to Shōni Tsunesuke, Kagesuke's brother and the *shugo* of Higo province.

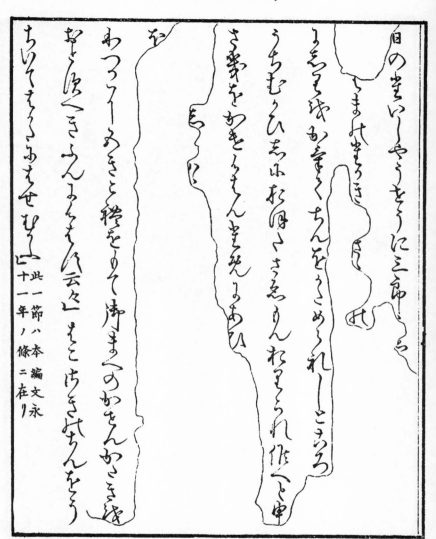

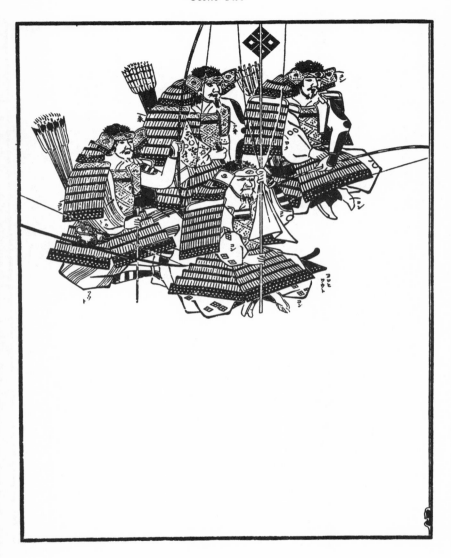

Dazai Shōni Saburō Saemon no jō (Kagesuke, age twenty-nine years) with horse and gear. An accurate portrait (nise-e) of his horse and accoutrements. He commands some five hundred horsemen.

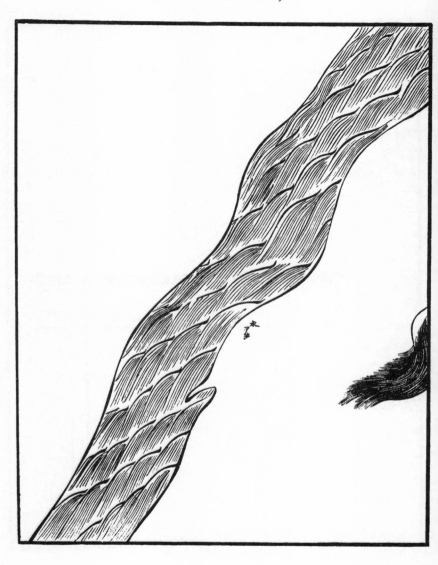

The torii of the Sumiyoshi shrine.[1]

---

[1]Written in red ink.

[3] Thinking that I was first to battle of all the warriors from Higo, I set off from the Hakata encampment. On my way to Akasaka, after passing the *torii* of the Sumiyoshi shrine, I met a warrior on a dapple grey horse at Komatsubara. He wore purple armor with a reverse arrowhead design, and a crimson billowing cape (*horo* 母衣) and, having just defeated the invaders (*kyōto* 凶徒) at their encampment, was returning with a hundred horsemen. The pirates (*zokuto* 賊徒) had fled. Two had been taken. He looked most brave and had two retainers walking before him on his left and right carrying heads—one pierced on a sword, the other on a *naginata* (長刀).[1] "Who passes here looking so brave?" I asked, and he replied "I am Kikuchi Jirō Takefusa of Higo province. Who are you?" "I am Takezaki Gorō Hyōe Suenaga of the same province. Watch me attack!" Saying so, I charged.

---

[1]As should be evident in the following scene, a *naginata* resembles a halberd, with a curved blade attached to a long wooden shaft.

そうろ乃ちんをうちいてひとみそうて　云々

のあるひやうくすゑあうゆける御らん候人とやてゑ

せむうふ」此一節ハ本編文永

十一年ノ條ニ在リ

Sukenaga

Suenaga

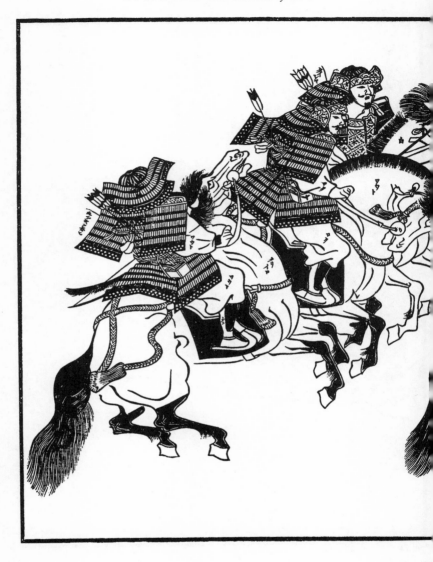

Heads (buntori) picked up by Takefusa's men.

[4] Defeated by Takefusa at Akasaka, the invaders (*kyōto* 凶徒) fled their encampment in two groups. The larger force retreated to Sohara; the smaller one fled to Tsukahara in Beppu. From Tsukahara, the smaller force attempted to link with the larger force at Shiohikata in Torikai. While pursuing the smaller force, my horse was slowed by the mud flats of the ebb tide (*hikata* 干潟) and could not gain on the fleeing enemy. The invaders established their camp at Sohara and planted many battle flags. Shouting a battle cry, I charged. As I was about to attack, my retainer Tōgenda Sukemitsu said: "More of our men are coming. Wait for reinforcements, get a witness and then attack!" I replied: "The way of the bow and arrow is to do what is worthy of reward. Charge!" The invaders set off from Sohara and arrived at the salt-house pines[1] of Torikai beach. There we fought. My bannerman was first. His horse was shot and he was thrown down. I Suenaga and my other three retainers were wounded. Just after my horse was shot and I was thrown off, Shiroishi Rokurō Michiyasu, a *gokenin* of Hizen province, attacked with a formidable squad of horsemen and the Mongols retreated toward Sohara. Michiyasu charged into the enemy, for his horse was unscathed. I would have died had it not been for him. Against all odds, Michiyasu survived as well, and so we each agreed to be a witness for the other. Also, a *gokenin* of Chikugo province, Mitsumoto Matajirō, was shot through his neck bone with an arrow. I stood as a witness for him.[2]

---

[1]Presumably a place name but the meaning is unclear.

[2]According to Miya Tsugio, the version of the scenes as they appear in the *Tankaku* copy is five, seven, eight, six, but his ordering schemata is based solely on the current state of the original manuscript and is by no means definitive.

まけふさ／せうかにあるきよちんをうけれとされぐ

ふくてよなりてかほをしゑすうそそにむよそひくて

せ／はへふのつ／くゑく云ちくこれそふの御きよん

みほとものみ二郎そひのお弥をゐそをさるれなり／く

きう人ふ豊俵
此一節ハ本編文永
十一年ノ條ニ在リ

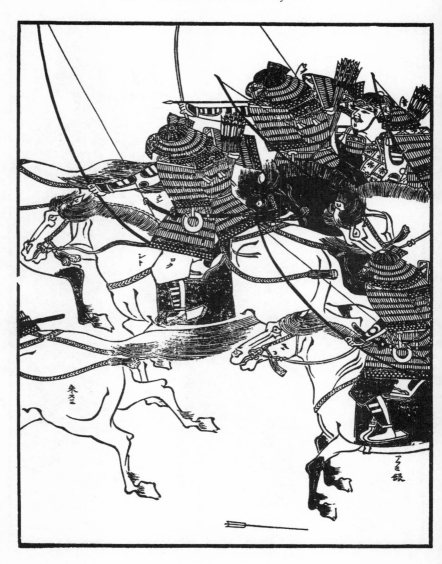

Shiroishi Rokurō Michiyasu with a hundred horsemen, attacking from the rear.

His riding horse being killed.
Suenaga's bannerman (hatasashi 旗指) Saburō Jirō Sukeyasu.
Tōgenda Sukemitsu.

Higo province's Takezaki Gorō Hyōe Suenaga. Age twenty-nine.[1]

---

[1]This caption appears on the original, but appears to be a later addition to the text, for it is not recorded in the *Tankaku* edition.

Cannonball (teppō)[1]

---

[1]Mongol armies clearly were aware of gunpowder, but the sophistication of their "guns" is open to considerable debate. For the best collection of relevant primary sources, see *Fukutekihen*, maki 2, pp. 38–44. Nevertheless, the above depiction of the projectile and the three Mongol soldiers who are resisting Suenaga represents a later additions to this scrolls. See "A Note on the Illustrations."

季長姉聟
三井三郎資長

Suenaga's younger brother-in-law, Mii Saburō Sukenaga.

[5] I intended to go to the Kantō [to plead my case] but the Juei priest told me that travel [to Kamakura] would generate suspicion (*gofushin* 御不審). [He said:] "Even though [Kamakura] had not forbidden people [from traveling east], such prohibitions are likely in the future.[1] [Therefore] no one shall provide you with traveling money (*yōtō* 用途)." I had no one to rely upon but myself. At the hour of the rabbit,[2] on the third day of the sixth month [of 1275], I left Takezaki. Others were suspicious [of me]. To my immense chagrin, not a single relative saw me off. Only two low-ranking followers (*chūgen* 中間), Yasaburō and Matajirō, accompanied me. In order to procure funds (*yōtō*), I had to sell my horse and saddle. I vowed to become a Buddhist priest and never to return if I were unable to present my case in Kamakura. Just at that time, I came across a pilgrim about to set off for Kumano shrine. Such believers are the basis of the faith—perhaps he could pray for me. Knowing that if he saw me I probably wouldn't be able to give him some funds for my safe journey (*hanamuke* はなむけ), I decided to provide him with a small offering (*gofuse* 御布施). Giving a mere hundred coppers (*ikketsu* 一結) to my retainer, I had him ask the pilgrim to pray deeply for me.

Passing by, I made my way to the barrier. There I visited Mii Shinsaemon Sueshige, my *eboshi* godfather[3] and the acting shugo [of Nagato province], who summoned female entertainers (*yūgimi* 遊君).[4] Regretting our parting, he told me to take the coastal road (*kaidō* 海道) to Kamakura, presented me with a palomino pony and cash, and sent me on my way.

On the tenth day of the eighth month, I worshiped at Mishima shrine in Izu.[5] As before, I had my retainer present an offering (gofuse 御布施)

---

[1]This passage refers to the events of 1275. The Kantō designates Kamakura, headquarters of the *bakufu* while the Juei gobo was most likely an elder of Suenaga's clan. The Juei gobō and not Kamakura forbade Suenaga from traveling east. He literally said that Kamakura "has not expressly forbidden you [from traveling east] but such an order [i.e. prohibition] cannot be issued at once." This proved perspicacious, for exigencies of guard duty prevented warriors from traveling either to Kyōto or to Kamakura a mere nine months later. See Document 35.

[2]Five A.M. For a list of all hours and their modern equivalents, see appendix 2.

[3]*Eboshi* 烏帽子 constituted formal headgear worn by nearly all adult males at the time. Sueshige was referred to as an *eboshi oya* 烏帽子親, or *eboshi* parent. During a coming-of-age ceremony, which commonly occurred when warriors were thirteen to eighteen years old, the man designated as *eboshi* parent would place the *eboshi* on the young man's head and determine his adult name.

[4]This man was a retainer of Nikaidō Takauji, the Nagato *shugo* from 1256 to 1276 who resided in Kamakura. See Document 35.

[5]Interestingly enough, it took Suenaga two months and one week to travel form Kyūshū to Izu, which reveals something about the speed of non-vital communications in the late thirteenth century.

and prayed with all of my heart for [success in the way of] the bow and arrow. On the eleventh day of the same month, I visited the shrine of the Hakone avatar, had another offering contributed, and prayed fervently.

[6] On the twelfth day of the eighth month I arrived in Kamakura. In the spirit of my purification at Mishima shrine, I bathed in the salt waters of Yuinohama, and then, even before stopping at the inn, I went to [the Tsuruoka] Hachiman shrine and had an offering presented, praying with all my heart for [success in the way of] the bow and arrow.

[7] Thereupon visited any number of officials and told them my tale but they ignored me because I appeared to be a minor warrior with only one low-ranking follower (*chūgen* 中間). Since there were no officials who would see me, I realized that I could only rely upon the support of the gods (*shinmei no kago* 神明の加護). So once again I visited Hachiman and prayed with all of my heart. On the third day of the tenth month, I had the opportunity to speak at the office of appeals that was administered at that time by Akita no Jō no suke Adachi Yasumori.[1]

[There I said:] "I Takezaki Gorō Hyōei Suenaga, a *gokenin* of Higo province, state my case. Last year on the twentieth day of the tenth month, during the battle with the Mongols, I set off toward the harbor of Hakozaki, and heard reports the pirates (*zokuto* 賊徒) were going to attack Hakata. As I left for Hakata, the general (*taishō*) of the day, Dazai no Shōni Saburō Saemon Kagesuke, who had fortified his encampment at Hakata's Okinohama, said that [we should] fight together. Because of this, most of the members of my clan remained behind in camp. I went before Kagesuke, faced him and [explained]: "Because my [land] dispute (*honso* 本訴)[2] has not been settled, I have only five mounted warriors.[3] Therefore, I have no choice but to fight visibly against the enemy. Other than advancing and having my deeds known, I have nothing else to live for. I want to lead the charge and have this reported to the lord."[4] Kagesuke replied: "I don't expect to survive tomorrow's battle but if I do I

---

[1]Yasumori was first appointed as the *shugo* of Higo sometime between 1272 and 1274, which explains how Suenaga, a Higo warrior, managed to have an audience with him. See *Zōtei Kamakura bakufu shugo seido no kenkyū*, (Tōkyō daigaku shuppan, 1971), pp. 229–230. For more on Yasumori's prominent institutional, political, and social position within the Kamakura *bakufu*, see the introduction.

[2]Some debate exists as to whether this term should be *honso*, or *honjo* (本所), which designates "homelands." See *Takezakijō*, p. 120. I have followed Ishii Susumu's interpretation.

[3]He literally says "I had few mounted retainers (*wakatō* 若党)–in fact, only five horsemen."

[4]*Kimi no kenzan ni goiresōrō beki* 君の見参に御入れ候べき.

will speak of your deeds." Thereupon I set off from the Hakata encampment and made my way to Shiohikata of Torikai, where I led the charge. My horse and my bannerman's horse were shot and killed and I Suenaga, Mii Saburō, and one other mounted retainer (*wakatō* 若党) were wounded. Shiroishi Rokurō Michiyasu, a *gokenin* of Hizen Province stood as my witness. Kagesuke recorded me as being first in his report (*hikitsuke* 引付).[1] I then asked Tsunesuke[2] to note in his document (*kakikudashi* 書下の状) that [my deeds] should appear in a [Kamakura] battle report (*onchūshin* 御注進),[3] and he wrote "If you have any questions regarding the first,[4] then [I will] explain the particulars," and left it at that. If [these documents] are not shown to the lord,[5] then I lose the honor of the [way of the] bow and arrow."

Lord Adachi Jō no suke said: "You have spoken of Tsunesuke's report. Do you know why [your deeds, so recorded, are not] worthy [of mention in a] battle report (*onchūshin* 御注進の分)?"

"How could I possibly know?"

Then tell me precisely what you do know. If you don't know [everything], then how can you possibly say that Kamakura's response has been insuficient?

"Tsunesuke wrote that if you have any questions regarding the first then he would fully examine the particulars if so ordered. I thought what he wrote in his document (*kakikudashi*) was worthy [of being recorded in a] battle report (*onchūshin no bun* 御注進の分), but [my being] first [in battle] is omitted from the report (*onchūshin*)." As I spoke, I took [Tsunesuke's] document (*kakikudashi*) and looked at it.

"Did you take any enemy heads? Were any of your men killed?" Yasumori asked.

"No heads taken. None were killed." I replied.

---

[1]*Hikitsuke* here clearly refers to a written document and not a judicial board, its other common thirteenth-century meaning.

[2]Kagesuke's brother, Tsunesuke, who was acting as *shugo* of Chikuzen province during the first invasions of 1274, even though he may not have been officially appointed at that time. According to Satō Shin'ichi, the last records of Tsunesuke's father, Kakuei, serving as *shugo* date from 1273, while the earliest records for Tsunesuke acting as *shugo* date from 1276. See *Zōtei Kamakura bakufu shugo seidō no kenkyū*, pp. 226–27 and 223–24.

[3]For other references to *onchūshin*, see Documents 9, 12, 21, and 23.

[4]This passage is difficult to decipher. Suenaga interpreted the phrase *saki ichidan* 先一段 as Suenaga being the first in battle, while Adachi Yasumori apparently believed that it referred to the petition that Suenaga originally submitted to Kamakura. This view was originally espoused by Aida, *Mōko shūrai no kenkyū*, pp. 470-71. Another plausible reading of this phrase is that it refers to the first passage of Tsunesuke's document.

[5]*Kimi no kenzan ni irazu* 君の見参に入らず.

"If that's the case, then you have not performed sufficient battle service (*kassen no chū* 合戦の忠). Other than being wounded, you did nothing at all. How can [Kamakura's response] be insufficient?" Yasumori countered.

"So I cannot have an audience with the lord because my deeds of being first in battle were not recorded in the battle report. But if you have any doubts about my truthfulness and need proof, why don't you dispatch an edict (*migyōsho* 御教書) to Kagesuke and ask him about it. If he writes an oath (*kishōmon* 起請文) declaring that my statements are false then not only can you ignore my military deeds, but you can take my head!"

"There is no precedent (*hikake* 引懸) for issuing an edict questioning Kagesuke. There is nothing I can do."

"I don't think that precedent matters here, for there is something that you have not considered."

"What is it? Tell me what it is I haven't considered," [replied Yasumori].

"If this concerned disputes over land rights (*shomu sōron* 所務相論) or if it were a battle involving only Japan (*honchō* 本朝) I know that I could not make such an unprecedented request. But this is a battle involving a foreign court (*ichō* 異朝). Precedent does not apply. It seems that I cannot be questioned or have [my reports] viewed by the lord[1] for lack of precedent! How then can I maintain my martial valor?"[2]

"What you say is true, but the law (*onsata no hō* 御沙汰の法) is perfectly clear. Without precedent, nothing can be done."

"My apologies for my rudeness but let me make myself perfectly clear. This is not a legal dispute. I desire to directly receive rewards. And, as I said before, if my assertion of being first to charge turns out to be false, then I revoke my claims for rewards and ask you to take my head. If what I say is true, then show [my battle report] to the lord[3] in order to spur on my battle valor.[4] If you ignore my request, it is as bad as [ignoring] a lament from a past life. What could exceed that?"

As I countered Yasumori for the third time, he relented. "Very well. I acknowledge your deeds in battle. I will state that your deeds should be seen [by higher authorities] and am sure that rewards shall be directly granted as you wish. Return now to your province at once and prepare to perform military service once again."

"As you will show [my report] to the lord, I will abide by your command. Nevertheless, since a judgment has not been reached regarding my disputed

---

[1] *Kimi no kenzan* 君の見参.

[2] *Yumiya no isami* 弓箭の勇み. Suenaga refers to warriors as practitioners of the way of the bow and arrow.

[3] *Kimi no kenzan ni makari iri* 見参にまかりいり.

[4] *Kassen no isami* 合戦の勇み.

holdings, I am landless (*musoku no mi* 無足の身). I don't know where to go to live. There are many I know well enough to enter their service [as a retainer], but I want to plant my own flag [and do things my way]. There is no such person [to act as a lord] and aid me (*fuchi suru* 扶持する), so I don't know where to go or what to do while waiting for the next great event."[1]

"Your situation," Yasumori reflected, "is most difficult indeed. I now must immediately report to the Yamanouchi lord.[2] He will hear of your battle deeds."

---

[1] The "great event" (*gojitsu no ondaiji* 後日の御大事) is another invasion.

[2] Hōjō Tokimune, the *shikken*, or regent to the Kamakura *shōgun*.

90

関東へ奏せむとする所に志ゆるゑの御房出て先あるま
しをのゝめるゑて仏不審をかゝる城出とめあるゝむ
ゆめふ一旦乃作りさゝろあるゝむすん云々同十一日そ
こねの権現さま いゝさゝく仏布施をまゝゝせゝく信
心をいゝゝきせい申し
同十二日かまゝゝゝゆ座く云々さゝくに八幡さま いゝゝゝ
て御布施をまいゝゝせゝく応了弓箭乃をせいを
申候し
かゝく媚きやうく川さゝく申次とゝゝくとも ちろきん
一人へゝゝゝゝゝゝゝゝゝ あひゝゝゝゝゝゝゝゝ
ゝゝゝゝゝゝゝゝやゝのあるゝ伝ゝゝくる

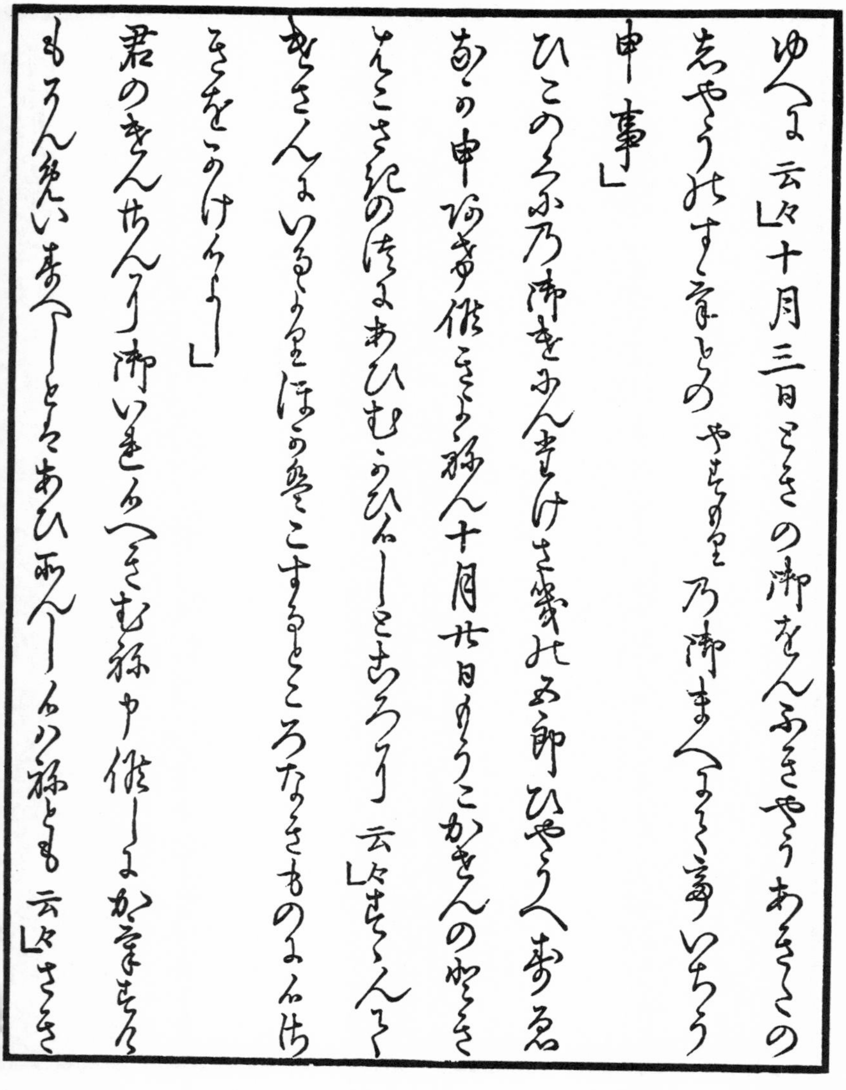

ゆへ云々十月三日こゝさの御をんふきやうあさくの

志やうみすとものやきする丞乃御ま へさき寿いちり

申事

ひこのゝふ乃御をゆんきけさ霙れゐ師ひやう へ寿名

あの申ひゞゝ催をゝ孫へ十月廿日りうこかをんのやさゝゝ

そゝさ紀の清よあひむうひねーとおろうり云々まそくんゝ

をさんよいるものをほの堅こすゝところなきものよん片

ををこあけうゝー」

君のきんちゝ御いきらへゝむ孫や催ーよか卒をゝ

もろん思い薄へーとゝあひあんゝゝかり孫とも云々さゝゝ

乃一きんハあさい給中あ君んく拍はきよあさくあそや

く候とんく内をくれんく」

君乃きんさんつくと次んきをせん乃めんわくをう

一たひん聖やか 云々やま乃うちとのくりいそくき海

いうきねほきにん御ハせんの事参面残くうけ

縮をるく候とくさんきくく風」

此六節ハ本編建治
元年ノ條二在リ

Ashina no hangan

Samurai of Lord Akita Jō no suke [Yasumori waiting] for various people to depart.

102

肥後国竹崎
五郎兵衛尉
季長

Takezaki Gorō Hyōe no jō Suenaga of Higo province.

Akita Jō no suke Yasumori

[8] On the fourth day of the same month, as I was reporting to Yasumori's Amanawa residence, the lackey (*kogirimono* 小切者) Notō Jirō, a gokenin of Hizen province came up to me and asked: "What happened yesterday at Yasumori's court of appeals (*teichū* 庭中)?"

"I repeatedly explained the situation to the administrators (*onbugyō* 御奉行) but they would not take up my case so I directly appealed [to Yasumori]."

"Yasumori told his retainers (*miuchi* 御内) that a warrior of unusual strength of will appeared in his court of appeals. This man declared that his rewards should be confiscated and his head should be chopped off if Saburō Saemon[1] were to say that his account [of battle] was false after being questioned [by Kamakura]. In a time of crisis, remember this man, Yasumori told Tamamura,[2] [adding that] he liked men from Tsukushi[3] because they speak of honor (*onmenboku* 御面目) even though [their documents] have not yet been reviewed. He recommended that this man [Suenaga] should be granted rewards." So Notō Jirō informed me. From then on, we spoke as usual.

On the first day of the eleventh month, at the hour of the sheep, I Suenaga was worshiping at [the Tsuruoka] Hachiman shrine when Tamamura Uma no Tarō Yasukiyo came up and summoned me alone to an audience hall.

"This [shōgunal] edict (*onkudashibumi* 御下文) confirming your land holdings has been granted from above as a reward for your battle service. Here."

Responding to his summons, I arose from the chamber (*ima futama* いま二間) and approached Yasukiyo. [Bowing deeply I] respectfully looked to Yasukiyo and received the document. As I was taking the document, Yasukiyo also said, "Yasumori personally requested that you be directly rewarded. Here." Again I respectfully received Yasumori's edict (*onkudashibumi*).[4]

"Now will you finally leave?"

Believing that Yasukiyo thought that I had spoken as I had done solely to receive more rewards, I said:

"As I said before, if I gain recognition from the Kamakura lord and am granted rewards then I will go back [to Kyūshū] the following day and will wait for the next crisis. If that is not the case then notify Kagesuke immediately [and have him punish me]."

"As a result of your complaint you have personally received your own

---

[1]Shōni Kagesuke.

[2]This man was a retainer of Yasumori.

[3]Kyūshū.

[4]In addition to receiving the *shōgun*'s edict, Suenaga received Yasumori's recommendation that he be rewarded.

edict (*onkudashibumi*). Now, one hundred and twenty others have been rewarded by Dazaifu.[1] Since you have had an audience, go back and be prepared to perform military service again. Here is a fully-equipped horse. How about returning now?"

I was speechless for having been so honored. Respectfully I received a chestnut horse with a saddle decorated with a small, comma-shaped heraldic device (*kotomoe* 小巴). Saeda Gorō, master of the stables, provided the horse's bridle and other well-made accoutrements. It was the first day of the eleventh month, at the hour of the sheep.[2]

---

[1]The Dazaifu was Kamakura's administrative headquarters in Kyūshū after the 1274 invasions.

[2]Some of the earliest copies of the scrolls, such as the Kyūshū University version, reproduce Passage 14 at the end of this scene, which probably represents its correct placement.

同四日あまるかその者ちふちん寿麻ゝひきん乃ろふの

御を人あり乃ゝゝゝ二節こゝゝりをのゝそめゝ川ゝゝゝ

礼志ゝす忍なゝふきいめんゝゝて 云々ろゝゝゝけあるゝま

小ともゝ忍のゝゝゝてまん志やゝ此忍をゝいまきんせゝろゝゝ

城をけゝゝむ睡や乃へ川きゝゝゝ出えくゝ節をゝてこれ城孩

そる十一月一日ひつの時をゝゝあり└

此一節ハ本編建治
元年ノ條ニ在リ

108

Jō no suke Yasumori

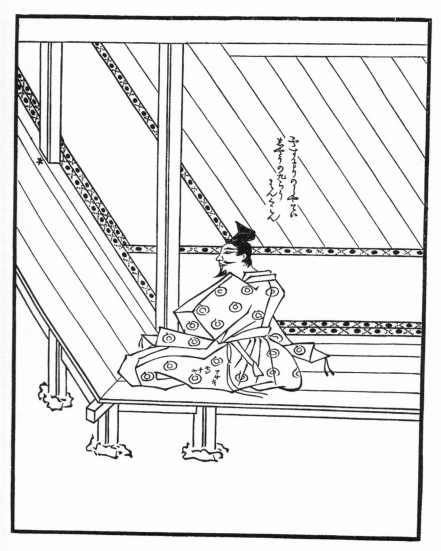

Yasumori's younger brother Jō no Kurō Hangan.

Suenaga
Saeda Gorō

The Second Scroll: The Invasion of 1281

Suenaga

Members of [Kawano] Michiari's house [customarily do] not wear formal headgear (eboshi) while battle is still being waged. This [they] say.

Iyo no Kawano Rokurō Michiari was thirty-two years old. His armor had been worn by Kawano Shirō Michinobu during the battles of the Heike when he joined the forces of the Genji.[1]

Michiari's heir, Kawano Hachirō.

---

[1] A reference to the Genpei wars of 1180–85. This passage, written in phonetic script, proves that the proper pronunciation for this Iyo warrior family is Kawano and not Kōno, as has been commonly assumed.

Michiari's bannerman.[1]

---

[1]Written in red.

妻戸ハ不ㇾ有ㇾ之慶後師書遠也

右原本以朱書ㇾ之

Such a side door does not exist here. The artist is mistaken.[1]

[1]Written in red.

[9][1] People thought highly of Kikuchi Jirō Takefusa.[2] He made a name for himself in the Bun'ei battles.[3] While passing in front of a stone wall where Takefusa had fortified his command post, I called out: "I know that the masts of the general's boat have been painted white. I am going [to sail forth], shoot at the enemy, and have my deeds reported to the lord.[4] If you survive, tell all."

---

[1]Miya Tsugio designates this passage as number 10, but it is labeled 9 here so as to correspond with the numbering schemata of Ishii. Miya's Passage 9 represents a repeat of Passage 7, which appears immediately after Suenaga received a horse from Saeda Gorō in Scene 10. From now on, all passage numbers will correspond to Ishii's numbers, and will be one less than those of Miya Tsugio.

[2]Other sources reveal that Kikuchi Takefusa had unusually close relations with high-ranking members of the Hōjō family. According to one surviving document, Takefusa dispatched his retainer to pay respects for the recently deceased Hōjō Masamura. Takefusa would have traveled to Kamakura in person, but could not because warriors from Kyūshū were forbidden to travel while on guard against the Mongols. See *Kamakura ibun*, vol. 15, doc. 11332, intercalary 5.29.[1273] Kikuchi Takefusa shojō.

[3]The first invasion of 1274.

[4]*Kimi no kenzan ni makari iresōrō* 君の見参にまかり入候.

人々於保睦の人をととふきちり乃二節さけすき文永乃

合戦みな綾あ弯となりて云々陶存席ハ出る得披

露らん人といひてう地ことをる四年ノ條ニ在リ此一節ハ本編弘安

Tōkichi Tarō. Age sixteen.

Hidaka Saburo. Age thirty.
Suenaga[1]

---

[1]Written in red.

[Kikuchi] Jirō Takefusa. Age thirty-seven.

The flag of Kikuchi Jirō.

Jirō

[10] Gōta Gorō Tōtoshi and Andō Saemon Jirō Shigetsuna, commanders (*ontsukai* 御使) dispatched from the Kantō, arrived at dawn on the fifth day of the seventh month. I said: "The enemy is separated from us by the sea. I cannot fight them during this crisis (*ondaiji* 御大事) without a ship." Gōta Gorō replied: "If you don't have a ship, then there is nothing that can be done." But at that time a *gokenin* of Hizen–I forget his name–said: "Let's find a good ship among the damaged craft in the harbor to the west of Takashima and drive off the pirates (*zokuto* 賊徒). [The Mongol survivors] are fleeing now!"

"That's right," I replied, "those troops would be infantry and their boats would be seaworthy craft. I want to cut down at least one [of the enemy]!"

"Inform the Shōni of our attack!" So said Gōta Gorō, who dispatched messengers with a command that read: "The pirates (*zokuto*) are fleeing. Dispatch forces to attack." Takuma Bettō Jirō Tokihide,[1] Ono Kojirō Kunitaka, and I Suenaga went around from boat to boat, looking for one to ride in, but could find none. Just as we gave up hope, a boat with the image of several coins emblazoned on the sail appeared. Gōta Gorō said: "That is the flag of Jō no Jirō.[2] Go there!" and dispatched us as messengers. I Suenaga boarded a messenger's skiff and set out to sea. Standing at the bow, I tried to get on Adachi's boat but couldn't, so I explained:

"I am a member of the *shugo*'s forces who has been ordered to get on board the next boat that arrives and fight." As I jumped on the boat, Kotabe no Hyōbu no bō had low-ranking followers (*shimobe* 下部) try to throw me off.

"This is the summoned boat [of Adachi Morimune]. Only members of his forces can board it. Stay off this boat!"

I yelled back to Kotabe, "In this vital matter I want to aid my lord.[3] Since I just got on the boat, I am not going to get off and wait for another that may never arrive. But if you give me a small boat, I will leave you."

"It is an outrage (*rōzeki* 狼藉) for you not to leave a boat when you have been ordered to disembark," he countered. And so when I had the opportunity I returned to my boat.

---

[1]See Document 31 for records pertaining to Tokihide.

[2]Adachi Yasumori. The Mongol accounts mention that Akita Jirō led reinforcements to the battlefield. See Ryusaku Tsunoda, *Japan in the Dynastic Histories* (Pasadena: P. D. and Ione Perkins, 1951), p. 87.

[3]Literally, "stand for the lord." *Kimi no ondaji tachisōrawan.* 君の御大事に たち候はむ.

同五日關東の沸つゝむかうて此五節をとて　あひそうて此

左衛門二郎志けつる　拂曉かをせをうり志に季長ゆをむて

海上をあるきてをあひくそ孫ひとを雪御大事かを穫ぬと

杉ゆえんと申す　云々、ゝを御兵邸房絶て乃沸ふねふん海

ての人よりほろ六のあまよ杉うすをせを申て志り人

をりてせきをろさむとをる役

君の唐大事まきちんをむさまゆるまのゝゑを　云々拍

ともの……ひょふかの……孫よ此…

此二節ハ本編弘安
四年ノ條二在リ

134

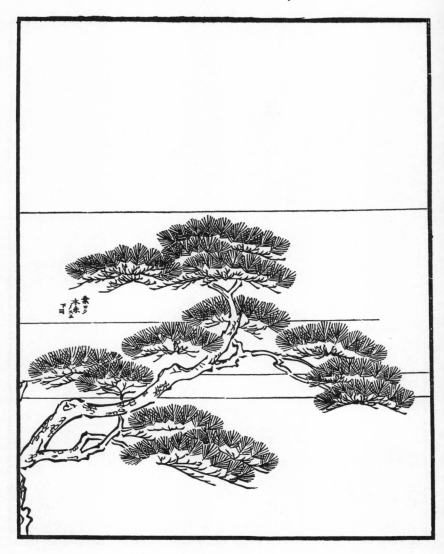

Suenaga boarded this boat at Ikinoshima. The others are Hida no Jirō Hidetada, Ono no Daishin Raijō, Yaigome no Gorō, and Miyahara Saburō. [They] set off for the sea battle of the shrine holdings (mikuriya 厨) at the hour of the cock on the fifth day of the seventh intercalary month, [and there] they fought.[1]

Hidetada had five relatives and retainers (wakatō) who boarded the pirates' ships and captured enemy heads (buntori), [but these deeds] were not recorded in documents of praise.

Received documents of praise.

Received documents of praise.

---

[1]For more on this encounter, see Documents 21–23, 40.

Raijō fought bravely in many battles, but because he was a retainer (hikan no kaku) of the Echizen lord, [his deeds] were not recorded in documents of praise.

くさの次郎
けねたつひやう
せん

The war boat (hyōsen 兵船) of Kusa no Jirō Tsunenaga.

142

あまくさの大や
けゝ十郎をねやす
日三郎たね村との
むやうせん

The war boat of Amakusa no Ōyano no Jūrō Taneyasu and Saburō Tanemura [of the same family].

Followers of the Kantō commander (ontsukai) Gōta no Gorō Tōtoshi riding in the war boat of Akitsuki no Kurō Tanemune, a gokenin from Chikuzen.

The war boat of the followers of Dazai Shōni Tsunesuke. [1]

[1]The *shugo* of Chikuzen province.

薩摩國守護下野守久親
同舎弟久長之手物兵舩

*The war boat of the followers of the shugo of Satsuma, Shimotsuke no kami
Hisachika, and his brother Hisanaga.*[1]

[1]Both members of the Shimazu family. As mentioned in the introduction,
some have construed this mention of Shimazu Hisanaga's name as proof that the
scrolls were created after 1316.

[11] [Text missing] "I was ordered to fight together with you. Send the boat over here." Straining to bring my boat nearby Takamasa's boat,[1] I took off my helmet. But there was no way for me to get on.

"I am acting on secret orders (*jintan* 甚深). Let me on the boat."

I brought my boat by Takamasa's.

"The *shugo* did not order you here. Get your boat out of here!"

Having no recourse, I replied: "As you know, I have not been called up by the *shugo*. I [am the deputy *shugo* but] arrived late. Heed my command."

"Lord Tsumori is on the boat. There is no more room," the crew of Takamasa's boat replied and started sailing away. Since there was nothing else I could do, I yelled:

"Since I am a warrior of considerable stature, let me alone get on your boat."

"We are heading off to battle. Why must you make such a fuss to Takamasa? Get on."

As they brought their boat nearby, I boarded. My retainers (*wakatō* 若党) saw this, and complained that I was abandoning them, but because of the nature of my request, only I Suenaga could embark but they could not. The way of the bow and arrow is to do what is worthy of reward. Without even a single follower I set off to engage the enemy. Since my retainers did not know that I had left my helmet behind, I picked up the shin guards that Morozane[2] had brought on the boat, tied them together and placed them on my head as a temporary helmet.

I told Takamasa: "I don't think that [the invaders] will fight with abandon, fearing not for their life, until we board their enemy ships. When we get close to their ships, take a "bear claw"[3] and capture them alive. They will prefer capture to death, for they want to return to their foreign lands (*ikoku* 異国). Once we have them hooked, stab them by impaling them where there is a joint in their armor (*kusazuri* 草摺)."

Takamasa replied: "Most of you are not prepared for battle. It seems like only Nonaka[4] wants to board the enemy ships."

I saw a nearby retainer (*wakatō* 若党) who had just taken off his helmet braided with yellow and white cords patterned with small cherry blossoms.

"Give me your helmet."

"I would like to gladly give you my helmet, but if I, without a helmet,

---

[1]The identity of Takamasa is unknown.

[2]One of Suenaga's retainers. See the depiction of this helmet in Scene 13.

[3]A grappling hook.

[4]Another of Suenaga's followers, a relative named Nonaka Tarō Nagasue. See Passage 13.

were to be killed because of you, Suenaga, then my wife and children would forever lament. Sorry, but I can't give it to you."

"Give it to me," I said again.

"I am sorry. I wrote an oath (*goseijō* 御誓状) that I signed, stating that only I or my lord (*nushi* 主) could wear this helmet."

Hearing this, I did not take the helmet. In order to lighten myself when I boarded the pirates' ships, I threw away some of my war arrows.

[12] At the dawn of the sixth, I arrived at Gōta Gorō's temporary lodging and explained in detail what had happened in battle.

"I knew this is what you would say," he said. "You haven't changed from [how you acted in] previous battles. Without your own boat, you repeatedly lied in order to join the fray. You are really the *baddest* man around (*dai mōaku no hito* 大猛悪の人)![1] I will notify our commanders about you. I also heard that Shikibu no bō will stand for you as a witness. If there are any further questions, have them contact me." And so Gōta Gorō also volunteered to stand as a witness for me.

---

[1]This term was clearly used as a compliment.

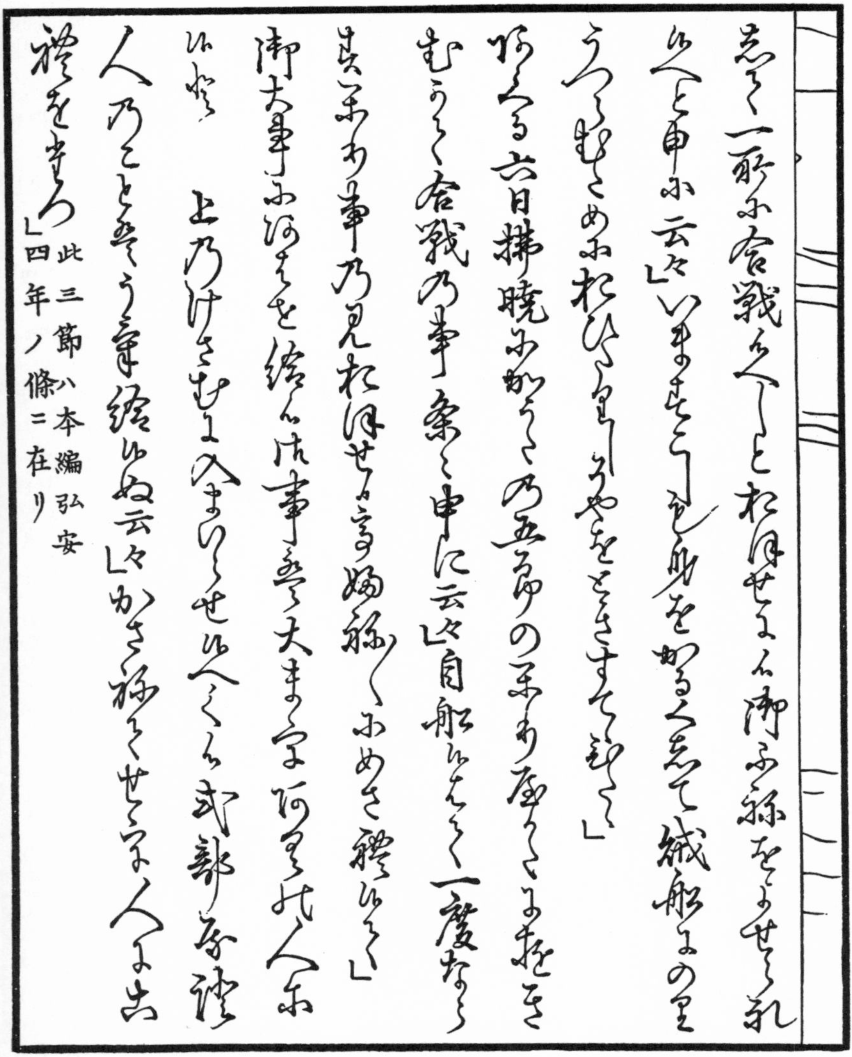

志く一形ふ合戦をくして松ほせよん御承弥をさすせられ

公と申ふ云々ゆまままそ一を死を切るくえて城船よの上

うくむさめお松ひくもり引やをををきすて初くく

松くる六日拂暁ふぬうその五百の手ち座くくよ在そ

むうくく合戦乃事案く申に云々自船くくく一度くく

其子あ事乃見れほせ言娟孫くふめさ禮ふくく

御大事ふ浅くを給ん几事ち大まま至阿ま此人ふ

にかくり 上乃けさむよ入まりくせよくくく武部序禮

人乃くとくう章絡むぬ云々くかき様くせくまく人よ出

此三節ハ本編弘安
四年ノ條ニ在リ

大
矢
野
兄
弟
三
人

種
保

The three Ōyano brothers. Shigemori.[1]

[1]The Ōyano eventually gained possession of Suenaga's scrolls.

Higo province. The first invaders taken.
Suenaga.[1]

---

[1]"Higo" is written in black ink, but all else is written in red. Notice (on the next page) how Suenaga's ersatz helmet, the shin guards mentioned in Passage 11, has just fallen off his head. Suenaga's name is no longer visible in the original.

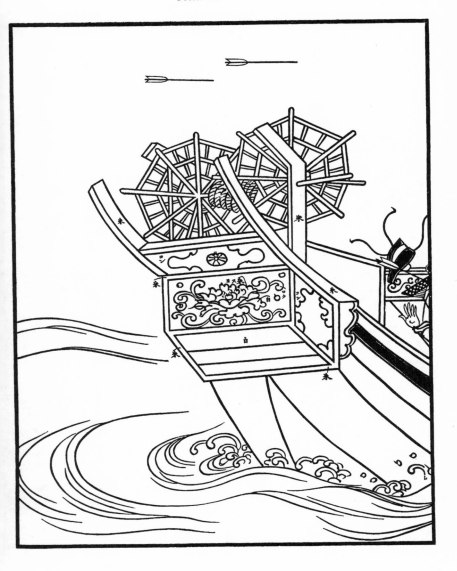

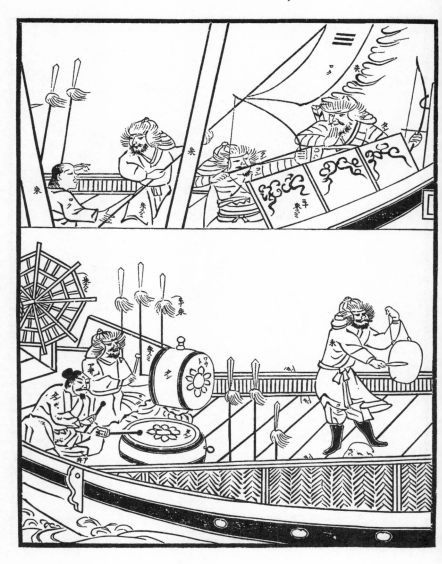

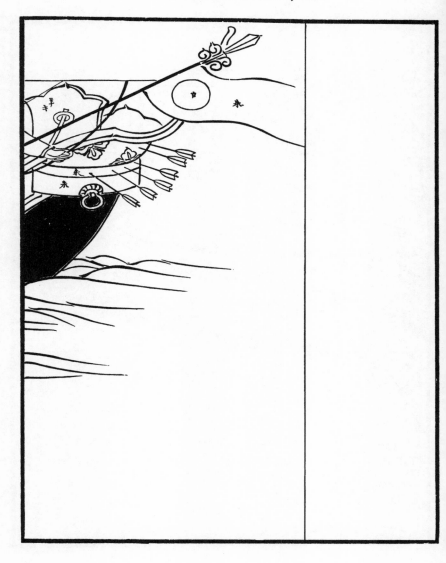

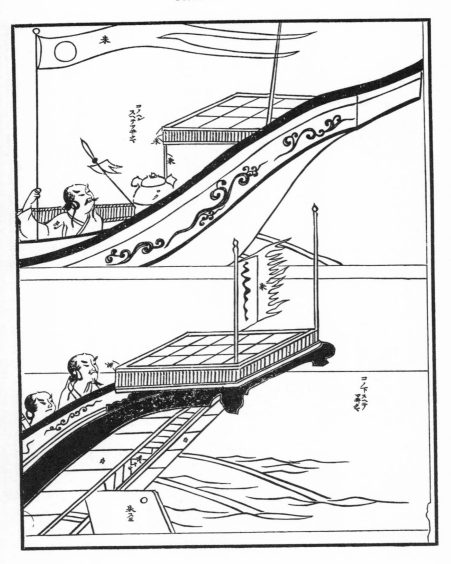

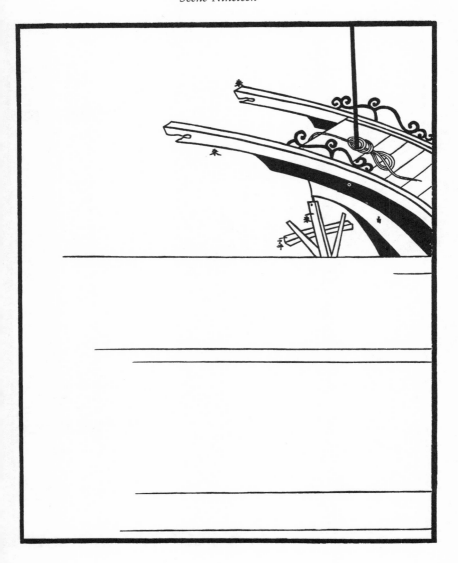

The Great God (Daimyōjin 大明神) of Shiga (志賀) Island.

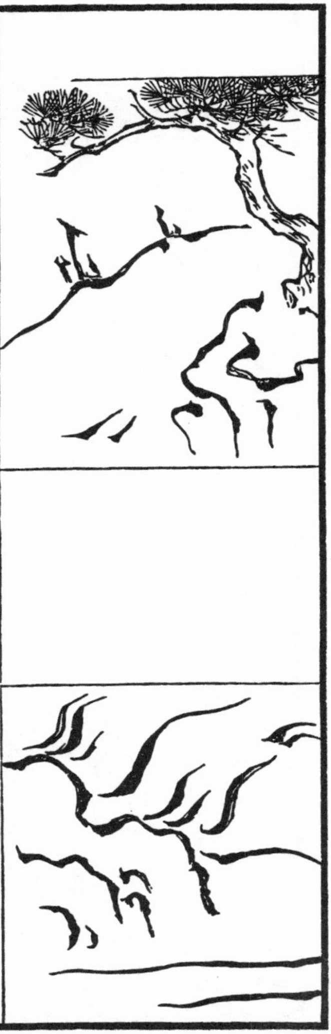

陣小をして合戦をいきを一ていまるきるんをかみりに云々

ちんさの足こるさるんか孫ふは此穏をきうゆ人ょら

彩彫てねひくみちゆ見をすてなきまく城れるゝこゝ

をくゝせ　云々土佐房道蔵うちゑ小の控人まは蔵宗

乃れての人まゝむゝの三郎蔵清をそそけさむよ

入くゝ同御ひきつけよ法くし一年ノ條二在リ

此二節八文永十

[13]   When I attacked the enemy and was wounded, a member of Hisanaga's forces,[1] Arisaka Iyajirō Yoshinaga, a *gokenin* of Shinano province, and Iwaya Shirō Hisachika, Hatakeyama Kaku Amidabu and Honda Shirō Saemon Kanefusa, who belonged to the forces of Hisanaga's nephew, Shikibu no Saburō, stood as witnesses for me. After Raijō had been wounded, I threw away my bow and picked up a *naginata*.[2] I tried to hurry my rowers by yelling "Get close! I want to board!" But when I said this the boatmen stopped using their oars and started pushing the boat back with their poles in order to flee. I had no choice but to switch boats again.

In the afternoon of the same day, I Suenaga and my men were wounded but survived and this was reported to the *shugo* at Ikinomatsubara.[3] We were the first from our province whose names were recorded in a report (*hikitsuke*). I joined the forces dispatched to Deer Island (*Shikanojima*)[4] and we fought a battle during the hour of the horse that day. My relative, Nonaka Tarō Nagasue, and my retainer, (*rōjū*) Tōgenda Sukemitsu, were wounded, and two of our horses were killed. A *gokenin* from Bungo, Hashizume Hyōgo Jirō, stood as a witness. Also, Morimune's man (*onte* 御手), Tamamura Saburō Morikiyo,[5] witnessed the death of Tosa no bō Dōkai. This was also recorded in the battle report (*onhikitsuke*).

---

[1]See the reference to Hisanaga in Scene 15.

[2]Ono no Daishin Raijō, a neighboring Higo warrior. See the introduction.

[3]The *shugo* refers to Adachi Morimune, the deputy *shugo* of Higo province. Adachi Yasumori was appointed the *shugo* of Higo from 1274 until 1281 but remained in Kamakura during the crisis. See *Zōtei Kamakura bakufu shugo seidō no kenkyū*, pp. 229–30. Ikinomatsubara also possessed considerable sacerdotal importance as well. See Document 64.

[4]Currently known as Shiga island.

[5]Presumably related to Yasumori's retainer Tamamura Uma no Tarō Yasukiyo.

The acting constable (shugonin)[1] of Higo province at this time, [Adachi] Jō no
Jirō Morimune.
Scribe
Suenaga's heads (buntori).

---

[1]This word *shugonin* apparently designates the acting *shugo*–often a deputy
shugo–when the official *shugo* was absent. See the reference to Morimune in
Passage 13.

Suenaga [of Higo][1]
Age thirty-six.

---

[1]Only the "Hi" of Higo province, written in red, is faintly legible in photographs of the original. See *Mōko shūrai ekotoba*, p. 115.

[14] Of Adachi Yasumori.

I speak of how I feel toward he . . . [who granted my rewards].[1] Well over one hundred [and twenty] men received praise but only I received an edict (*onkudashibumi*) and a horse. What could [exceed] my honor [as a man of the way] of the bow and arrow? [During the Bun'ei battles . . .].[2] How could I ever [repay] this? [You] shall be filial sons if [you] are always first in leading the charge during times of great importance for the lord.[3]

The first year of Einin [1293], ninth day, second month

[15] When I went to the Kantō, I had a dream (*gomusō* 御夢想) . . . [text missing]. On 5.23 [1275], the deity of the Kōsa shrine appeared, flew over the shrine, and settled in a cherry tree to the east. [I went to the] Kantō (関東) and thus received the lands of Kaitō (海東)–these are the same characters as those of the shrine where I worshiped . . . [text missing].[4] It was the . . . virtue of the deity that allowed Suenaga's honor [as a man] of the bow and arrow to flourish once I entered the Kaitō. This can be known, for I saw the deity in a cherry tree. Because of that, I received an edict (*onkudashibumi*) on the first day of the eleventh month of the same year, returned to Takezaki on the fourth day of the first month of the new year, and entered my Kaitō lands on the sixth day of the same month. Reflecting upon this, I knew that I had to praise the deity. Thus it is recorded.

The first year of Einin [1293], ninth day, second month

---

[1]As Passages 14 and 15 suffer from extensive damage, certain phrases remain cryptic. Likewise, Passage 14 may have originally appeared at the end of the first scroll.

[2]The text is missing, but has been drawn from the Kyūshū University copy of the text. See also Ishii, "Takezaki Suenaga ekotoba," p. 427.

[3]*Kimi no ondaiji aran toki wa saizen ni saki o kaku bekinari. Kore o kōnoko to subeshi* 君の御大事あらん時は、最前に先を懸くべきなり。これをけふのことすべし。 The last passage remains difficult to decipher, but presumably refers to "filial children" (*kōnoko* 孝の子).

[4]Suenaga believed that his receipt of the Kaitō lands was directly due to the intervention of the Kōsa deity for several reasons. The first is that the Kaitō district constituted Kōsa shrine lands. See *Mōko shūrai ekotoba*, p. 128, and Kuroda, *Nihon no rekishi 8*, pp. 184–85. Suenaga believed that the recurrence of the character "east" also proved divine intervention. The Kōsa deity appeared in a cherry tree to the east in his dreams; Suenaga traveled to the east to appeal his case; another word for Kamakura is the Kantō (関東) or "east of the barrier;" and finally, the lands that Suenaga received are known as Kaitō (海東), the "eastern ocean."

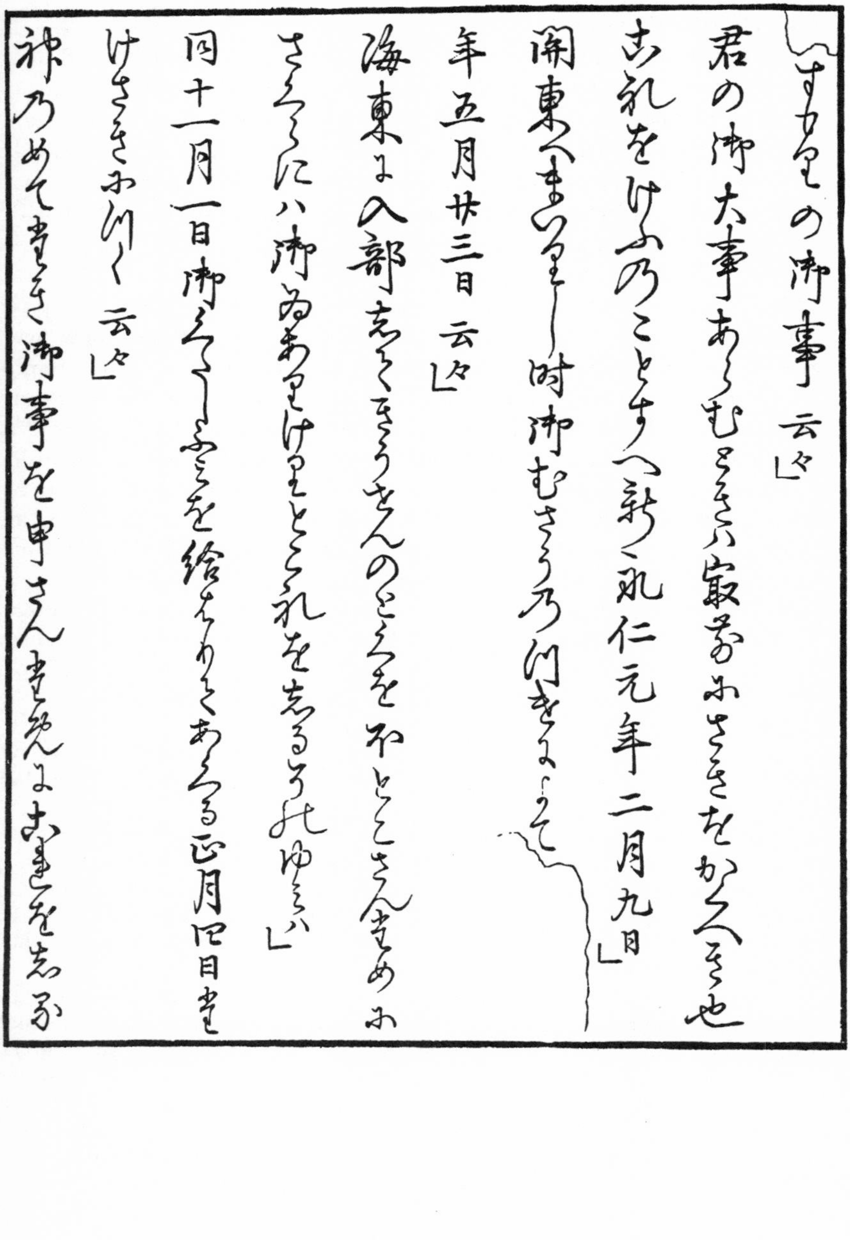

すかもの御事 云々

君の御大事あるむさゝふ寂寞ふさゝきをかくゑゝ也

これをけふのことよへ新く乱仁元年二月九日

関東へまゐらせ〳〵時御むさうの川をみて

年五月廿三日 云々

海東ハ部きくゑうをんのところを不とさん含めふ

さらに八御ゐあるをけふにとゝれを志るゝ此ゆくゝ八

同十一月一日御くゝふゝを給ゝりくあるゝる正月廿日き

けさきおり〳〵 云々

神乃めてきくゝ御事を申さんきゝえんよきゝを志る

ノ條ニ
在リ

一まのからゝそ永仁元年歳次癸巳二月九日∟此三節八本編建治元年

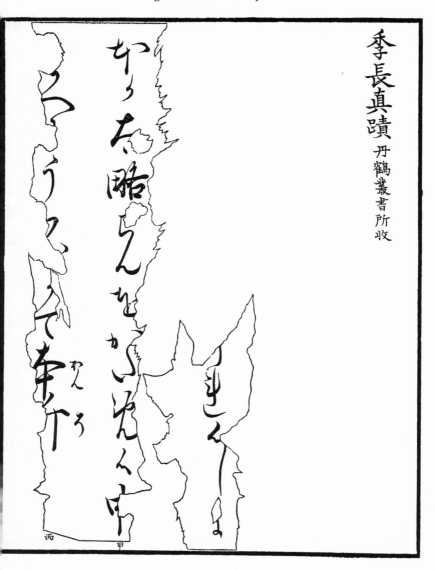

Poorly preserved textual fragments, possibly of Suenaga's hand.

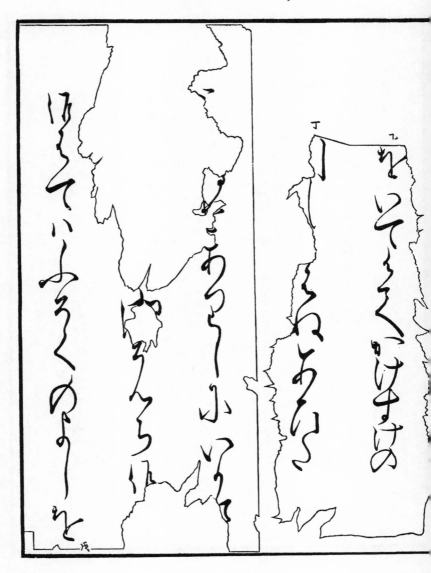

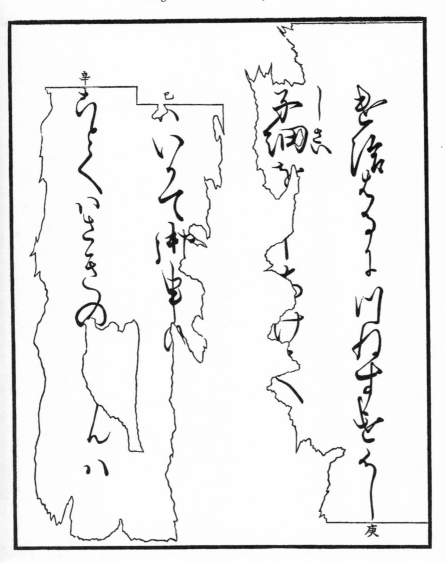

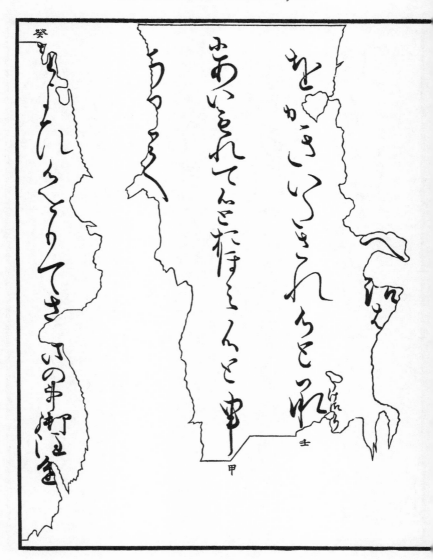

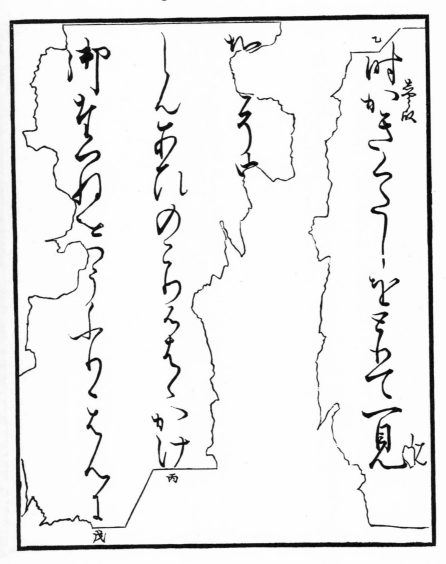

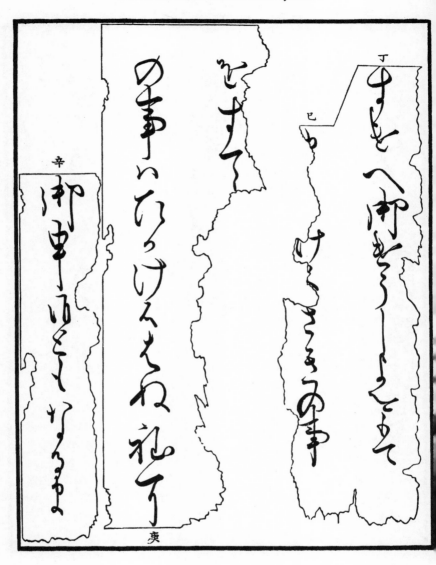

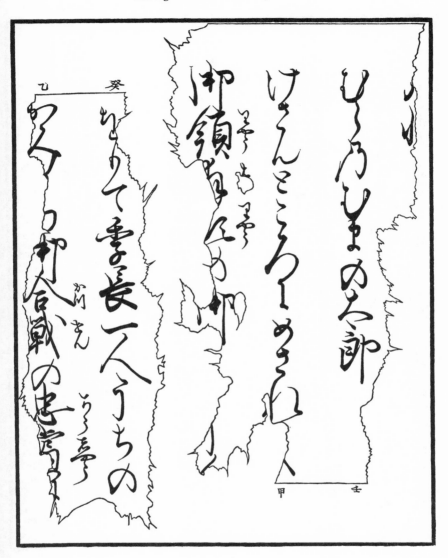

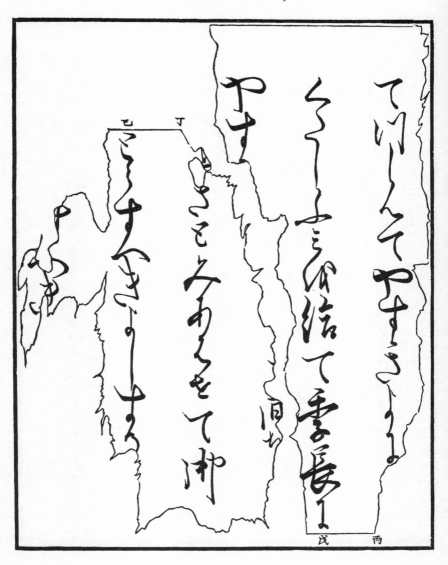

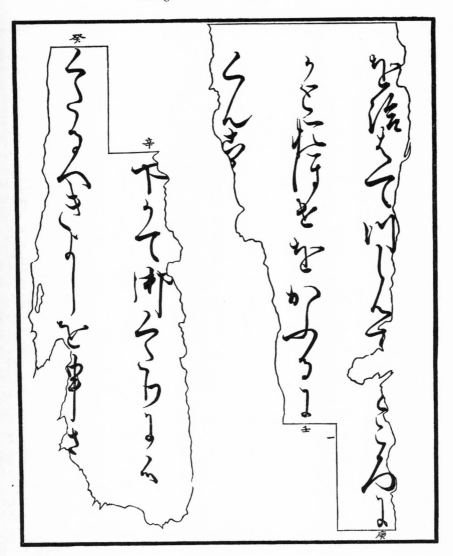

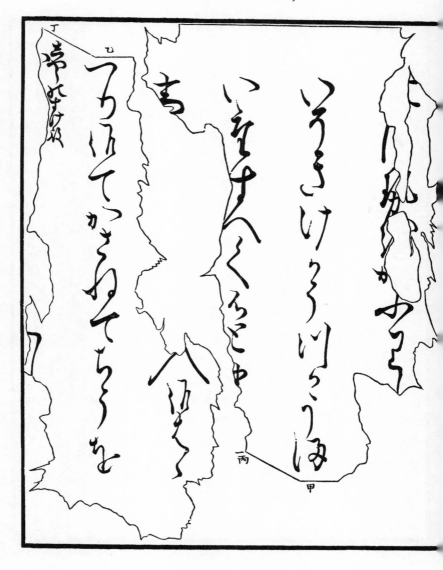

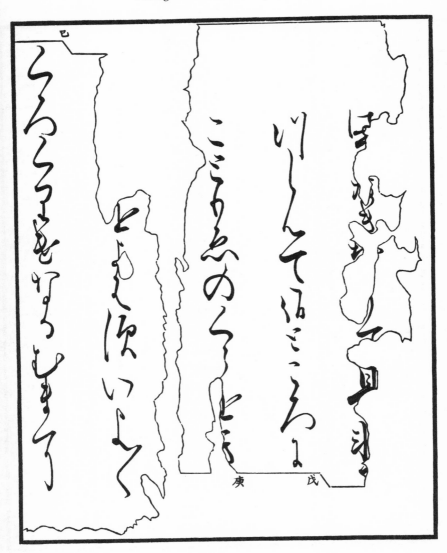

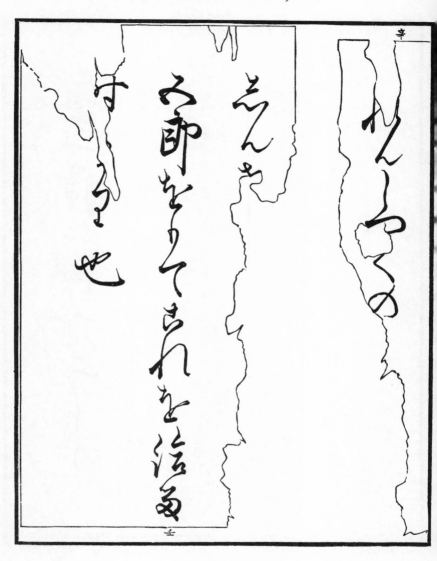

PART TWO

Records of the Invasions

A LETTER CONCERNING THE MONGOL THREAT

Document 1. *Excerpt of a letter written by the Zen priest Tōgen Eian in 1270.*[1]
*Tōgen Eian was well-aware of the international political situation. He also
believed in Japanese superiority and even composed a poem stating "Even if it is
the end of the world,[2] our country [Japan] is superior to all [the other] countries
[in the world]."[3] This letter shares this conceit.*

Because Japan's military skills (*Nihon koku no bugei* 日本国武芸) supersede
those of all other nations, our bows and arrows [are used with] peerless
skill, and our armor makes even the gods tremble . . . . the Mongols desire
to conquer Japan. Once Japan's warriors are under their control, they will
be able to conquer China (*Karado* 唐土) and India (*Tenjiku* 天竺). The
country of the Mongols would direct strategy while Japan would fight in
the field for their victory. With the strength [of Japan and the Mongols]
combined, no country could resist. That is why the Mongols now desire to
subjugate Japan.

---

[1]*Kamakura ibun*, vol. 14, doc. 10559, Tōgen Eian ikenjō. For more of Tōgen
Eian's documents, see also docs. 10557–58, Tōgen Eian ganmon; doc. 10630, Tōgen
Eian keihakumon; doc. 10880, 9.3.1271 (Bun'ei 8) Tōgen Eian ganmon; and vol. 15,
doc. 11267, 5.20.1273 (Bun'ei 10) Tōgen Eian ganmon utsushi. Tōgen was born in
Harima province and studied Tendai Buddhism before converting to Zen. After
spending time at Kenchōji, in Kamakura, he traveled to Kyōto, where he founded
Shōdenji. Tōgen studied under priests from the continent who resided in Japan and
became convinced that the Mongols were destined to fail in their invasion of
Japan. He died in 1277.

[2]*Mappō* 末法, the end of the Buddha's law.

[3]This poem appears in *Kamakura ibun*, vol. 14, doc. 10880, 9.3.1271 (Bun'ei
8) Tōgen Eian ganmon. For a summary of his life, his poems, and a picture of one
of his prayers, see Kuroda, *Nihon no rekishi 8*, pp. 66–67 and Yamaguchi Osamu,
Mōko shūrai–Genkō no shijitsu no kaimei (Kofusha sensho, 1988), pp. 88–89.

A MOBILIZATION ORDER ISSUED BY KAMAKURA

Document 2. *The following order was issued to gokenin with lands in Kyūshū. Each gokenin was commanded to travel there and report to the acting shugo in preparation for defense against the Mongols. This order was issued by the regent (shikken), Hōjō Tokimune, and his co-signer, Hōjō Masamura. Real power was wielded by Tokimune, heir to the main lineage of the Hōjō, the tokusō. Since the time of Tokimune's father, Tokiyori, lineage had become more important than institutional position. After Hōjō Tokiyori resigned as regent in 1246, he continued to dominate the bakufu for seventeen years, including his final seven years of "retirement," until his death in 1263. Hōjō Masamura had been appointed the renshō, or co-signer for the regent in 1256 and became regent himself after Tokiyori's death. Masamura remained, however, a caretaker until Tokimune was old enough to be appointed regent, in 1268. Masamura relinquished his post as shikken but remained the renshō until he died in 1273.[4]*

We have heard reports that the Mongols are to attack. Hence *gokenin* shall be dispatched to Chinzei [Kyūshū]. Immediately travel to your holdings in Higo province and follow the commands of the acting *shugo* (*shugonin*). Defend against the foreigners and protect your holdings from bandits (*akutō* 悪党). This order is so conveyed.

The eighth year of Bun'ei [1271], thirteenth day, ninth month

Sagami no kami (monogram)[5]
Sakyō Gon no Taifu (monogram)[6]

[To:] The sons of Koshiro Uemon no jō[7]

---

[4]*Kamakura ibun*, vol. 14, doc. 10873, 9.13.1271 (Bun'ei 8) Kantō migyōsho. See also a nearly identical directive, doc. 10874, 9.13.1271 (Bun'ei 8) Kantō migyōsho. According to the *Sonpi bunmyaku*, Masamura perished on 5.21.1273. See vol. 4, p. 20. For references to his death, and orders forbidding Kyūshū gokenin to travel to Kamakura and pay their respects, see *Kamakura ibun*, vol. 15, doc. 11332, intercalary 5.29.[1273] Kikuchi Takefusa shojō.

[5]Hōjō Tokimune.

[6]Hōjō Masamura.

[7]The Koshiro were originally *gokenin* from Musashi province, belonging to the Kodama band (*tō* 党), who were rewarded with lands in Higo as a result of their valor during the battles of 1247, when Hōjō Tokiyori destroyed the Miura. See Seno, *Chinzei gokenin no kenkyū*, p. 262.

Organizing Defenses

Document 3. *Kamakura had not yet devised a system of overall command against the Mongols. Ōtomo Yoriyasu, the shugo of Bungo and Chikugo provinces, was responsible for organizing and leading gokenin from his provinces into Chikuzen and Hizen, the strategic regions of Northern Kyūshū that were controlled by the Shōni.[8] Here, he has one of his deputies, the Bungo gokenin Nokami Sukenao, inquire of another of his representatives, Odawara Kageyasu, regarding the current dispositions of the Bungo (and Chikugo?) forces.[9]*

Hashiuragaki 端裏書: A circulated document (*kaibun* 廻文) from the *shugo*'s office concerning the important provinces of Chikuzen and Hizen. Arrived 2.16 Bun'ei 9 [1272].[10]

Concerning the defense of the strategic provinces of Chikuzen and Hizen: warriors from the east are already traveling [there]. According to an order recently received from the Kantō, *gokenin* [from each province of Kyūshū] must be organized and led [by their *shugo*], and perform guard duty by the final day of the coming third month. Some have [already] received [a report of] the location [where they should defend], while others have dispatched their representatives (*ondaikan* 御代官), [who] have already

---

[8]Shōni Sukeyoshi (Kakuei) was *shugo* of both Hizen and Chikuzen provinces, although he passed his posts to his son Tsunesuke sometime prior to 1276. Ōtomo Yoriyasu was also appointed as the *shugo* of Chikugo province from 1272 until 1277 as well.

[9]*Kamakura ibun*, vol. 14, doc. 10964, 2.1.[1272 (Bun'ei 9)] Bungo no shugo Ōtomo Yoriyasu kaibun.

[10]*Hashiuragaki* constitute summaries of a document, or related commentary, later written on the outside fold of these records by either the recipient or by archivists. As these statements sometimes provide important information, they have been translated. The circulated document, or *kaibun*, also known as a *kaimon* or a *mawashibumi*, was sent to two or more individuals. See "*kaibun*," in *Komonjo yōgo jiten*, comp. Arai Eiji et al. (Kashiwa shobō, 1983). In this case, the two officials involved are Yoriyasu's representatives in Bungo, Nokami Sukenao and Odawara Kageyasu. See *Hennen Ōtomo shiryō*, comp. Takita Manabu vol. 1 (Fuzanbo, 1942), p. 445, and *Chūkai, Genkō bōrui hennen shiryō–Ikokhen keigo banyaku shiryō no kenkyū*, comp. Kawazoe Shōji (Fukuoka: Fukuoka kyōiku iinkai, 1971), pp. 127–28. According to *Kamakura ibun*, vol. 20, doc. 15700, 10.16.1285 (Kōan 8) Bungo no kuni ōtabumi an, p. 370, the *gokenin* Nokami Tarō Sukenao shared rights with Uda Fujita Shirō Moriaki, holy name Dōen, to 11 *chō* 6 *tan* of Nokami village, in Bungo province.

crossed [the provincial] boundary [into Chikuzen and Hizen]. Immediately inquire to the person [in charge of these forces].[11] [You] shall serve and not be remiss. Respectfully.

(The ninth year of Bun'ei [1272]), first day (*sakujitsu* 朔日), second month

[Ōtomo] Yoriyasu (monogram)[12]

[To:] Nokami Tarō dono[13]

DOCUMENTS 4–6. RESPONDING TO THE FIRST BATTLES

Document 4. *Ōtomo Yoriyasu received the following Kamakura bakufu edict, which was issued by Hōjō Tokimune and co-signed by Hōjō Yoshimasa.[14] Yoshimasa had been appointed to this post on 6.7.1273, after Hōjō Masamura's death, and remained co-signer until he took Buddhist vows in 4.1277. The co-signer post remained vacant until 1283, while Yoshimasa died in 1281. One can infer from this order that the bakufu desired to increase the size of the armies that it mobilized, and tried to rectify this situation by promising even non-gokenin rewards for their military service.*

Written during the time of the Chinzei kanrei.[15]

As the Mongols have attacked Tsushima and Iki Islands, forces are being dispatched. Even non-*gokenin* residents (*jūninra* 住人等) of Kyūshū will be rewarded if they perform military service. Let this be known. This order is so conveyed.

The eleventh year of Bun'ei [1274], first day, eleventh month

---

[11]According to Kawazoe, this document refers to Odawara Kageyasu, another of Yoriyasu's representatives. The document as it appears in *Kamakura ibun* suffers from an error in transcription, and substitutes the charcter of "place" for "person," but the versions printed in the compilations of Kawazoe and Takita Manabu (see note 10) are correct.

[12]Ōtomo Yoriyasu.

[13]Nokami Sukenao.

[14]*Kamakura ibun*, vol. 15, doc. 11742, 11.1.1274 (Bun'ei 11) Kantō migyōsho an. This document is a later copy of the original. Hereafter copies of the original monogram will be referred to as *arihan*, which merely means that a monogram existed, but no attempt was made to copy it.

[15]This passage was added by a later copyist in order to identify the document and should not be confused with the original text.

Musashi no kami (copy of monogram)[16]
Sagami no kami (arihan)[17]

[To:] Ōtomo Hyōgo no kami nyūdō dono[18]

Document 5. *Kamakura feared that the Mongols would sweep through Japan upon landing in Kyūshū and ordered absentee shugo to travel to their appointed provinces and take command of local gokenin. Although the Takeda had been invested with the post of shugo of Aki province since the 1240s, it was not until the crisis of 1274 that Takeda Nobutoki was ordered to personally travel to Aki and organize those gokenin residing in his province. From this time until 1293, when the Hōjō became shugo of Aki, Kamakura relied upon the Takeda to remain there and assume control of its warriors.*[19]

Hashiuragaki: Copy of a Kamakura order (*buke ongechijō an*) concerning Mongol guard duty.

According to a report (*chūshin* 注進) by [Shōni] Kakuei, the Mongols have attacked Tsushima and Iki Islands and already battle [is being] waged. Quickly depart for Aki [province] prior to the twentieth day of this month. If the invaders attack, mobilize the *jitō gokenin* and those residents (*jūnin* 住人) who possess full administrative authority over their lands throughout the province and offer resistance. There must be no further negligence. This order is so conveyed.

The eleventh year of Bun'ei [1274], first day, eleventh month

Musashi no kami (arihan)[20]
Sagami no kami (arihan)[21]

[To:] Takeda Gorōjirō dono[22]

[16]Hōjō Yoshimasa.
[17]Hōjō Tokimune.
[18]Yoriyasu.
[19]*Kamakura ibun*, vol. 15, doc. 11741, 11.1.1274 (Bun'ei 11) Kantō migyōsho an. Not all *shugo* resided in the provinces. Suenaga's narrative reveals that the *shugo* of Nagato, Nikaidō Takauji, remained in Kamakura throughout 1275.
[20]Hōjō Yoshimasa.
[21]Hōjō Tokimune.
[22]Takeda Nobutoki.

Document 6. *Compare this order, issued to a gokenin, to Document 5, which was issued to the shugo of Aki province. Kamakura expressly ordered these men to fight under their shugo's command, which suggests that military service under such constables was not automatic.*[23]

According to a report by [Shōni] Kakuei, the Mongols have attacked Tsushima and Iki Islands and already battle [is being] waged. *Gokenin* are being dispatched [to western Japan]. Quickly depart for your Iwami [province] holdings prior to the twentieth day of this month. If the invaders attack [Iwami], you shall follow the mobilization [orders] of the acting *shugo* (*shugonin*) and offer resistance. There must be no further negligence. This order is so conveyed.

The eleventh year of Bun'ei [1274], first day, eleventh month

Musashi no kami (monogram)[24]   Sagami no kami (monogram)[25]

RECEIPTS OF GUARD DUTY

Document 7. *Ōtomo Yoriyasu, the eastern Chinzei commissioner and shugo of Bungo province, verified the battle service of Togō Gorō Korechika, who apparently fought at the same area in 1274 that Suenaga mentions in Passage 4 of his scrolls.*[26] *These documents, known as "receipts," or fukukanjō (覆勘状), were originally given to gokenin as proof of their service on guard duty. In this case, however, a receipt was issued by the shugo to Togō Gorō, a gokenin under his command, as proof of battle service against the Mongols. This document represents an important precurser to documents of praise (kanjō 感状), which were presented by commanders to their troops from 1333 onward. In contrast to later commanders, however, thirteenth-century shugo only had the authority to issue reports to Kamakura and could not personally bestow rewards.*

Orikaeshi hashiuragaki: A document concerning the Mongol battles from the Eastern *shugosho* (守護所).[27]

---

[23]*Kamakura ibun*, vol. 15, doc. 11743, 11.1.1274 (Bun'ei 11) Kantō migyōsho. See also doc. 11744, 11.3.1274 (Bun'ei 11) Kantō migyōsho an.

[24]Hōjō Yoshimasa.

[25]Hōjō Tokimune.

[26]*Kamakura ibun*, vol. 15, doc. 11771, 12.7.[1274 (Bun'ei 11)] Ōtomo Yoriyasu fukukanjō utsushi. This particular document is a copy (*utsushi* 写) dating from 1702.

[27]This passage was written on the back fold of the document when it was

[A report] concerning your [battle] service (*chūsetsu* 忠節) against the Mongols at the Torikai beach encampment in Chikuzen province has already been dispatched to the Kantō. This is so conveyed.

(The eleventh year of Bun'ei [1274]), seventh day, twelfth month

[Ōtomo] Yoriyasu

[To:] Togō Saemon Gorō dono

DOCUMENTS 8–11. EARLY ATTEMPTS TO VERIFY BATTLE SERVICE

Kamakura struggled to formalize a means of verifying military service in the aftermath of the first invasions. Gokenin dispatched various written records pertaining to their service to Kamakura, but some of these documents were deemed unacceptable by the bakufu.

Document 8. *Kamakura became aware that not all gokenin fought as valiantly as Suenaga or Togō Gorō Korechika of Document 7. Shortly after the 1274 conflict, Hōjō Tokimune and Yoshimasa had this document dispatched to Ōtomo Yoriyasu, which demanded that the names of those who did not perform military service be recorded.* [28]

It has come to our attention that in the previous year, when foreign pirates attacked, a great number of men faced the battlefield but did not attack; or claiming to guard [provincial] boundaries, they did not advance. This most certainly invites punishment for poor service (*fuchū no toga* 不忠之科). From now on, those who do not perform service (*chūsetsu* 忠節) shall be duly noted and punished. This purport shall be announced to the *gokenin*. This order is so conveyed.

The first year of Kenji [1275], seventeenth day, seventh month

Musashi no kami (arihan)[29]   Sagami no kami (arihan)[30]

---

copied. Ōtomo Yoriyasu was the eastern *shugo*, or official in the Chinzei commission (*bugyō* 奉行), while the western *shugo* was Shōni Kakuei. See *Chūkai, Genkō bōrui hennen shiryō*, p. 145. This designation continued until 1284. The Chinzei *bugyō* was replaced by the Chinzei *tandai* on 3.7.1293. See Documents 37–40.

[28]*Kamakura ibun*, vol. 16, doc. 11962, 7.17.1275 (Kenji 1) Kantō migyōsho an.

[29]Hōjō Yoshimasa.

[To:] Ōtomo Hyōgo no kami nyūdo dono[31]

Document 9. *A summons written by Odawara Kageyasu, a retainer of Ōtomo Yoriyasu (the "eastern Chinzei commissioner" and shugo of Bungo province), requesting that three warriors report to Yoriyasu so that he could question them, write a report, and forward it to Kamakura. Such an investigation was required to satify the bakufu's lingering doubts about their military service.*[32]

There has been a further inquiry [from the *bakufu*] regarding the particular [nature of] battle service (勲功) [by those men listed below, who fought against] the Mongols. [In order for the *shugo* Ōtomo Yoriyasu to create] a report (*onchūshin* 御注進) [for Kamakura], you shall dispatch a representative (*ondaikan* 代官) [for further questioning] prior to the tenth of this month. By [Yoriyasu's] authority (*onsata* 御沙汰). Respectfully.

(The first year of Kenji [1275]), sixth day, eleventh month

[Odawara] Kageyasu (monogram)

[To:] Matama Matajirō
Imi Hyōe Jirō dono
Togō Saemon Gorō dono[33]

Document 10. *Kamakura did not accept a "receipt," or fukukanjō, as adequate proof of military service. Instead, the bakufu required a detailed narrative of one's military valor, which led to the development of a new type of document, the petition for military reward, or gunchūjō (軍忠状). Here, Ōtomo Yoriyasu, the shugo of Bungo and Eastern Chinzei Commissioner, requested that Togō Saemon Gorō submit a precise record of his deeds instead of relying merely on the shugo's receipt of his actions (Document 7).*[34] *Takezaki Suenaga also attempted to rely upon a similar document (kakikudashi 書下) to "prove" his military service to Kamakura officials, but met with little success.*[35]

---

[30]Hōjō Tokimune.

[31]Ōtomo Yoriyasu.

[32]*Kamakura ibun*, vol. 16, doc. 12107, 11.6.[1275 (Kenji 1)] Chinzei higashi kata bugyō meshibumi.

[33]Togō Korechika.

[34]*Kamakura ibun*, vol. 16, doc. 12130, 11.23.[1275 (Kenji 1)] Ōtomo Yoriyasu kakikudashi.

[35]See Suenaga's audience with Adachi Yasumori in Passage 7 of the first scroll.

Concerning battles against the Mongols. Last year, most [of your] reports were forwarded [to Kamakura]. Nevertheless, you must immediately record [and dispatch] a detailed account of your [military] service (*gohōkō no shidai* 御奉公之次第). This is so conveyed.

(The first year of Kenji [1275]), twenty-third day, eleventh month

Ōtomo Yoriyasu (monogram)

Arrived the seventh day, twelfth month of the same year[36]

[To:] Togō Saemon Gorō dono[37]

Orikaeshi hashigaki A document written by the administrative board of the Eastern Commissioners [to the] Togō (*higashikata bugyosho kakikudashi* 東方奉行所書下　とこを)[38]

Document 11. *Togō Saemon Gorō proved unwilling or unable to provide a written record of his military service, as was requested in Document 10. Nor did Gorō respond to the summons issued by Ōtomo Yoriyasu's representative, Odawara Yoriyasu (Document 9). Here, Ōtomo Yoriyasu personally summoned Togō Saemon Gorō to dispatch a representative, who could be questioned about his battle deeds.*[39]

Concerning battles against the Mongols. In order to continue with [my] investigation (*tazunesata gatame ni* 為尋沙汰), immediately dispatch a representative [for questioning]. Respectfully.

The third year of Kenji [1277], fifteenth day, sixth month
arrived the twenty-second day[40]

[Ōtomo] Yoriyasu (monogram)

---

[36]This passage was written after Togō Korechika received the document from Ōtomo Yoriyasu and should not be confused with the original text.

[37]Togō Korechika.

[38]This passage was written on the right side of the folded document and should not be confused with the original.

[39]*Kamakura ibun*, vol. 17, doc. 12752, 6.15.1277 (Kenji 3) Chinzei higashi kata bugyōsho Ōtomo Yoriyasu meshibumi.

[40]This passage was written after the Togō received this document.

[To:] Togō Saemon Gorō dono

Orikaeshi hashigaki A summons (*meshibumi* 召文)   from the administrative board of the Eastern Commissioners.[41]

DOCUMENTS 12–13. A FAILED ATTEMPT TO ACHIEVE AUTONOMY

Document 12. *A duplicate copy (an* 案*) of the petition (mōshijō* 申状*) that the priest Zenki dispatched to Ōtomo Yoriyasu.*[42] *This document reveals that a warrior could conceive of both a clan-wide chieftain and a familial chieftain existing at the same time. Shiga Zenki desired to fight directly under the command of his distant relative and "chieftain" (sōryō* 惣領*) of all the Ōtomo, Yoriyasu, and not with his family chieftain, Shiga Yasutomo. Furthermore, from this document, one can infer that warriors would not receive recognition for battle service if forced to serve under their familial sōryō. Zenki did not mind serving under Yasutomo for most of the time, but he desired to at least have the opportunity to receive public recognition from Ōtomo Yoriyasu for his service against the Mongols. Shiga Zenki based his claim of independence upon one edict that he had received from Yoriyasu, issued before they had been blocked by Shiga Yasutomo. Zenki never received further recognition or rewards and ultimately was reduced to pawning some of his own holdings. Shortly before his death, Zenki conveyed his lands to one of Yasutomo's sons, whom he had adopted as his heir.*

Hashiuragaki: The defense statement of Shiga *ashari* (阿闍梨) concerning public duties.

The priest Zenki, holder of the Chikaji (近地) *myō jitō shiki* (名地頭職) [located] within half of Shiga village–to the south–in Ōno estate respectfully states:
Please forbid mobilization orders (*saisoku* 催促) from Shiga Tarō Yasutomo, the chieftain (*sōryō* 惣領) of half of [Shiga] village, and instead allow [Zenki] to be mobilized directly by the chieftain (*sōryō* 惣領) [of all Ōtomo relatives, and] *shugo* [Ōtomo Yoriyasu], and to serve under him concerning preparations [for defense against] foreigners.[43]

---

[41]This passage constitutes a later commentary and should not be confused with the original.

[42]*Kamakura ibun*, vol. 16, doc. 12303, intercalary 3.15.1276 (Kenji 2) Sō Zenki moshijō an. For contrary examples, see Documents 53–55.

[43]Preparations against foreigners may in fact refer to the invasion of Korea, preparations which began during the previous month. See *Kamakura ibun*, vol. 16,

Appended: One edict (*ongechijō* 御下知) from the *shugo*.

The above mentioned *myō jitō shiki* was granted [to Zenki] according to the wishes of [his grandmother], the Zen nun Kasahaya (風早), who divided the [Shiga] half of the village and [granted] Zenki [his] hereditary lands.[44] [Zenki] does not dispute that he is to serve under Yasutomo's command while performing guard duty (*ōbanyaku* 大番役), [sending the proper] ratio [of troops based on his] paddy [lands].[45] But for the additional [service of] defense against the foreign [invaders], Zenki desires to personally receive mobilization orders from the chieftain (*sōryō* 惣領) [of all the Ōtomo who is also the] *shugo*.[46] Even though it is impossible to know whether the [fortunes of war entail military] valor [or] failure,[47] if [Zenki] performs some suitable (*bungen* 分限) great deed (*taikō* 大功), [he wishes to] either receive a Kantō battle report (*onchūshin*), or to have his name clearly recorded in a document (*onhikitsuke*). Nevertheless, Zenki's Kyōto legacy[48] joined [the forces of your] weak representative (*daikan*), Yasutomo.[49] [Yasutomo] dispatched a letter of interference[50] and requested that the

---

doc. 12271, and Documents 17–18 herein.

[44]The Zen nun Kasafusa Shinmyō was the wife of Ōtomo Yoshinao. She was the mother of five of Yoshinao's twelve sons. One of these sons, Yoshiaki (能郷), founded the Shiga family, whose genealogy can be found in *Bungo no kuni Ōno no shō shiryō*, comp. Watanabe Sumio (Yoshikawa kōbunkan, 1979), pp. 205–7. Shinmyō explicitly provided for both of her Shiga grandsons in her testaments. See *Kamakura ibun*, vol. 12, doc. 8851, 8.6.1262 (Kōchō 2) Ami Shinmyō yuzurijō, and doc. 8969, 7.2.1263 (Kōchō 3) Shiga Yasutomo Shinmyō rensho yuzurijō an. Although she divided Shiga village between the two brothers, she only granted one unit of *myō* paddies to Shiga Zenki. A provincial register of land holdings in Bungo province dating from 1285 reveals that Yasutomo possessed 33.12 *chō* of land to Zenki's 3.3. See *Kamakura ibun*, vol. 20, doc. 15700, 10.16.1285 (Kōan 8) Bungo no kuni ōtabumi an, p. 367, and *Bungo*, pp. 241–52. While ensuring that Zenki would have complete control over his own lands, she explicitly stated that Zenki's brother, Yasutomo, shall have authority (*sata* 沙汰) over him as family chieftain (*sōryō* 惣領).

[45]This passage cannot be deciphered in Zenki's petition, but becomes clear when compared with Kasafusa's testament. See *Kamakura ibun*, vol. 12, doc. 8969, 7.2.1263 (Kōchō 3) Shiga Yasutomo Shinmyō rensho yuzurijō an.

[46]Ōtomo Yoriyasu.

[47]Literally, the "process of [military] service or loss."

[48]The meaning is not clear. Perhaps Zenki's Kyōto legacy refers to a Kyōto dalliance that resulted in a son?

[49]Fighting words by Zenki. Yasutomo took umbrage at being called "weak." See his rebuttal of two months later. *Kamakura ibun*, vol. 16, doc. 12332, 4.1276 (Kenji 2) Shiga Yasutomo chinjō an

[50]*Kossakujō* 乞索状, which is defined in the *Sata mirensho* as "a letter in which somebody writes in order to interfere after he has seen another man's

chieftain (sōryō) [of all of the Ōtomo, and] shugo stop dispatching separate mobilization orders [to Zenki].[51] Zenki knew absolutely nothing [about Yasutomo's actions]. In order to receive the mobilization [orders] of the chieftain [and] shugo, [Yoriyasu], and to perform outstanding service concerning preparations [for defense against] foreigners, respectfully stated thus.[52]

The second year of Kenji [1276], fifteenth day, intercalary third month

The priest Zenki (arihan)

Document 13. *Zenki appended the following document to his petition, sent to him by Ōtomo Yoriyasu, which engendered his dreams of autonomy and his brother Yasutomo's ire. As should be clear, this document merely affirms that Zenki is to serve under his brother.*[53]

Hashiuragaki: This is a copy of Ōtomo dono's order (*ongechi*).

---

letter" (*Kossakujō wa tanin no jō o shoken ari, gojitsu kamae-idasu jō nari*). For a convenient translation, see Carl Steenstrup, "*Sata mirensho*: A Fourteenth-Century Law Primer," *Monumenta Nipponica* 35 (1980): 432.

[51]Again, the shugo mentioned here is Ōtomo Yoriyasu.

[52]Although Zenki resisted serving under Yasutomo for guard duty (see *Kamakura ibun*, vol. 16, doc. 12332, 4.1276 (Kenji 2) Shiga Yasutomo chinjō an), he was apparently unsuccessful in receiving any recognition for his battle service. By contrast, Shiga Yasutomo received rewards for valor against the Mongols. See *Kamakura ibun*, vol. 27, docs. 20929–30, Ahō (Shiga Yasutomo) yuzurijō an. Zenki fell on hard times. Although he had been designated as the head priest of Tomaridera by Shinmyō in 1265 (see *Kamakura ibun*, vol. 12, doc. 9245, 3.23.1265 (Bun'ei 2) Ami Shinmyō kudashibumi), he was forced to sell this position to a nun for 450 *kanmon* (貫文) of cash in 1283. These lands were ultimately restored to him after Kamakura's debt relief (*tokusei* 徳政) of 1297, but soon thereafter Zenki granted them to Yasutomo. See *Kamakura ibun*, vol. 26, doc. 19426, 8.5 1297 (Einin 5) Zenki yuzurijō, and vol. 27, doc. 20411, 3.25.1300 (Shōan 2) Ōtomo Sadachika saikyojō. Zenki also pawned his documents to Hiyoshi shrine for 42 *kanmon* of cash and borrowed 10 *kanmon* for his adopted son's coming-of-age ceremony. See *Kamakura ibun*, vol. 27, doc. 20959, 1.16.1302 (Shōan 4) Bō keijō an. Ironically, this adopted son was none other than one of Yasutomo's progeny, Tomoaki (Enjō). Zenki had promised to convey his lands to one of Yasutomo's sons as early as 1271. See *Kamakura ibun*, vol. 14, doc. 10795, 3.5.1271 (Bun'ei 8) Sō Zenki keiyakujō, and finally vol. 29, doc. 22648, 5.20.1306 (Kagen 4) Tora-ō-maru (Shiga Tomoaki) keijō, and *Nanbokuchō ibun Kyūshū hen*, vol. 2, docs. 2303–4, 2.9.1347 (Jōwa 3) Shiga Enjō yuzurijō an, for proof of Enjō's succession.

[53]*Kamakura ibun*, vol. 16, doc. 11883, 5.12.[1275 (Bun'ei 12)] Ōtomo Yoriyasu kakikudashi an.

In order to be prepared against the Mongols, it has been reported [that you] shall serve with Shiga Tarō [Yasutomo], the holder of all the *myō* lands (*sōmyō* 惣名) [of the southern half of Shiga village]. This purport shall be known. This is so conveyed.

(The twelfth year of Bun'ei [1275]), twelfth day, fifth month

The former Dewa no kami (arihan)[54]

Jurisdictional Disputes on the Eve of the Second Invasion

Document 14. *Kamakura possessed accurate intelligence regarding the second Mongol invasion, and attempted to quell both familial rivalries and jurisdictional disputes during this time of national emergency. This document, dispatched from Hōjō Tokimune to Ōtomo Yoriyasu, admonished gokenin who disobeyed their shugo.*[55]

Concerning the guarding of Chinzei, it has been reported that the Mongol foreign pirates will attack during the fourth month of the next year. Quickly report to [*shugo*] headquarters (*yakusho* 役所) and be highly prepared. In recent years, reports have been heard that *shugo* and *gokenin* are in considerable discord over administration (*shomu no sōron* 所務之相論) and jurisdiction in criminal matters (*kendan no sata* 検断之沙汰), and are not prepared [to defend Chinzei]. It is the height of disservice (*fuchū* 不忠) [for such warriors] not to reflect on the great crisis [that confronts] the realm,[56] [but instead are only] concerned with their own petty disputes. *Gokenin* and lower-ranking warriors (*gunpyō* 軍兵) shall follow the orders of the *shugo* and perform the service (*chū*) of defensive battle. [They] also shall not pick favorites [among] the acting *shugo* (*shugonin*).[57] The service, or lack thereof [of *gokenin* and lower-ranking warriors] shall be reported. [Suitable] rewards and punishments will be duly meted out. Those who disobey this order shall be severely punished for disservice (*fuchū*). This purport shall be announced throughout the province. This order is so conveyed.

The third year of Kōan [1280], eighth day, twelfth month

---

[54]Ōtomo Yoriyasu.

[55]*Kamakura ibun*, vol. 19, doc. 14207, 12.8.1280 (Kōan 3) Kantō migyōsho.

[56]*Tenka tainan o kaerimirezaru no jō* 不顧天下大難之状.

[57]The passage literally states "shall not also discuss *shugonin* who are favored and shunned."

Sagami no kami (arihan)[58]

[To:] Ōtomo Hyōgo no kami nyūdō dono[59]

Documents 15–19.
Guard Duty and the Aborted Invasion of Korea

Document 15. *This document, issued by Shōni Tsunesuke (1225–89), constitutes the oldest surviving record that he issued as the head of the Dazaifu and as shugo of Chikuzen, Buzen, and Hizen provinces. Tsunesuke would, however, be divested of some of his shugo posts as the bakufu assumed increasing responsibility for the governance of the provinces of Kyūshū (Documents 27–29). This document was probably addressed to the Shimazu Hisatsune, who held the shugo office of Satsuma province, and reveals that Kyūshū gokenin were mobilized throughout the year and served on guard duty on a rotating basis.*[60]

Concerning guard duty against the Mongols, [my] messenger Minbu Jirō Hyōe no jō Kunishige shall contact you. Please announce widely what you hear [from him]. Respectfully.

Fourth day, second month

Dazai Shōni Tsunesuke (arihan)

Submitted to: Takei Matatarō dono

Guard duty against the Mongols:
The three months of spring: Chikuzen and Higo provinces.
The three months of summer: Hizen and Buzen provinces.
The three months of autumn: Bungo and Chikugo provinces.
The three months of winter: Hyūga, Ōsumi, and Satsuma provinces.

The twelfth year of Bun'ei [1275], second month

Document 16. *Kamakura's defenders were not overawed by the initial Mongol attack, for they soon prepared for an invasion of Korea.*[61] *Ōtomo Yoriyasu dispatched*

---

[58]Hōjō Tokimune.
[59]Ōtomo Yoriyasu.
[60]*Kamakura ibun*, vol. 15, doc. 11805, 2.1275 (Bun'ei 12) Shōni Tsunesuke shojō an.
[61]Although this document does not appear in *Kamakura ibun*, Kamakura

the following document to his representative, the Bungo gokenin Nokami Sukenao. Each gokenin was responsible for overseeing the mobilization of troops and sailors from within his domains for the Korean invasion and for reporting the composition of these forces to the shugo.[62]

Preparations for the advance into foreign countries:

— Submit a list of large and small boats within your holdings and the names and ages of sailors and oarsmen. You shall make preparations to dispatch these men to Hakata by the middle of next month.

— When crossing into foreign lands, record the names and ages of upper and lower [class] men, their arms, and their armor (*heigu* 兵具).

The preparations mentioned above should be completed prior to the twentieth day of this month and a report dispatched [to Yoriyasu]. You have the authority to severely punish those who flee. This is so conveyed.

The second year of Kenji [1276], fifth day, third month

The former Dewa no kami (monogram)[63]

[To:] Nokami Tarō dono[64]

Documents 17 and 18. *The following documents reveal the resources that were available to a gokenin of comparable stature to Takezaki Suenaga. Here, Jōyū, the manager (azukari dokoro 預所) of Kubota estate in Higo province, has recorded the men, equipment, and horses that he could muster for the Korean invasions. He created this list in response to a request by Adachi Morimune, the brother of Adachi Yasumori, and deputy shugo of Higo since 1274. The defensive tone of Jōyū's reply suggests that a response was expected prior to the tenth day of the third month of 1276.*[65]

apparently first issued an order to subjugate Korea on 10.2.1275 (Kenji 1). See *Chūkai, Genkō bōrui hennen shiryō*, p. 148.

[62]*Kamakura ibun*, vol. 16, doc. 12252, 3.5.1276 (Kenji 2) Ōtomo Yoriyasu kakikudashi.

[63]Ōtomo Yoriyasu.

[64]Nokami Sukenao.

[65]*Kamakura ibun*, vol. 16, doc. 12271, 3.30.1276 (Kenji 2) Higo Kubota no shō Sō Jōyū ukebumi. Such responses to orders, and lists of troops, carried little prestige and were rarely preserved. This document survived because it was later used to record the history of Hakozaki shrine. See *Nihonshi shiryō 2 chūsei*, ed. Rekishigaku kenkyūkai (Iwanami shoten, 1998), p. 145. One can infer from Document 41 that laborers had to depart to Hakata prior to the twentieth day of the third month.

Hashiuragaki: A reply from the Kubota *azukari dokoro.* An acknowledgement of orders (*ukebumi* 請文) by the priest and *azukari dokoro* of Kubota estate in Higo province, Jōyū.

On the twenty-ninth day of this month, an order, written on the twenty-fifth, was received [directly from Morimune that stated] in order to conquer foreign lands, we should submit a list of [our] forces, weapons, and [the number of our] horses.

In accordance with previous missives, I had already counted the number of troops and weapons [that comprise] my own forces (*gushinsei* 愚身勢) and reported [them] to the *ōryōshi*,[66] Kawajiri Hyōe no jō, prior to the tenth day [of this month]. Since I received a second notification, I personally have recorded [the composition of my forces once again]. This purport should be made known. Respectfully [stated by] Jōyū.

The second year of Kenji [1276], thirtieth day, third month

The priest and *azukari dokoro* of Kubota estate Jōyū

Document 18. *Jōyū's list of followers, horse, and weapons.*[67]

The followers, weapons, and horses of the priest and *azukari dokoro* of Kubota estate in Higo province.

1. Myself, age thirty-five.
   One *rōjū* (郎従), three *shojū* (所従),[68] and one horse.

2. Weapons:
   One suit of full armor (*yoroi* 鎧), one suit of simplified armor (*haramaki* 腹巻), two bows, two quivers of war arrows (*ōya* 征矢), and one sword (*tachi* 大刀).

In accordance with the command, recorded thus.

The second year of Kenji [1276], thirtieth day, third month

Perhaps *gokenin* that were to be dispatched to Korea had to reply prior to the tenth day of the third month.

[66] 押領使, a provisional constable appointed in emergency situations from the ranks of *gokenin*. See *Nihonshi shiryō* 2, p. 145.

[67] *Kamakura ibun*, vol. 16, doc. 12275, 3.20.1276 (Kenji 2) Higo Kubota no shō Sō Jōyū chūshinjō.

[68] The distinction between these two types of retainers is unclear.

The priest and *azukari dokoro* of Kubota estate Jōyū

Document 19. *The following consists of an excerpt from a letter by the priest Nichiren to a woman from the Toki family. The Toki were powerful deputies to the Chiba, the hereditary shugo of Shimosa province. This passage describes the immediate aftermath of the first Mongol invasion and how more Kamakura warriors were dispatched westward, in preparation for an attack on Korea. This document was written on the twenty-seventh day of the third month. The year, although unspecified, must be 1276.*[69]

Concerning Yuki,[70] Tsushima, and Dazaifu, the people of Kamakura are as joyful as those [residing in] Heaven [because of the victory over the Mongols] but those who must depart for Tsukushi[71] [lament unceasingly]. When the men, who must go, part from [their] women, who must remain behind, it is as [difficult as] ripping off skin [from flesh]. Face to face, looking into each other's eyes, they sorely lament. Gradually distance [grows as they pass through] Yui no hama, Inafura,[72] Koshigoe, Sakawa, and the slopes of Hakone. As each day or two passes, they gradually walk further and further away, step by step, passing through rivers and mountains and even beyond the clouds. Those who must stay behind [break into] tears; those that go along [break into] laments. Their sorrow knows no bounds . . . These warriors–if they attack–may be captured alive in the mountains or on the seas or meet a horrible end either in their boats or in Korea (*Kōrai*).

DOCUMENTS 20–24. THE INVASION OF 1281

Gokenin and their witnesses came to record more precise and verifiable narratives of their battle service in the aftermath of the second invasions.

Document 20. *This copy (an 案) of an original document (kakikudashi), issued by Ōtomo Yoriyasu, the shugo of Bungo, provides a useful example of how the process of rewards and claim verification would proceed. When Takezaki Suenaga reported to Adachi Morimune in Scene 21, Morimune's scribe probably recorded*

[69]*Kamakura ibun*, vol. 16, doc. 12270, 3.27 Nichiren shojō. See also *Chūkai, Genkō bōrui hennen shiryō*, pp. 155–56, and *Nichiren bunshū*, ed. Kabutoki Shōkō, (Iwanami bunkō, 1968), pp. 78–80.

[70]Written phonetically but must refer to Iki Island.

[71]Kyūshū.

[72]Perhaps refers to Inamura. All of the stations mentioned here are stations that one passes when traveling out of Kamakura along the Tōkaidō.

a document quite similar to this. This document also reveals that witnesses could not belong to the same family as the claimant, and that the oaths of all witnesses were to be dispatched to the shugo.[73]

Yashirō Yoshiaki, son and representative of Uda Shirō nyūdō Dōen, a *gokenin* of Bungo province, states that during the Mongol battles of the eighth day of the sixth month of this year he and his base followers (*genin* 下人) were wounded.[74] According to his petition, witnesses saw them depart for the battlefield and fight defensively. In order to assess whether or not discrepancies exist, oaths shall be taken from those [witnesses] unrelated (*hiensha* 非縁者) [to Yoshiaki who are] in accord. Oaths that clearly state [Yoshiaki's battle valor] shall be presented and witnesses' statements shall be dispatched immediately to the *shugo*'s office. This is so conveyed.

The fourth year of Kōan [1281], second day, twelfth month

The former Dewa no kami[75]

[To:] Kogo Saemon no jō dono[76] Hoashi Hyōe no jō dono[77]

Document 21. *The Satsuma province gokenin Hishijima Tokinori submitted the following document to Shimazu Hisatsune (Hisachika), who was the shugo of Satsuma through the time of the Kōan (1281) battles.*[78] *While this document has been classified as the oldest surviving petition for rewards (gunchūjō 軍忠状), a close reading reveals that it was issued in response to Hisatsune's request for*

---

[73]*Kamakura ibun*, vol. 19, doc. 14514, 12.2.1281 (Kōan 4) Ōtomo Yoriyasu kakikudashi an.

[74]The Uda shared 11.6 *chō* of lands in Nokami village, Kusu district, Bungo province, with the *gokenin* Nokami Tarō Sukenao. See the reference to Uda Fujita Shirō Moriaki, holy name Dōen, in *Kamakura ibun*, vol. 20, doc. 15700, p. 370.

[75]Ōtomo Yoriyasu.

[76]According to the Bungo register of *gokenin*, found in *Kamakura ibun*, vol. 20, doc. 15700, 10.16.1285 (Kōan 8) Bungo no kuni ōtabumi an, p. 369, the *gokenin* Kogo Saemon Michishige (holy name Shingen) was the *jitō* of eighty *chō* of land in Kogo, Kusu district, while one can infer from doc. 15701, 10.16.1285 (Kōan 8) Bungo no kuni zudenchō, p. 377, that Michishige was one of nine *gokenin* who shared seventy three *chō* of land in Kogo, Kusu district (*gun*) in Bungo province.

[77]*Kamakura ibun*, vol. 20, doc. 15700, 10.16.1285 (Kōan 8) Bungo no kuni ōtabumi an, p. 370, reveals that Hoashi Rokurō Hyōe no jō Michisada, holy name Sairen, was the *jitō* of 17.6 *chō* of Hisatomi *myō* land, in Bungo province, while doc. 15701, 10.16.1285 (Kōan 8) Bungo no kuni zudenchō, p. 377, simply designates him as Hoashi Rokurō Saemon Michisada (Sairen).

[78]For more on the Hishijima, see Documents 42 and 44.

additional information and should be classified as an appeal.[79] *Tokinori desired that a record of his actions be forwarded by the shugo to Kamakura so that he might become eligible for rewards.*[80] *Shugo could forward documents to Kamakura but lacked the authority to grant rewards.*

The Satsuma *gokenin* Hishijima Gorōjiro Minamoto Tokinori respectfully states:

As a result of my battle service (*kassen no chūkin* 合戦之忠勤), I desire to receive a battle report (*onchūshin* 御注進) [from Kamakura] that has the details [of my actions recorded].

Appended: A copy of the verification report (*shōjō an* 證状案) [of military service received] from Ōi no suke dono.[81]

Concerning the above, on the twenty-ninth day of the past sixth month, when several thousand of the Mongol pirates' boats attacked Iki Island, Tokinori together with his relative Kawada Uemon no jō Morisuke crossed over to his island and defended it. Ōi no suke dono's verification report (*onshōjō* 御證状) makes this clear. Next, during the battle of Takashima on the seventh day of the next seventh month,[82] we attacked from the land. As before, Tokinori now wishes to receive a judgment [from Kamakura in favor of granting him rewards] as a result of his battle service. Respectfully stated thus.

The fifth year of Kōan [1282], second month

Document 22. *The oath of Ōi no suke Nagahisa. Close relatives to the shugo proved valued witnesses, because they were perceived to be more reliable than other warriors. Just as Takezaki Suenaga emphasized that Shōni Kagesuke, the younger brother of the shugo, witnessed his deeds, so too did Hishijima Tokinori highlight the importance of this statement, Shimazu Nagihisa's "verification report" of Document 21. This document represents a copy of the oath that was*

---

[79]*Shugo* commonly made such requests. For a similar situation, see Documents 7 and 10. For more on the classification of this document, see Urushihara Tōru, *Chūsei gunchūjō to sono sekai* (Yoshikawa kōbunkan, 1998), pp. 116, 124–32, 145–46.

[80]*Kamakura ibun*, vol. 19, doc. 14583, 2.1282 (Kōan 5) Hishijima Tokinori gunchūjō an.

[81]"Oi no suke dono" refers to Shimazu Nagahisa, who was the younger brother of Satsuma's *shugo*, Hisatsune. Nagahisa later changed his name to either Hisatoki, Takahisa, or both. For more on the genealogical obscurity of this person, see Urushihara, *Chūsei gunchūjō to sono sekai*, p. 146. Tokinori refers to this document as a verification report instead of a mere witness's statement because Nagahisa was such a close relative of the *shugo*.

[82]He is referring to the intercalary seventh month. See Document 22.

presented in Hishijima's previous document. When appealing to the shugo, Tokinori apparently no longer possessed his original documents, which is why he had Nagahisa write another copy of his oath some two months after his initial submission of reports.[83]

It is true that Hishijima Gorōjirō Tokinori, a *gokenin* of this province [of Satsuma, fought] as he has stated during the battles against the Mongols, and that on the twenty-ninth day of the past sixth month, Gorōjirō [Tokinori], together with his relative, Kawada Uemon no jō Morisuke, boarded Nagahisa's boat and crossed over to Iki Island. Likewise, I witnessed the fact of Gorōjiro attacking from the land during the battle of Takashima, on the seventh day of the seventh intercalary month. If some part of this account is a lie, may the body of Nagahisa endure the divine punishment of the greater and lesser gods [that exist] throughout the country of Japan. Respectfully.

The fifth year of Kōan [1282], fifteenth day, fourth month

Ōi no suke Nagahisa

Document 23. *Togō Korechika submitted the following petition to Kamakura in an attempt to receive rewards. His account describes the same battle of Takashima that is mentioned in Documents 21–22. This document also reveals that Korechika did not even know the first name of one of his witnesses, Kazusa Saburō nyūdō.*[84]

The Bungo *gokenin* Togō Saemon Gorō Ōkami Korechika hōsshi (holy name Shukumyō) respectfully states:

I desire to receive immediately a [Kamakura] battle report (onchūshin 御注進) [that mentions my deeds], and to be singled out for rewards, as is customary [for service in] battles against the Mongols at Takashima, in Hizen province, on the seventh day of the seventh intercalary month of the past year of 1281.

Concerning the above, when the Mongol invaders (kyōto 凶徒) arrived on the shores of Takashima, in Hizen province, Shukumyō galloped to Hoshishika, of the same province, and on the seventh day, at the hour of

---

[83]*Kamakura ibun*, vol. 19, doc. 14611, 4.15.1282 (Kōan 5) Shimazu Nagahisa shōjō. For more on this document, see Urushihara, *Chūsei gunchūjō to sono sekai*, pp. 131–32.

[84]*Kamakura ibun*, vol. 21, doc. 15867, 3.1286 (Kōan 9) Shami Shukumyō (Ōkami Korechika) gunchūjō.

the serpent,[85] crossed over to this island and performed battle service on its eastern beaches. Shukumyō's son, Shirō Koretō managed to decapitate (*buntori* 分取) the enemy.[86] In addition, my retainer (*rōjū* 郎従) Saburōjirō Shigetō was wounded. The bannerman, one of the base (*genin* 下人), Yaroku Suemori, was [also] wounded. These actions were witnessed by Shite Chikugo no bō Enhan, of the same province, and Kazusa Saburō nyūdō real name not known. Shukumyō desires to receive a [Kamakura] report [chronicling his deeds], and to be singled out for rewards with due haste. Respectfully stated thus.

The ninth year of Kōan [1286], third month

Shami Shukumyō (monogram)

Document 24. *The following copy (utsushi) of a document, dispatched by Shōni Kagesuke to Kamiyama Shirō, a witness for Kasai Norikage, shows that witnesses' statements had to be recorded as oaths in order to be considered as "proof" of battle service. This document also provides insight into the nature of battles on the high seas before the typhoons slammed into the Mongol fleet.*[87]

The *jitō* Kasai (香西) Kotarō Norikage of Ki no shoya, Chikugo province, states that on the fifth day of the seventh intercalary month of 1281, in the seas off the coast of Mikuriya-kozaki in Hizen province, he managed to pursue a large vessel, one of three Mongol pirate crafts, and do battle. [After] boarding [that] enemy ship, Norikage decapitated [the enemy],[88] while his younger brother, Hironori, pursued the foreign pirates into the sea. Some relatives and followers (*hikan*) were wounded, while [other] retainers (*rōjū*) were either killed, wounded or managed to decapitate the enemy.[89] Witnesses have stood [for Norikage] attesting that they saw [his

---

[85]Nine to eleven in the morning. For more on the hours of the day, see appendix 2.

[86]*Buntori* literally means capture a part of an enemy. Usually means taking a head, although it could merely designate taking a piece of enemy armor.

[87]*Kamakura ibun*, vol. 20, doc. 15150, 4.12.1284 (Kōan 7) Shōni Kagesuke shojō utsushi, and *Fukutekihen*, maki 4, pp. 28–29.

[88]Literally, he performed *buntori*, which generally involved the "capture" of an enemy's head. See Document 23.

[89]Again, performed *buntori*.

actions]. Nevertheless, an oath should be written [by these witnesses] that verifies the truth of Norikage's battle service. [Respectfully].

The seventh year of Kōan [1284], twelfth day, fourth month

Kagesuke ([ari]han)

[To:] Kamiyama Shirō dono

DOCUMENTS 25–32. INVESTIGATING CLAIMS & GRANTING REWARDS

A comparison with Documents 8–11 reveals the improvements that Kamakura made in verifying battle service.

Documents 25 and 26. *The following two documents reveal that Nokami Sukenao, the Bungo gokenin who was Ōtomo Yoriyasu's deputy, proved to be a popular witness because of his ties with Yoriyasu. Yoriyasu signed this document as shami, indicating that he had taken religious vows.*[90]

Oda Saemon no jō Kaneshige states that you are a witness (*shōnin* 證人) for his deeds (*gunkō* 軍功) against the Mongols. In order to question you regarding the particulars [of Kaneshige's service], report to [Dazai]fu by the middle of this month. If, however, you are designated to guard vital [areas of Northern Kyūshū], you can come to the [Dazai]fu on that occasion. This is so conveyed.

The seventh year of Kōan [1284], nineteenth day, sixth month

Shami (monogram)[91]

[To:] Nokami Tarō dono[92]

Document 26. *Another document dispatched to the ubiquitous Nokami Sukenao by Ōtomo Yoriyasu.*[93]

---

[90]*Kamakura ibun*, vol. 20, doc. 15214, 6.19.1284 (Kōan 7) Ōtomo Yoriyasu kakikudashi.

[91]Ōtomo Yoriyasu.

[92]Likewise, see *Kamakura ibun*, vol. 20, doc. 15215, 6.19.1284 (Kōan 7) Ōtomo Yoriyasu kakikudashi, for an identically worded document issued to Mori Saburō, who stood as a witness on behalf of Nokami Sukenao.

[93]*Kamakura ibun*, vol. 20, doc. 15493, 3.27.1285 (Kōan 8) Ōtomo Yoriyasu

Hoashi Yoichi Saburō Michitoshi[94] states his battle [service] against the Mongols. In order to determine the particulars, report to Hakata prior to the tenth day of the coming month. This is so conveyed.

The eighth year of Kōan [1285], twenty-seventh day, third month

Shami (monogram)[95]

[To:] Nokami Tarō dono

Documents 27–29. *Kamakura solidified its control over Kyūshū in the aftermath of the second invasions. Hōjō Tokisada had been appointed to replace Shōni Tsunesuke as the shugo of Hizen province sometime after the second month of 1281 (Kōan 4).[96] The following three documents were issued to the Hizen province gokenin Yamashiro Matasaburō Shigeru.*

Document 27. *Even though Tokisada accepted the veracity of various eyewitness accounts, he still required an oath to be dispatched from all relevant witnesses before he would consider recommending a warrior for rewards.[97]*

The Hizen province *gokenin*, Hakazaki Gotō Saburō nyūdō Jōmyō,[98] has dispatched numerous battle verification reports (*kassen shōmon* 合戦證文). [What] has been seen [is accepted as being] true. Hisakijima Matasaburō's oath (*kishōmon*) shall be dispatched [to the office of the Hizen *shugo*]. This is so conveyed.

The fifth year of Kōan [1282], second day, third month

kakikudashi .

[94]Hoashi Michitoshi's identity is not known, although he was obviously a relative of Hoashi Michisada, who was mentioned in Document 20.

[95]Ōtomo Yoriyasu.

[96]Tsunesuke's last document as the *shugo* of Hizen appears on 2.18.1281. See *Kamakura ibun*, vol. 19, doc. 14251, 2.18.1281 (Kōan 4) Shōni Tsunesuke shojō. For the first document of Hōjō Tokisada, the younger brother of the previous *shikken*, Hōjō Tokiyori, as *shugo* of Hizen, see doc. 14418, 8.10.1281 (Kōan 4) Hōjō Tokisada kakikudashi. Tokisada remained the *shugo* of Hizen until his death in the eighth month of 1289. This office became a Hōjō sinecure fom the time of Tokisada until the fall of the *bakufu*.

[97]*Kamakura ibun*, vol. 19, doc. 14586, 3.2.1282 (Kōan 5) Hōjō Tokisada kakikudashi.

[98]The Hakazaki were a Hizen *gokenin* family, closely related to the Gotō, who held lands in Hakazaki estate, near Takeo shrine.

223

Taira (monogram)[99]

[To:] Yamashiro Matasaburō dono[100]

Document 28. *Here is the document that Hōjō Tokisada dispatched to Yamashiro Shigeru's witnesses, demanding that they submit oaths.*[101]

Yamashiro Matasaburō Shigeru, a *gokenin* of Hizen province, speaks of witnesses (*shōnin*) [for him during] the battle of Iki Island. [Shigeru's] petition is thus. Regarding a detailed record of witness (*kenjō* 見状), trust the veracity of what has been seen. Written oaths that record [witnesses' accounts of Shigeru's deeds] shall be submitted [to the office of the *shugo*]. This is so conveyed.

The fifth year of Kōan [1282], twenty-fifth day, ninth month

Taira (monogram)[102]

[To:] Funahara Saburō dono
Tachibana Satsuma Kawakami Matajirō dono

Document 29. *Shugo were responsible for investigating battle reports. Discrepancies warranted further questioning.*[103]

A discrepancy exists regarding the particulars [of your deeds during] the Mongol battles of the past year. Dispatch Hyōei Tarō prior to the coming twenty-sixth and have him clearly state [the particulars]. This is so conveyed.

The sixth year of Kōan [1283], nineteenth day, third month

---

[99]Hōjō Tokisada, the *shugo* of Hizen province.

[100]According to Seno, the Yamashiro were a powerful *gokenin* from the Shimo Matsura region of Hizen province. See Seno, *Chinzei gokenin no kenkyū*, p. 186. For documents pertaining to an inheritance dispute among the Yamashiro during the years of 1238–44, see Mass, *Development of Kamakura Rule*, docs. 138–44, pp. 270–75.

[101]*Kamakura ibun*, vol. 19, doc. 14702, 9.25.1282 (Kōan 5) Hizen no kami Hōjō Tokisada kakikudashi.

[102]Hōjō Tokisada.

[103]*Kamakura ibun*, vol. 20, doc. 14807, 3.19.1283 (Kōan 6) Hōjō Tokisada (Tametoki) kakikudashi.

Taira (monogram)[104]

[To:] Yamashiro Matasaburō dono[105]

Document 30. *Once a claim was verified, shugo forwarded petitions and witnesses's statements to Kamakura.*[106]

Petitions and oaths of witnesses have been inspected concerning the battle at Iki Island's Seto-ura, when foreign pirates attacked during the second day of the seventh month of the past year. They shall be dispatched to the Kantō. Respectfully.

The fifth year of Kōan [1282], ninth day, ninth month

Taira (monogram)[107]

[To:] Ryūzōji Kosaburō Saemon no jō dono[108]

Document 31. *Kamakura lacked adequate resources to reward its warriors for their military service. The holdings of those killed in factional infighting were quickly distributed to other warriors in belated recognition for their service against the Mongols. Here, the bakufu confiscated the lands of the illustrious Shōni Kagesuke, who had been killed during the Shimotsuki disturbance of 1285, and granted them to Takuma Bettō Tokihide, one of Takezaki Suenaga's comrades (Passage 10). The following edict represents a copy (an 案) of the original document that had been dispatched by Hōjō Sadatoki, who was appointed regent (shikken) in 1284. His co-signer, Hōjō Naritoki, had been appointed in 1283.*[109]

Immediately appoint the Takuma Bettō Tokihide, lay priest religious name

---

[104]Hōjō Tokisada, who later changed his name to Tametoki.

[105]Yamashiro Shigeru.

[106]*Kamakura ibun*, vol. 19, doc. 14696, 9.9.1282 (Kōan 5) Hizen no kami Hōjō Tokisada shojō. In order to be consistent, however, this document should be classified as a *kakikudashi*.

[107]Hōjō Tokisada.

[108]Ryūzōji Iekiyo.

[109]*Kamakura ibun*, vol. 21, doc. 16008, 10.28.1286 (Kōan 9) Kantō gechijō an. Naritoki, the son of Hōjō Shigetoki, succeeded Hōjō Yoshimasa as co-signer in 1283 and died in 1286. Sadatoki, the son of Tokimune, became regent in 1284, resigned as regent in 1301, but continued to wield power in the *bakufu* until his death in 1311.

[left blank], to the *jitō shiki* of Shitosha, Chikuzen province the legacy of the former governor (zenshi 前司) of Buzen Provinces, Kagesuke.[110]

The above is hereby granted as a reward for battle service against the Mongols in 1281. You shall forthwith enjoy the profits of the land (*ryōshō* 領掌) in accordance with precedent.[111] This order is thus.

The ninth year of Kōan [1286], twenty-eighth day, tenth month

Sagami no kami Taira ason (arihan)[112]

Mutsu no kami Taira ason (arihan)[113]

Document 32. *Jitō rights were more commonly granted through the chancellory of the shōgun's house (mandokoro 政所) in the aftermath of the first invasion. Although the mandokoro had once been a significant organ of governance, it fell out of use after the death of the third shōgun, Minamoto Sanetomo, in 1219, and thereupon merely became the documentary vehicle for granting and confirming right of jitō shiki. The mandokoro tended to be monopolized by the Hōjō regent, in this case Tokimune, and his co-signer, Hōjō Yoshimasa, who both signed this document as bettō. Yamashiro Shigeru received this document.*[114]

The office (*mandokoro* 政所) of the *Shōgun* orders:
To Eri [in] Hizen Province

Appointed: To the office of the *jitō*
Kamemaru[115]

The above was granted to Kamemaru's late father Yamashiro Yasaburō

---

[110]Kagesuke's title of "former governor" did not imply administrative control over the region.

[111]*Ryōshō* should best be thought to denote a usufructary right, whereby the profits of an estate, and the ability to manage it, could be used without impairing the substance of their possession.

[112]Hōjō Sadatoki.

[113]Hōjō Naritoki.

[114]*Kamakura ibun*, vol. 16, doc. 12077, 10.29.1275 (Kenji 1) Shōgun (Minamoto Koreyasu) ke mandokoro kudashibumi. For insightful commentary on the role of the *mandokoro*, see Mass, *Development of Kamakura Rule*, pp. 75–80. For references to Hōjō Yoshimasa, see Document 4; for Yamashiro Shigeru, see Documents 27–29.

[115]The childhood name of Yamashiro Shigeru.

as a reward for his battle service against the Mongols this past year. You shall forthwith administer [this land] in accordance with precedent. It is commanded thus. Wherefore, this order

the first year of Kenji [1275], twenty-ninth day, tenth month

> anzu, Sugano
> chikeiji

ryō Saemon shōjō Fujiwara
bettō　　　　Sagami no kami Taira (monogram)[116]
　　　　　　Musashi no kami Taira[117]

DOCUMENTS 33–34. MAINTAINING VIGILANCE

Document 33. *Shortly after the 1274 invasion, rumors were rife that the Mongols would strike again. Kamakura expected an attack after Hōjō Tokimune ordered the execution of a Mongol emissary at Tatsunoguchi in Kamakura during the fourth month of 1275. Here, Ōtomo Yoriyasu dispatched the following document to his Bungo deputy, Nokami Sukenao.*[118]

Concerning guard duty against the Mongols. A report arrived from the western *shugonin*[119] which states that he has heard of some suspicions [that the Mongols might again attack] during the ninth or tenth month. In order to be prepared, please depart first, sometime during this month, make your way to the *shugo* office in Chikugo province, and build [fortifications] there. Those who cannot serve because of serious illness should, however, dispatch an oath (*seijō* 誓状) swearing to that effect. All healthy sons, relatives, and retainers (*wakatō*) shall be dispatched [to Chikugo] without exception. If you do not report prior to the first day of the tenth month, then you shall be liable [to extend your period of guard duty] for the number of days that you were late. Those who are negligent with the aforementioned [service] shall be reported to the Kantō. Have all [warriors] mobilized together. This is so conveyed.

[116]HōjōTokimune.
[117]Hōjō Yoshimasa.
[118]*Kamakura ibun*, vol. 16, doc. 12022, 9.22.1275 (Kenji 1) Bungo no shugo Ōtomo Yoriyasu kakikudashi. For helpful annotations, see also *Chūkai, Genkō bōrui hennen shiryō*, pp. 144–45.
[119]The western *shugo* of the Chinzei commission (*bugyō* 奉行) was the head of the Shōni. See *Chūkai, Genkō bōrui hennen shiryō*, p. 145. Whether this individual was Kakuei or his son Tsunesuke is by no means clear. See also Documents 7 and 37–40.

The first year of Kenji [1275], twenty-second day, ninth month

The Former Dewa no kami (monogram)[120]

[To:] Nokami Tarō dono[121]

Document 34. *The recipient of this document, although unknown, is probably a member of the Nokami family, for they received another document from Ōtomo Yoriyasu on the same day (Document 16). Yoriyasu was apparently waiting for Bungo troops to report to him in the vicinity of Kashii shrine, in Chikuzen province.*[122]

In order to be prepared for the foreign [invaders], dispatch your son as your representative [to Hakata] prior to the fifteenth day of this month. Respectfully.

The second year of Kenji [1276], fifth day, third month

Reports state that he is at Kashii shrine[123]

The Former Dewa no kami (monogram)[124]

DOCUMENTS 35–40. RESTRICTING TRAVEL TO KYŌTO AND KAMAKURA

In order to prevent gokenin from abandoning guard duty in order to launch appeals, the bakufu devised increasingly sophisticated institutions for adjudicating litigation in Kyūshū.

Document 35. *Takezaki Suenaga's decision to report to Kamakura in 1275 (see Passage 5 of his scrolls) proved to be fortuitous. Another gokenin, Tahara Yasuhiro of Bungo province, was unable to travel either to Kyōto or to Kamakura because he was required to perform additional guard duty a mere nine months after*

---

[120]Ōtomo Yoriyasu.
[121]Nokami Sukenao.
[122]*Kamakura ibun*, vol. 16, doc. 12253, 3.5.1276 (Kenji 2) Ōtomo Yoriyasu kakikudashi.
[123]This passage was not originally written on the document, but was later added by its recipient.
[124]Ōtomo Yoriyasu.

Suenaga had set off on his journey.[125] *Although Yasuhiro dispatched a messenger to plead his case, he also had Hōjō Muneyori, the recently appointed shugo of Nagato province, write this letter on his behalf to Taira Yoritsuna.*[126]

Ōtomo Sakan Kurōdo [Tahara] Yasuhiro states that he performed outstanding service during the battles of two years ago [1274]. He laments that even though he must travel to [either Kyōto or Kamakura] in order to appeal [his lack of rewards], for the following two months there can be no let up in defense efforts against the foreigners [in Kyūshū]. [As Yasuhiro cannot leave], first [he will] dispatch a messenger, who will state the particulars [of his grievance]. [I am] interceding (*kunyū* 口入) [on his behalf]. Stated thus so that, just between us (*uchiuchi* 内々), you will understand [the situation]. Respectfully.

Eighth day, third month   Shūri no suke (monogram)[127]

[To:] Taira Saemon no jō dono[128]

Document 36. *The bakufu forbade Kyūshū warriors from leaving the island in order to appeal rulings after the invasion of 1281. The following record reveals that Kamakura first dispatched edicts to its branch office in Kyōto, the Rokuhara tandai* (六波羅探題), *which thereupon conveyed them to Kyūshū. Policies concerning prisoners and wall repair are also discussed.*[129]

---

[125]The Tahara were a collateral lineage of the Ōtomo, closely related to the Shiga, who appear in Documents 12–13.

[126]This document is reproduced twice in the *Kamakura ibun*. See vol. 16, doc. 12257, 3.8.[1276] Hōjō Muneyori shojō, and vol. 20, doc. 14802, 3.8.[1283] Hōjō Kanetoki shojō. The 1276 date and attribution to Muneyori is correct. See *Chūkai*, *Genkō bōrui hennen shiryō*, pp. 145–47. Hōjō Muneyori was the younger brother of the regent at the time, Tokimune. He replaced Nikaidō Takauji (堂氏), the absentee *shugo* of 1275 (see Scene 5) on 1.11.1276. For such a powerful person, closely related to the *shikken*, to be appointed as the *shugo* of Nagato reveals the importance that Kamakura attached to this most western province of Honshū. Muneyori died during the sixth month of 1279. See *Chūkai*, *Genkō bōrui hennen shiryō*, p. 147 and *Zōtei Kamakura bakufu shugo seidō no kenkyū*, pp. 186–87.

[127]Hōjō Muneyori.

[128]Taira Yoritsuna, the powerful *bakufu* official who would later attack and kill Adachi Yasumori. Yoritsuna, the father of Sadatoki's wet nurse, was ultimately suspected of trying to make his own son *shōgun* and was killed on Sadatoki's orders in 1293.

[129]*Kamakura ibun*, vol. 19, doc. 14456, 9.16.1281 (Kōan 4) Rokuhara migyōsho.

Regulations:

Even though [you have] repelled [Mongol] pirate ships, you must not willfully embark on the long journey to the capital. In cases of particular emergency [exceptions may be granted] depending on the circumstances if you explain the particulars.

You must entrust each surrendered foreigner [to a warrior responsible for guarding him, as] it is not yet decided what to do with them. All boats [arriving from the continent] that appear in bays and harbors should always be inspected, regardless if by day or night or whether the ships are large or small. Such men must not willfully float away [from Japanese waters]. Be prepared [to enforce these regulations on] even those who claim to be fishermen, or to be traders with the continent.

You must prohibit those foreigners who are coming to, and entering [Japan], for the first time.

You must serve without negligence [as has been the case] to date. Fortifications must be repaired and guard duty must be performed.

Those who are negligent concerning these regulations shall later have [cause for] regret. This is so conveyed.

The fourth year of Kōan [1281], sixteenth day, ninth month

Sakan shōgen (monogram)[130]

[To:] Nokami Tarō dono [131]

Document 37. *Because warriors were forbidden to travel to either Rokuhara or the Kantō to launch appeals, Hōjō Sadatoki and Naritoki, the Kamakura shikken and his co-signer, established a judicial apparatus for Kyūshū, the Chinzei dangisho* (鎮西談義所), *which was staffed by Ōtomo Yoriyasu, Shōni Tsunesuke, Utsunomiya Michifusa, and Shibuya Shigeaki. This council replaced the Chinzei bugyō, which had been administered by Yoriyasu and Tsunesuke until it was abolished in 1284, and marks an important precursor to the Chinzei tandai of 1293.*[132] *The following document was issued to Ōtomo Yoriyasu, one of the four members of the Chinzei council.*

---

[130]Hōjō Tokikuni, a Rokuhara *tandai*. He was appointed to this post in 1275, and was summoned to Kamakura and executed for his "evil deeds" in 1284. See *Chūkai, Genkō bōrui hennen shiryō*, p. 199.

[131]Nokami Sukenao.

[132]*Kamakura ibun*, vol. 21, doc. 15945, 7.18.1286 (Kōan 9) Kantō migyōsho an. A useful summary of the *Chinzei dangisho* appears in *Chūkai, Genkō bōrui hennen shiryō*, pp. 219–22. See also Document 40. For the earlier *Chinzei bugyō*, see Documents 7 and 9.

Concerning appeals by residents of Chinzei. An order has been issued that the acting *shugo (shugonin* 守護人*)* [of Chinzei] are to investigate these matters. Nevertheless, there have been reports that *jitō gokenin*, temple and shrine administrators (*bettō* 別当), shrine attendants (*kannushi* 神主), priests (*kuzō* 供僧), shrine officials, and even various *myōshu* (名主)[133] and estate officers (*shōkan* 庄官) have traveled to the Kantō to appeal their cases. From now, unless there are special orders to the contrary, they shall not travel to the Kantō or Rokuhara. If appeals [are to be submitted], they should be judged by the council (*yoriai* 寄合) [composed] of Shōni nyūdō, Hyōgo nyūdō, Satsuma nyūdō, and Kawachi Gon no kami nyūdō.[134] The particulars of cases that are difficult to judge shall be recorded. Even if [the case] is an appeal, [matters] shall be quickly investigated and reported. Nevertheless, if [any plaintiff] feels enmity for one of the commissioners (*bugyōnin* 奉行人), then [only] the remaining members [of the council] shall investigate [the case]. This purport shall be announced [throughout the Chinzei provinces]. This order is so conveyed.

The ninth year of Kōan [1286], eighteenth day, seventh month

Sagami no kami (arihan)[135]
Mutsu no kami (arihan)[136]

[To:] Ōtomo Hyōgo no kami nyūdō dono[137]

Document 38. *Once the Chinzei dangisho had been established (Document 37), warriors apparently desired to follow the commands of these men, and not*

---

[133]*Myōshu* designated powerful provincials who possessed considerable local authority, but who had not been classified as *gokenin* by the Kamakura *bakufu*. For more on their status, see Conlan, "State of War," pp. 135–37.

[134]These men are Shōni Tsunesuke, Ōtomo Yoriyasu, Utsunomiya Michifusa, and Shibuya Shigeaki respectively. Tsunesuke and Yoriyasu were the Chinzei commissioners, while Michifusa would later be appointed as *shugo* of Chikugo province. See *Zōtei Kamakura bakufu shugo seidō no kenkyū*, p. 218. References to Shigeaki can be found in the genealogy of the Takagi (高城), which reveals that he was related to one of the lineages of the Shibuya, *gokenin* of Satsuma province. See the Takagi genealogy, found in the Japanese portion of Asakawa Kan'ichi, *The Documents of Iriki* (The Japan Society for the Promotion of Science, 1955), p. 321.

[135]Hōjō Sadatoki.

[136]Hōjō Naritoki.

[137]Ōtomo Yoriyasu.

their shugo, which reveals that powers of lordship naturally accrued to judicial authority. Here, Hōjō Sadatoki and Naritoki reiterated that gokenin and other warriors were still to follow the commands of their shugo. This edict was dispatched to Shimazu Tadamune, the shugo of Satsuma.[138]

Concerning defense against the foreign pirates. Chinzei *jitō gokenin* and those possessing complete administrative authority [over their lands] must follow the orders of *shugo*. It has been already commanded that [these men must] aid in defense preparations and perform outstanding service in defensive battles. Even though the Chinzei commissioners have been designated, there are families [that now] ignore the *shugo's* commands. Even though they [may have] previously fought in battle, these men shall not be rewarded, but instead punished for disservice (*fuchū* 不忠). This purport should be announced immediately throughout the province of Satsuma. This order is so conveyed.

The ninth year of Kōan [1286], thirtieth day, twelfth month

Sagami no kami (arihan)[139]
Mutsu no kami (arihan)[140]

[To:] Shimazu Saburō Saemon no jō dono[141]

Document 39. *Hōjō Kanetoki,*[142] *formerly one of the Rokuhara tandai, was dispatched to his new post as Chinzei tandai in 1293. This document, written by the shikken Hōjō Sadatoki, represents an attempt to shore up shugo authority while at the same time asserting the Chinzei tandai's primary role in directing defenses against the Mongols. Shimazu Tadamune, the shugo of Satsuma, appears to have had particular difficulties in ensuring compliance from the gokenin of Satsuma.*[143]

---

[138]*Kamakura ibun*, vol. 21, doc. 16082, 12.30.1286 (Kōan 9) Kantō migyōsho an, and *Chūkai, Genkō bōrui hennen shiryō*, pp. 230–31.

[139]Hōjō Sadatoki.

[140]Hōjō Naritoki.

[141]Shimazu Tadamune.

[142]Kanetoki (also known as Moritoki), the son of Hōjō Muneyori, remained at this post until 1295, when he returned to Kamakura, became a member of the council (*hyōjō*), and died during that same year. See *Sonpi bunmyaku*, vol. 4, p. 18, in *Shintei zōho Kokushi taikei* (Yoshikawa kōbunkan, 1964). Little is known about Ietoki, save that he returned with Kanetoki to Kamakura in 1295.

[143]*Kamakura ibun*, vol. 23, doc. 18131, 3.21.1293 (Shō-ō 6) Kantō migyōsho. A copy of this document, with a mistaken date, appears in vol. 21, doc. 16081,

In order to guard against the foreign pirates, Kanetoki and Tokiie have been dispatched to the Chinzei. Strategies for defensive battle shall be conducted in unison (*ichimi dōshin* 一味同心) after council [deliberation] (*hyōjō* 評定) [with these men]. Moreover, please follow Kanetoki's plans during the course of battle. Next, those *jitō gokenin* and men [with] complete jurisdiction over shrine and temple estates who disobey the acting *shugo's* requests, and are not in accord, shall be reported. That the [*shugo*] shall possess the authority [to mobilize men] shall be especially announced throughout the province of Satsuma. This order is so conveyed.

The sixth year of Shō-ō [1293], twenty-first day, third month

> Musashi no kami (monogram)[144]
> Sagami no kami (monogram)[145]

[To:] Shimotsuke Saburō saemon no jō dono[146]

Document 40. *The establishment of the Chinzei tandai provided gokenin who had not yet received rewards with a new opportunity to appeal. The following document, written by the Hizen gokenin and shrine attendant Fujiwara Sukekado, reveals his dissatisfaction with the Chinzei dangisho for not recommending him for rewards as a result of his battle service at Takashima in 1281.*[147] *Hundreds of warriors had been rewarded by Kamakura in 1289, but somehow, Fujiwara Sukekado had been omitted from their ranks.*

The Hizen *gokenin* and head (*daigūji* 大宮司) of Kurokami Takeo shrine, Fujiwara Sukekado, respectfully states:

[Sukekado] desires to immediately receive rewards as a result of his battle service, and in accordance with custom, [regarding] the battles against the foreign pirates of the previous year of 1281.

[Concerning the] above, when the foreign pirates attacked, [Sukekado]

12.30.1286 (Kōan 9) Kantō migyōsho|an. Nevertheless, because the original document exists, and Kanetoki, one of the Rokuhara *tandai*, can be independently verified as departing for Kyushu in 1293, the latter designation is correct. See also *Chūkai, Genkō bōrui hennen shiryō*, pp. 266–67.

[144]Hōjō Nobutoki.

[145]Hōjō Sadatoki.

[146]Shimazu Tadamune.

[147]*Kamakura ibun*, vol. 25, 8.1296 (Einin 4) Fujiwara Sukekado mōshijō. For other documents pertaining to Takeo shrine that have been translated, see Mass, *Development of Kamakura Rule*, docs. 57, 67, and 98, pp, 210–11, 219–20, and 242, and Mass, *Lordship and Inheritance*, docs. 55–56, pp. 177–79.

boarded a pirate ship at Chizaki'oki (千崎息). Although wounded, Sukekado managed to capture one enemy alive, and to take one head.[148] In addition, during the attack on Munehara (棟原), on Takashima, [Sukekado] captured two alive while performing battle service. The *Chinzei dangisho* was responsible for [investigating] the particulars. Witnesses were questioned, and a report was [created], but [Sukekado] was omitted [from the ranks of those who] received equal[ly divided] rewards (*heikin onshō* 平均恩賞).[149] This is a cause of great lament. What could exceed this? It has been customary for many to receive rewards after launching appeals. Furthermore, as a report from the [Da]zaifu makes perfectly clear, Sukekado was personally wounded. How could [Sukekado] be omitted from [the list of those who received] equal[ly divided] military rewards? [Sukekado] has even heard that all of those who performed defensive warfare [and] guard duty received rewards. Why has Sukekado, who was personally wounded, not received any rewards? Many years and months have passed [since the invasions]: shouldn't [the Chinzei *tandai*] feel great pity? In short, on various fields of battle [Sukekado] has decapitated the enemy, captured [them] alive, and been personally wounded. Witness's statements and the report (*chūshin*) of the [Da]zaifu make this clear. In addition, as a result of my battle service, and in accordance with custom, [Sukekado] desires to receive equal military rewards. Thus respectfully stated as such.

The fourth year of Einin [1296], eighth month

DOCUMENTS 41–43. FORTIFICATIONS AND GUARD DUTY

Although Kamakura aborted its Korean expedition, the bakufu nevertheless managed to build extensive fortifications extending for ten kilometers along the harbors of Northern Kyūshū. These walls were built by warriors drawn from several Kyūshū provinces. Originally, the structures were made of earth, but later replaced with stone.[150] Men from each region varied their construction

---

[148]Literally, "perform *buntori*."

[149]1289, Kamakura split up a number of large estates in Kyūshū and granted portions to hundreds of warriors. These rewards, known either as *heikin onshō* or *heikin gunshō* (平均軍賞) constituted only miniscule amount of land. See *Kamakura ibun*, vol. 22, docs. 16917–27, 3.12.1289 (Shō-ō 2) Mōko kassen gunkōshō haibunjō.

[150]In some cases, the stone walls were constructed in front of the older earthen walls. For recent excavations of the walls at Nishijin (西新), see the western edition of the *Asahi Shinbun* for the evening of 11.11.1999. This article has also been reproduced in the January 2000 Fukuoka section of the *Gekan bunkazai hakkutsu*

techniques according to the terrain and availability of rocks. In some cases, nearby stones were used, whereas in others, boulders were transported from the island of Nokonoshima.[151] *These walls were made of sandstone and granite and were roughly two to three meters wide and two to three meters high. Many allowed for a commanding view of the coastline.*[152] *Even though the Kamakura bakufu collapsed in 1333, its successor, the Ashikaga bakufu, demanded guard duty be performed through 1348.*[153] *Political turmoil coupled with the final collapse of the Yuan dynasty in 1368 led to the abandonment of guard duty. Having served their purpose, the walls gradually fell into disrepair, finally sinking into the sand by the year 1700.*[154]

Document 41. *This document is the first reference to constructing a wall. Shōni Tsunesuke issued the following document the the Fukae, a gokenin family from Hizen province. Almost a month was required for this document to reach them.*[155]

Hashiuragaki: Fukae and the others from Tōgō estate, as well as Echū Jirō Saemon nyū[dō] and Arima Saemon listed their holdings (*chūmon densū* 注文田数). Arrived on the second year of Kenji [1276], fourth month, fifth day. The stone walls [were] built by the Shōni lord.[156]

As for the construction of a stone wall in strategic areas (*yōgai ishitsuiji* 要害石築地) in order to guard against the foreigners: commissioners (*bugyō*) shall levy corvees throughout the province on an equal basis, except for those who will be setting off for Korea (*Kōrai*). Prior to the twentieth day of this month, dispatch laborers to the harbor at Hakata where [they shall be placed under] the authority of [*shugo*] administration (*yakusho* 役所). Respectfully.

The second year of Kenji [1276], tenth day, third month

shutsudo jōhō (月刊文化財発掘出土情報). I am indebted to Joan Piggott for bringing this article to my attention.

[151]Yanagida Yoshitaka, "Genkō bōrui to chūsei no kaigan sen," in *Yomigaeru chūsei I Higashi ajia no kokusai toshi Hakata* (Heibonsha, 1988), p. 187.

[152]Ibid., p. 183. For a most comprehensive map of the location of the walls, see pp. 192–93.

[153]For the last references to guard duty at Hakata, see *Nanbokuchō ibun*, vol. 3, docs. 2453–54, 3.12.1348 (Jōwa 4) Fujiwara Michiatsu mōshijō, and 3.12.1348 (Jōwa 4) Tachibana Satsuma Kimiyuki mōshijō.

[154]See Yanagida, "Genkō bōrui to chūsei no kaigan sen," p. 194.

[155]*Kamakura ibun*, vol. 16, doc. 12260, 3.10.1276 (Kenji 2) Shōni Tsunesuke ishitsuijiyaku saisokujō.

[156]This passage was written by the recepient of the document.

Shōni (monogram)[157]

[To:] The *jitō* of Fukae village[158]

Documents 42–43. *Gokenin were liable to serve on guard duty for periods ranging from a month, for the residents of nearby provinces, to as long as half a year for those coming from Southern Kyūshū.*

Document 42. *The following was penned by a representative for the shugo of Satsuma, and dispatched to Hishijima Sukenori, who received praise for the half-year of service performed by his representative, Shinren.*[159]

Concerning the completion of Hakozaki guard duty by Satsuma province [*gokenin*]. You have performed [guard duty] from the tenth month until the first day of the fourth month [of this year].

The third year of Kōan [1280], first day, fourth month

The representative (*ondaikan*) Shinren (monogram)

[To:] Hishijima Tarō dono[160]

Document 43. *Here, Fukabori Tokinaka, a Hizen province gokenin, personally performed guard duty for one month.*[161]

Concerning Hakata guard duty against foreigners. From the twenty-[seventh] day of the eighth month until the twelfth day [of the ninth month][162] you have performed guard duty. Respectfully.

[157]Shōni Tsunesuke.

[158]The Fukae (Yasutomi) were originally scribes from Kamakura who had traveled to Northern Kyūshū. Ultimately, they came under the control of the Ryūzōji. See *Chūkai, Genkō Bōrui hennen shiryō*, pp. 148–49.

[159]*Kamakura ibun*, vol. 18, doc. 13906, 4.1.1280 (Kōan 3) Shinren Hakozaki ban'yaku fukukanjō.

[160]Hishijima Sukenori, the father of Hishijima Tokinori. See Documents 20–21 and *Chūkai, Genkō bōrui hennen shiryō*, p. 242.

[161]*Kamakura ibun*, vol. 19, doc. 14100 9.12.1280 (Kōan 3) Shōni Tsunesuke keiko ban'yaku fukukanjō.

[162]This portion of the document is missing, but can be reconstructed from a copy of the same document. See *Kamakura ibun*, vol. 19, doc. 14101, 12.1280 (Kōan 3) Shōni Tsunesuke keiko ban'yaku fukukanjō an.

The third year of Kōan [1280], twelfth day, ninth month

[Shōni] Tsunesuke (monogram)

[To:] Fukabori dono[163]

DOCUMENTS 44–47. REPAIRING THE WALL

Document 44. *Gokenin were responsible for constructing a portion of the wall in addition to their guard duty, as the following document from the deputy shugo of Satsuma to Hishijima Sukenori attests.*[164]

[You have] served since the beginning [in constructing the] 6,132-yard-long Hishijima portion[165] of the stone wall [that is the responsibility of those who possess holdings] inside Mitsuie'in.[166] This is so conveyed.

(The seventh year of Kōan [1284]), twenty-first day, intercalary fourth month

Munetada (monogram)[167]

[To:] Hishijima Tarō dono[168]

---

[163]Fukabori Yagorō Tokinaka. The Fukabori were related to the Miura, of Sagami province, but were granted *jitō shiki* to the harbor of Sonogi estate, in Hizen province, in 1255. See *Chūkai, Genkō bōrui hennen shiryō*, pp. 183–84.

[164]*Kamakura ibun*, vol. 20, doc. 15182, intercalary 4.21.[1284 (Kōan 7)] Shimazu Munetada fukukanjō. Nevertheless, this designation appears mistaken, for according to Kawazoe, Munetada was a deputy *shugo* for the Shimazu. See *Chūkai, Genkō bōrui hennen shiryō*, pp. 207–8.

[165]Five *jō* (丈) four *shaku* (尺) and four *sun* (寸), which equals approximately 51.4 *chō* in length. One *chō* consists of 119.303 yards.

[166]The Hishijima held *myōshu shiki* at Mitsuie'in in Shimazu estate. Four *myōshu*, the Hishijima, Nishimata, Kawada, and Maeda, were in fact responsible for constructing the walls. Hence, the Hishijima's actual burden has been estimated to be 16 *chō*, or nearly 1,910 yards. See *Chūkai, Genkō bōrui hennen shiryō*, pp. 177–78 and 207–8. For documents pertaining solely to Hishijima *myō*, see *Kamakura ibun*, vol.16, doc. 11867, 4.11.1275 (Bun'ei 12) Minamoto Sukenori mōshijō; doc. 11876, 4.26.1275 (Bun'ei 12) Minamoto Sukenori mōshijō; vol. 26, docs. 20216, 8.1299 (Shōan 1) Minamoto Tadanori yuzurijō, and 20217, 8.1299 (Shōan 1) Minamoto Tadanori okibumi.

[167]Munetada was apparently an otherwise unknown deputy of Shimazu Tadamune, the *shugo* of Satsuma.

[168]Hishijima Sukenori.

Repairing the Wall

Documents 45–46. *A copy of the order from Hōjō Kanetoki, the newly appointed Chinzei tandai, to Shimazu Tadamune, the shugo of Satsuma, demanding that he ensure that the stonewalls remain in good repair.[169] Tadamune dispatched a copy of Kanetoki's message with his own two days later. Both documents were copied by the Satsuma gokenin Hishijima Sukenori.*

Concerning the construction of stone walls and other vital [fortifications]: Even though the Kantō has issued many orders, it has been reported that [this construction] has not been attended to. Immediately complete this task. Those areas that are difficult [to complete] shall be reported. This shall be announced throughout the province of Satsuma. This is so conveyed.

The sixth year of Shō-ō [1293], twenty-first day, fourth month.

Echigo no kami (gohan)[170]

[To:] Shimōsa Saburō Saemon no jō dono[171]

Document 46. *Shimazu Tadamune's document.[172]*

Concerning the construction of the Hakozaki stone walls and other vital [fortifications], a copy of the order (migyōsho) of Echigo no kami, dated the the twenty-first day of this month, is as such. As for the three feet (shaku) of the Kasa area and the Urashiba [portion of the wall] that remain in disrepair [in spite of] repeated requests [to do something], you must complete this task prior to the twentieth day of the coming fifth month. Those late [in accomplishing this task] shall be reported. This is so conveyed.

Twenty-third day, fourth month

Saemon no jō (arihan)[173]

[To:] The *jitō gokenin* of Satsuma province

[169]*Kamakura ibun*, vol. 23, doc. 18178, 4.21.1293 (Shō-ō 6) Hōjō Kanetoki kakikudashi an.
[170]Hōjō Kanetoki.
[171]Shimazu Tadamune.
[172]*Kamakura ibun*, vol. 23, doc. 18179, 4.23.[1293 (Shō-ō 6)] Shimazu Tadamune shigyōjō an.
[173]Shimazu Tadamune.

238

Document 47. *Even after the Kamakura bakufu had been destroyed in 1333, its successor, the Ashikaga bakufu, continued demanding that Kyūshū warriors contribute to the upkeep of the Hakata fortifications. A copy of the following edict, issued by Ashikaga Tadayoshi to Ōtomo Ujiyasu, reveals that the Ōtomo and the Shōni were once again solely responsible for administering Northern Kyūshū.*[174]

Reports have been heard that [parts of] the stone walls (*ishitsuiji* 石築地) that guard the Chinzei have collapsed. Together with Dazai Shōni Yorihisa,[175] you shall immediately announce to those who are responsible (*honyaku'nin* 本役人) [for repairing the walls] that they shall complete repairs by the end of this year. If any of them have difficulties [in repairing the walls, they] shall have their names reported. Punishments shall be meted out. Thus.

The fifth year of Kenmu [1338], first day, intercalary seventh month

gohan[176]

[To:] Ōtomo Shikubu no jō dono[177]

DOCUMENTS 48–49. PROVISIONS

The Kamakura bakufu dramatically expanded its jurisdiction over all lands, including previously immune estates (shōen 荘園), in order to secure adequate provisions immediately before the Mongols attacked in 1281.[178]

---

[174]*Nanbokuchō ibun*, vol. 1, doc. 1213, intercalary 7.1.1338 (Kenmu 5) Ashikaga Tadayoshi migyōsho an. Tadayoshi was brother to the first Ashikaga *shōgun*, Ashikaga Takauji, while Ujiyasu was appointed to the *shugo* of Bungo, Hizen, and briefly, Hyūga provinces during the years of 1336–37.

[175]Yorihisa had been appointed the *shugo* of Higo, Chikuzen, and Buzen provinces in 1336.

[176]A copy of the monogram of Ashikaga Tadayoshi.

[177]Ōtomo Ujiyasu.

[178]An excerpt from this diary, written by Otsuki Akihira, who was the chief secretary (*shoki kyokuchō* 書記局長) of the Council of State (Dajōkan). This diary is known as "Excerpts of the diary of 1281," or *Kōan yonnen* (1281) *nikkishō* (弘安四年日記抄). Only one year of Akihira's diary survives because it was excerpted and used as a precedent in determining a response to a Korean attack on Tsushima island in 1419. For references to the text, see *Chūkai, Genkō bōrui hennen shiryō*, pp. 191–92 and *Nihonshi shiryō 2 chūsei*, pp. 147–48 . Finally, for the disputes of 1419, see *Nihonshi shiryō 2 chūsei*, pp. 334–37. I am indebted to Katsuyama Seiji for being able to view photographs of this manuscript.

Document 48. *Otsuki Akihira, the chief secretary of the Council of State, copied the order that had been dispatched from Hōjō Tokimune, in Kamakura, to the Rokuhara tandai, Hōjō Tokimura and Tokikuni. Akihira's commentary is as follows.*[179]

In order to guard against foreigners, the nine provinces of Chinzei along with Inaba, Hoki, [Izumo], and Iwami shall not pay taxes (*nengu* 年貢) [to the capital]. Instead, [produce] shall be appropriated (*tenjō subeshi* 点定). A document from Kamakura arrived last night stating that all estates should follow [Kamakura's] orders (*gechi*) [text missing]. The foreign pirates have yet to cross [national] boundaries: [Kamakura must] wish for the destruction of the capital! The laments of those of high and low station are without compare. I must check the veracity [of this report] and then record [the Kamakura document].

Document 49. *A copy of the Kamakura edict to the Rokuhara tandai.*[180]

As battle [is being waged] with foreigners, provisions (*hyōrōmai* 兵粮米) at [this] time [are most] vital.[181] As for the Chinzei, and throughout the provinces of Inaba, Hōki, Izumo, Iwami [text missing] . . . if [surplus] rice and grains exist [from] estates possessing complete rights and authority (*honsho ichienryō no tokubun* 本所一円領得分), and the wealthy [text missing], [then they] shall be appropriated. Let this purport be conveyed [text missing] to the *Tōgū daibu*.[182] Thus.

The fourth year of Kōan [1281], twenty-eighth day, sixth month

Sagami no kami [183]

---

[179] For more on Tokikuni, see Document 36. For Tokimura, see note 184.

[180] *Kamakura ibun*, vol. 19, doc. 14355, 6.28.1281 (Kōan 4) Kantō migyōsho an.

[181] This passage is difficult to decipher, for the text is missing. This interpretation is based on the reconstruction that appears in *Nihonshi shiryō 2 chūsei*, pp. 147–48.

[182] The *Tōgū daibu* (東宮大夫) was also the *Kantō mōshitsugi*, Kamakura's diplomatic liaison in Kyōto, a post held in 1281 by Saionji Sanehira. The post of *Tōgū daibu* was otherwise responsible for administrating affairs of the crown prince.

[183] Hōjō Tokimune.

Records of the Invasions

[To:] Mutsu no kami dono[184]
Echigo Sakan daibu shōgen dono[185]

DOCUMENTS 50–52. FEARS OF FUTURE INVASIONS

Document 50. *Kamakura feared an attack on the western provinces of Honshū in 1281. Hōjō Tokimune appoints Hōjō Tokinari (Kanetoki) as shugo of Harima province in order to bolster defenses, and expressly orders Harima gokenin to obey Kanetoki's orders.*[186]

In order to be fully prepared for the foreign pirates, [I am] dispatching Sagami Shichirō Tokinari to Harima province.[187] If you hear that pirate ships have entered the shipping lanes of the San'yō ocean,[188] follow Tokinari's orders and perform defensive battle service. This order is so conveyed.

The fourth year of Kōan [1281], eleventh day, intercalary seventh month

Sagami no kami (monogram)[189]
[To:] Terada Tarō nyūdō dono[190]

Document 51. *The bakufu also orders eastern gokenin to travel to western Honshū, and to defend these regions if the Mongol fleet managed to pass through the strategic Shimonoseki straits that separate Kyūshū from Honshū.*[191] *The Kodama, gokenin of Mutsu province, are commanded to report to their Aki holdings, where they would remain.*[192]

---

[184]HōjōTokimura, who became appointed as the northern Rokuhara *tandai* on 5.16.1278, was the son of Hōjō Masamura. See *Sonpi bunmyaku*, vol. 4, p. 20, and for more on Masamura, Documents 2 and 4. Tokimura perished in battle, at the age of sixty-four, on 4.23.1305.

[185]HōjōTokikuni.

[186]*Kamakura ibun*, vol. 19, doc. 14388, intercalary 7.11.1281 (Kōan 4) Kantō migyōsho.

[187]Tokinari was the first name of the future Rokuhara *tandai*, Hōjō Kanetoki. See *Chūkai, Genkō bōrui hennen shiryō*, pp. 192–93. For more on Kanetoki, see Documents 39, 45–46, and 52.

[188]The waters off of northwestern Honshū (i.e. the provinces of Izumo and Iwami).

[189]HōjōTokimune.

[190]The Terada were Harima *gokenin*.

[191]These straits were the site of the famous battle of Danoura in 1185.

[192]*Kamakura ibun*, vol. 19, doc. 14389, intercalary 7.11.1281 (Kōan 4) Kantō

Be fully prepared for the foreign pirates. Dispatch your son to [your] holdings in Aki province by the middle of the coming eighth month. If the pirate ships enter [the straits of] the Moji (門司) barrier,[193] [your son] must immediately follow the mobilization of the acting *shugo*,[194] join the encampment of Nagato province forces, and perform defensive battle service. This order is so conveyed.

The fourth year of Kōan [1281], eleventh day, intercalary seventh month

Sagami no kami (monogram)[195]

[To:] Kodama Rokurō dono and [the family of] Shichirō[196]

Document 52. *The Chinzei tandai Hōjō Kanetoki orders signal fires to be established in 1294 on the outlying islands of Northern Kyūshū as a precaution against further Mongol attacks. Hōjō Sadamune, the shugo of Hizen province, transmitted a copy of Kanetoki's order to the Hizen gokenin Ōshima Michikiyo.*[197]

Hashiuragaki: Arrived on the second year of Einin [1294], twentieth day, third month

Concerning signal fires, a copy of an order (*gohōsho* 御奉書) from the Echigo provincial governor (*kokushi* 国司)[198] is as follows: "Already by the hour of the horse[199] on the twenty-sixth day of the third month, Chikuzen

---

migyōsho. For similar orders, see also *Kamakura ibun*, vol. 19, doc. 14390, intercalary 7.11.1281 (Kōan 4) Kantō migyōsho an.

[193]Moji designates a region on the Kyūshū side of the straits, while Shimonoseki is located on the Honshū side.

[194]Literally *shugonin*, which could designate an acting or deputy *shugo*.

[195]Hōjō Tokimune.

[196]Kodama Shigeyuki and Iechika. For their continued guard duty of the Kodama in Aki during 1320, see *Kamakura ibun*, vol. 36, doc. 27549, 8.17.1320 (Gen-ō 2) Rokuhara migyōsho.

[197]*Kamakura ibun*, vol. 24, doc. 18499, 3.6.1294 (Einin 2) Chinzei migyōsho (an incorrect designation, for the *shugo* Sadamune clearly dispatched this document). I would like to thank Saeki Kōji for showing my this original document, and others of the Kurishima collection, on 6.9.2000.

[198]Hōjō Kanetoki, who was also the Chinzei *tandai*. His document is functionally similar to an edict (*migyōsho*) but because of his rank, his document is technically only a *gohōsho*. For more on the relationship of status to the designation of particular documents, see *Komonjo yōgo jiten*, p. 393.

[199]Eleven in the morning until one in the afternoon. See appendix 2.

province has been ordered to ignite signal fires. It shall be announced to all the regions of all the islands [of Hizen] that Hizen's signal fires must be ignited at the same time. If it rains on that day, the signal fires should be ignited on the twenty-seventh of the same month." Because signal fires shall be ignited on the high regions of each island, starting at Iki island, [the islanders of] Ōshima must be on the lookout[200] for the smoke of Iki Island. At that time [when smoke is seen], without fail [you] shall gather much kindling, pile it up, and earnestly ignite [a blaze]. [The residents of] each [island] shall strive to be on the lookout for hazy glow [of signal] fires [from the other]. It has already been announced that if fires are visible from Ōshima, [new fires] shall be ignited on Takashima. It is of greatest importance to guard against the foreigners. There must be no further negligence. This is so conveyed.

The second year of Einin [1294], sixth day, third month

Shūri no suke (monogram)[201]

[To:] Ōshima Matajirō dono[202]

DOCUMENTS 53–55. GUARD DUTY, GOKENIN STATUS, AND THE PARAMETERS OF FAMILIAL AUTHORITY

In contrast to the case of Documents 12–13, where Shiga Yasutomo's chieftair authority was upheld by the bakufu over his brother Zenki, here Sata Sadachika managed to wrest autonomy from his cousin Chikaharu.

Document 53. *Kamakura's confirmations proved decisive in determining gokenin status. Chiba Munetane, the shugo of Ōsumi, declares Sata Sadachika to be a gokenin based on his possession of a bakufu document of confirmation.[203]*

---

[200]Literally, "protect" the smoke of Iki Island. This phrase is repeated again below.

[201]Hōjō Sadamune became the *shugo* of Hizen province after his father, Hōjō Tokisada, perished in 8.1289, and continued serving through 1295. For more on Hōjō control over the post of Hizen *shugo*, see Documents 27–29.

[202]Ōshima Michikiyo. The Ōshima possessed the *jitō shiki* of Ōshima island which constituted a portion of the Uno mikuriya. They also adopted the name Ōi and would later join the Matsura band (*tō* 党) from the mid-fourteenth centur₁ onward. See Seno, *Chinzei gokenin no kenkyū*, p. 172.

[203]*Kamakura ibun*, vol. 20, doc. 15003, 11.18.1283 (Kōan 6) Ōsumi no shug₁ Chiba Munetane gechijō.

Concerning the dispute between Nejime Yashirō Chikaharu, the Ōsumi *gokenin* and *hon jitō* (本地頭) of Minamimata-sata village, and Sata Yakurō Sadachika,[204] *gokenin* of the same province and the western *hon jitō*, over guard duty against the foreigners. Both sides have made many claims, [but] in short, Sadachika is an independent *gokenin*, for he possesses a confirmation edict (*ando no onkudashibumi* 安堵御下文) [from Kamakura]. He thus shall perform guard duty independently. Ordered and commanded thus.

The sixth year of Kōan [1283], eighteenth day, eleventh month

Munetane (monogram)[205]

Document 54. *Once the shugo Chiba Munetane had declared Sata Sadachika to be a gokenin, he had his deputy announce this to the other gokenin in Ōsumi province.*[206]

Concerning the dispute between Sata Yashirō dono[207] and Yakurō dono[208] over guard duty, [the *shugo's*] edict (*ongechi* 御下知) reads as follows: "Both sides have made many claims, [but] in conclusion Sadachika is an independent *gokenin*, for he possesses a confirmation edict (*ando no kudashibumi*) [from Kamakura]. He thus shall perform guard duty independently. Ordered and commanded thus." Nevertheless, this purport should [be known throughout the province]. Respectfully.

The sixth year of Kōan [1283], twenty-second day, eleventh month

Dōi (monogram)[209]

[To:] Taji Kojirō dono

Document 55. *Both Sata Yakurō Sadachika and his brother, Ishi-ō, managed to assert autonomy, and gokenin status, based upon a bakufu confirmation. The*

---

[204]Both these men ultimately adopted the name of Sata in order to distinguish themselves from the Nejime. See *Chūkai, Genkō bōrui hennen shiryō*, pp. 204–6.

[205]Chiba Munetane, the *shugo* of Ōsumi province from 1283 until 1291.

[206]*Kamakura ibun*, vol. 20, doc. 15008, 11.22.1283 (Kōan 6) Ōsumi no shugodai Dō'i kakikudashi.

[207]Sata Yashirō Chikaharu.

[208]Sata Yakurō Sadachika.

[209]The deputy *shugo*, Dō'i, otherwise unknown.

following receipt of guard duty service from Chiba Munetane reveals that both served separately on guard duty. Ultimately, however, Sadachika gained control over Ishi-ō's lands by declaring him to be insane.[210]

Concerning guard duty against the foreigners. For the past ninety days, from the first day of this past sixth month until the last day of the eighth month, you have served [your share of] guard duty–fifty-four days. Sata Ishi-ō's days are excluded. Respectfully.

The sixth year of Kōan [1283], twenty-second day, tenth month

Munetane (monogram)[211]

[To:] Sata Yakurō dono[212]

THE FALL OF THE ADACHI

Document 56. *The following document reveals much about the nature of military service and the state of judicial affairs in Kyūshū during the tumultuous year of 1285. After Adachi Yasumori was assassinated in Kamakura during the "Frosty Moon Disturbance," his son Morimune joined forces with Shōni Kagesuke and fought against the bakufu at Iwato, where they were defeated and killed. Many gokenin, such as Sata Sadachika (Documents 52–54), took advantage of this incident to perform military service under the command of their shugo.*[213] *Sadachika fought against Morimune and Kagesuke because he happened to be in Hakata, filing a lawsuit, which reveals that a system of adjudication for Kyūshū gokenin functioned well before Kamakura created the Chinzei dangisho and other regional judicial institutions (see Documents 36–37).*[214]

[210]*Kamakura ibun*, vol. 20, doc. 14979, 10.22.1283 (Kōan 6) Ōsumi no shugo Chiba Munetane fukukanjō. Sata holdings were divided so that three-fifths belonged to Sadachika and the rest belonged to Sata Ishi-ō. See *Kamakura ibun*, vol. 19, doc. 14339, 6.2.1281 (Kōan 4) Kantō gechijō. By 1285, Sadachika claimed that Ishi-ō had "become crazed and insane, and, being of no use to the Kantō, had fled his lands and moved to another province." See *Kamakura ibun*, vol. 20, doc. 15720, 10.1285 (Kōan 8) Kenbu Sadachika shoryō chūshinjō an, p. 396. See also *Chūkai, Genkō bōrui hennen shiryō*, pp. 203–4.

[211]Chiba Munetane.

[212]Sata Yakurō Sadachika.

[213]In this case, Chiba Munetane, the *shugo* of Ōsumi.

[214]*Kamakura ibun*, vol. 21, doc. 15764, 12.18.1285 (Kōan 8) Chiba Munetane kakikudashi. Cogent analysis of the significance of this document in understanding the development of Chinzei institutions appears in *Chūkai, Genkō bōrui hennen*

Hashiuragaki: A document (*kakikudashi*) written [during the] battle [against] Echizen dono [Adachi Morimune]

Because [news of] a disturbance (*sōdō* 騒動) [erupted] concerning the chastisement of the previous governor of Echizen Morimune arrived here [in Hakata] precisely at the time when you were here [engaged in] litigation, you have joined our forces. This is most splendid. Now that all is calm in the world, those who are not performing guard duty should return to their home provinces. Respectfully.

The eighth year of Kōan [1285], eighteenth day, twelfth month

Munetane (monogram)[215]

[To:] Sata Yakurō dono[216]

DOCUMENTS 57–65. RELIGION AND WAR

Both the Court and Kamakura initiated prayers against the Mongol invaders.

Document 57. *The court took the lead in promulgating prayers throughout Japan shortly after the Mongols dispatched their first diplomatic missive to Japan. The following document was issued by the reigning sovereign, Kameyama. This document originally appeared in the Kichizokuki, the diary of Yoshida Tsunenaga (1239–1309). He added his commentary to this document, which had been written by Taira Tōbō, the Lesser Controller of the Right (ushōben 右少弁) and chamberlain (kurōdo 蔵人) for Kameyama.[217] From this document, one can also infer that Koryo messengers warned Japan of an imminent invasion.[218]*

A sovereign's edict (*senji* 宣旨)[from] the eighth year of of Bun'ei [1271], twenty-first day, ninth month.

---

shiryō, pp. 213–14.

[215]Chiba Munetane.

[216]Sata Yakurō Sadachika.

[217]*Kamakura ibun*, vol. 14, doc. 10882, 9.21.1271 (Bun'ei 8) Kameyama tennō senji.

[218]*Kichizokuki* (吉続記), the diary of Yoshida Tsunenaga (1239–1309), records the period when Tsunenaga was appointed chamberlain (*kurōdo* 蔵人) of the inner palace in 1267 until he advanced to become a Major Counselor (*dainagon* 大納言) in 1302. Fragments of fourteen of these years survive. Tsunenaga was appointed to the office of Lesser Controller of the Left (*sashōben* 左少弁) in 1270, and it is at this post that he records court edicts most relevant to the Mongol invasions. Tsunenaga's diary mostly illuminates court ritual and courtier affairs, and has been published in the *Shiryō taisei* (史料大成).

In recent days, the heavens above have displayed [a great] disturbance. [The sovereign feels] not the slightest at ease. In addition, messengers from the Western Domains[219] have told of the Northern Barbarian[220] plot [to conquer Japan]. This fact [of an invasion] stems from a profound reason that cannot be easily discerned.[221] The many are afraid [and wish that] this menace [will] forever cease. You shall please [have prayers offered for] peace. A Ninnō-e[222] curse (*juganmon* 呪願文) [against the Mongols] shall be created and recorded.

The Kurōdo Saemon gon no suke Taira Tōbō received [this].[223]

Concerning the main country of the Mongols, no one has yet read their history.[224] The current Northern Barbarian document is most suspicious. Perhaps it is someone's indirect admonishment.

Document 58. *In contrast to the reigning emperor, who issued prayers for the sake of the country, Kamakura's offerings proved to be of a more limited scale.*[225] *Here, the shrine attendant of Itsukushima shrine, Fujiwara Chikasada, issues the following command to his subordinates.*

A sword[226] has been offered to the shrine from the Kantō to pray for the destruction of foreign [invaders]. Wait until an auspicious day to present

---

[219] Another name for Koryo.

[220] Mongol.

[221] This meaning of this sentence stems from the term *kii* (希夷), which comes from the writings of Lao Tzu.

[222] The Ninnō-e constituted one of the most important state rituals, whereby the Ninnō-e, or "Benevolent Kings Protecting Their Countries" Sutra (or Prajñāpāramitā sūtra), was read by ranking priests. This sutra described how a king could protect his country from all calamities by means of the power of the Bodhisattvas of the Five Quarters.

[223] Taira Tōbō held the office of Ushōben (右少弁) and was of the Kammu Heishi lineage. Many of his relatives had been invested with the office of secretariat, or chamberlain (*kurōdo*), a post that Tōbō himself held for both the retired sovereign Gosaga and the reigning ruler, Kameyama. See *Sonpi bunmyaku*, vol. 4, p. 6. For documentary references to Tōbō, see *Kamakura ibun*, vol. 14, doc 10658, 7.27 Go Saga Jōkō inzen. See also *Kamakura ibun*, vol. 15, doc. 11190 2.18.1273 (Bune'ei 10) Kameyama tennō senji, and docs. 11213, 11709, and 11855.

[224] This passage represents the commentary of Yoshida Tsunenaga.

[225] *Kamakura ibun*, vol. 15, doc. 11766, 12.2.1274 (Bun'ei 11) Fujiwara Chikasada kakikudashi.

[226] Descriptions of the sword (*chōbukurin shishi shitan* 長伏輪獅子牡丹) are cryptic and hereby omitted.

the sword and record the rites that you perform. This sword shall be added to the repository of shrine treasures. Thus.

The eleventh year of Bun'ei [1274], second day, twelfth month

[To:] The office (*mandokoro* 政所) of Itsukushima shrine

Document 59. *The bakufu ordered Buddhist temples to recite prayers for victory over the Mongol invaders. The shugo of each province requested that each temple record and submit their prayers to the shugo, who would forward them to Kamakura. This document, was issued by the shugo of Bungo, Ōtomo Yoriyasu, to the priests of Rokugō mountain.*[227]

Concerning prayers for the destruction of foreigners. Abide by the Kantō edict (*migyōsho*), pray with fervor, and record the rites that you perform.[228] This is so conveyed.

The seventh year of Kōan [1284], twenty-fifth day, third month

[To:] The priests of Rokugō mountain

Document 60. *Here, the shikken, Hōjō Sadatoki, orders the shugo of Aki to bestow a sword and horse to Itsukushima shrine in exchange for curses against the Mongols.*[229] *Responsibility for providing these offerings lay with the shugo of Aki province, although the bakufu continued to oversee the process by dispatching special representatives and by demanding written receipts of its offerings.*

Concerning the subjugation of foreign countries. One sword and one divine horse shall be presented to the First Shrine (*Ichinomiya* 一宮) of each province. Immediately provide [these offerings] for the provinces of Noto and Aki. A receipt [of these offerings] shall be dispatched [to Kamakura]. This order is so conveyed.

The sixth year of Shō-ō [1293], eleventh day, second month

[227]*Kamakura ibun*, vol. 20, doc. 15124, 3.25.1284 (Kōan 7) Ōtomo Yoriyasu shigyōjō.
[228]For the record of their prayers, see *Kamakura ibun*, vol. 20, doc. 15312, 9.1284 (Kōan 7) Bungo Rokugōzan kitō kansū mokuroku.
[229]*Kamakura ibun*, vol. 23, doc. 18109, 2.11.1293 (Shō-ō 6) Kantō migyōsho an.

Mutsu no kami (gohan)[230]
Sagami no kami (gohan)[231]

[To:] The former governor (*zenshi* 前司) of Bizen[232]

Document 61. *Orders from the shugo (Document 60) are conveyed to their deputy, who dispatched the following to Itsukushima shrine.*[233]

Concerning the subjugation of foreign countries. An order dispatched from Kamakura, dated the eleventh day of this past second month, shall be posted to all the shrine attendants. It states as follows: " One sword and one divine horse shall be presented to the First Shrine (*Ichinomiya* ― 宮) of Aki province so that they can engage in full ceremonies and pray with exemplary fervor." Their receipt [of these items] shall be forwarded [to Kamakura]. Thus.

The sixth year of Shō-ō [1293], twenty-first day, fourth month
(gohan ari)

[To:] Nagao Hyōe Gorō dono

Document 62. *Kamakura also provided funds to the shrines, but stipulated how they should pray for military success.*[234]

Concerning those prayers for the subjugation of foreign countries: excerpts of the Great Hannya sutra shall be read (*tendoku* 転読) at Aki province's Itsukushima shrine.[235] Likewise, it is [your] responsibility to forward 12 *kan* (貫) [of cash] to the shrine family for the head shrine attendant (*gokannushi*

---

[230]Hōjō Nobutoki.

[231]Hōjō Sadatoki.

[232]Identity unknown. In all probability, someone from the Nagoe Munenaga branch of the Hōjō. See *Zōtei Kamakura bakufu shugo seido no kenkyū*, pp. 118–19, 173–74.

[233]*Kamakura ibun*, vol. 23, doc. 18176, 4.21.1293 (Shō-ō 6) Bō shigyōjō an.

[234]*Kamakura ibun*, vol. 23, doc. 18128, 3.20.1293 (Shō-ō 6) Kantō migyōsho an.

[235]The *Mahāprajñāparamitā Sutra* (or Great Wisdom sutra), 600 volumes, which was first translated into Chinese by the T'ang monk Xuan Zang in the seventh century. This massive sutra explains how the all observed phenomenon are in fact subjective perceptions. By setting one's mind free of the illusion that objective phenomena truly exists, this sutra was widely believed to emancipate people from evil. Shrine attendants read this sutra, which reveals the sometimes hazy boundary between Shintō and Buddhism at this time.

御神主). A receipt [of these offerings] shall be forwarded [to Kamakura]. This order is so conveyed.

The sixth year of Shō-ō [1293], twentieth day, third month

> Mutsu no kami (gohan)[236]
> Sagami no kami (gohan)[237]

[To:] The former governor (*zenshi* 前司) of Bizen[238]

Document 63. *Saitō Motoari, a member of the hikitsuke who was apparently dispatched to Aki as a special messenger, verifies that Itsukushima shrine has received Kamakura's offerings.*[239]

Bestowed to Itsukushima shrine

Total:

> One sword by Totan.
> One bow two sections [wrapped in] bamboo and rattan.[240]
> One quiver of war arrows with white tails.

For prayers to subjugate the foreigners, the above offerings have been received. Thus.

The sixth year of Shō-ō [1293], sixteenth day, fourth month

The representative (*ontsukai* 御使) Ukan shōgen Fujiwara Motoari
(monogram)[241]

---

[236]Hōjō Nobutoki.

[237]Hōjō Sadatoki.

[238]Identity unknown. See Document 60.

[239]*Kamakura ibun*, vol. 23, doc. 18171, 4.16.1293 (Shō-ō 6) Aki no Itsukushimasha no shinmotsu hōkenjō. The *hikitsuke* constitutes an investigative office, which became the principle organ of judicial inquiry for the *bakufu* shortly after its establishment in 1249.

[240]This probably designates a ceremonial bow wrapped in rattan (藤 *tō*) and bamboo, which represents an early version of an ornamental wrapped bow (*shigetō no yumi* 重藤弓).

[241]According to the *Sonpi bunmyaku*, vol. 2, p. 327, Saitō (Fujiwara) Michiari held the lower fifth rank and was a member of the Kantō *hikitsuke*.

Document 64. *The following document*[242] *conveys sentiments that closely resemble those of Takezaki Suenaga at the epilogue of his picture scrolls. The priest Tahōbō managed to secure considerable patronage from Kamakura because of his dreams. Perhaps Takezaki Suenaga was one of the Higo gokenin, wearing full armor, who participated in these ceremonies at Ikinomatsubara.*

Hashiuragaki: A copy

Respectfully stated:
[I offered a] prayer to the Kumano avatars of Ikinomatsubara, Sawara district, Chikuzen province. Forces from abroad issued a curse (*chōbuku*) to destroy Japan. I had a dream, sign of the Kumano avatars, whereby their forms[243] appeared at Ikinomatsubara and said, "The following gods–Suwa Daimyōjin, Kashima no Daimyōjin, Mishima no Daimyōjin, Aki [province's] Itsukushima no Daimyōjin, the [gods of the] Izumo shrine (*onyashiro*), Hakozaki Hachiman, Sumiyoshi Daimyōjin, Kawakami Yodohime, Kawara Daibōsatsu, the Eight Great Dragon Kings (*Hachidai ryū-ō*), and the Dragon King of the ocean (*Umi no kairyū-ō*)–are deflecting the curse (*chōbuku*) back to the other countries (*takoku*). [You] Tahōbō will have this dream." When I reported this to the Kantō, the *shugo* at the time, Lord Nagasaki[244] ordered that a shrine (*yashiro* 社) be built at Ikinomatsubara. Just as twelve realms and twelve [fundamental] doctrines exist, so too [does the dream] coming from Kumano [mentions twelve deities].[245] I offered a prayer [to Kumano] for an end to turmoil and [the

---

[242]*Kamakura ibun*, vol. 24, doc. 18341, 8.15.1293 Tahōbō ganmon. See also *Chūkai, Genkō bōrui hennen shiryō*, pp. 277–78.

[243]Tahōbō refers to the twelve Kumano avatars. Nevertheless, it is not clear if he is seeing all twelve or merely one in his dream, for medieval Japanese makes no distinction between singular and plural deities.

[244]This refers either to Nagasaki Mitsutsuna, the younger brother of Taira Yoritsuna, or to Mitsutsuna's son, Takatsuna, a powerful force in the *bakufu* until its destruction in 1333. The Nagasaki were retainers of the Hōjō and so must have been the deputy *shugo* of Higo.

[245]The above passage remains difficult to decipher. One finds references to twelve *onmuku*, which presumably designates the twelve realms of existence according to Buddhist beliefs. *Muku* perhaps designates *mukui*, which can then be equated with the 12 causes and effects (*jūni innen*). See *Mikkyō jiten*, comp. Sawa Takeshi (Kyōto: Hōzōkan, 1975) pp. 346–47. *Onajiki onjutai* seems to refer to twelve fundamental doctrines of Buddhism. Kawazoe, in *Chūkai, Genkō bōru hennen shiryō*, p. 278, admits that he is baffled by this passage. A parallel is apparently drawn between fundamental aspects of Buddhist doctrine and the appearance of twelve different deities (the list of eleven and the Kumano avatars in Tahōbō's dream. The final connection is, of course, that twelve Kumano avatars

restoration of] prosperity to Japan (*Nihon koku* 日本国). Higo *gokenin*, wearing battle garb, participated in the ceremonies. Offered to the twelve Kumano avatars at Ikinomatsubara.

The first year of Einin [1293], fifteenth day, eighth month

Document 65. *Otherwordly support was believed to have vanquished the Mongols in 1293 and 1314 as well. Significantly, both years coincide with the time that Suenaga amended the regulations to his shrine. These beliefs appear to have strengthened as the fourteenth century progressed, as evidenced by the following document, written during the third intercalary month of 1314 by the reigning emperor, Hanazono.*[246]

Clear weather. The Nyoen holy man (*hijiri* 上人) arrived . . . [and] told me that the doors to the third building of the Sumiyoshi shrine had been [flung] open and the chain around them had been cut. That chain was made of iron and was six inches (*sun*) thick–clearly not something that people could easily break. The holy man [Nyoen] visited the shrine and peered inside. Truly it was most mysterious indeed. This had to be [the gods] quelling foreign countries (*ikoku chōbuku*). During the previous Mongol invasions, signs [had emanated] from this shrine. That evening Shigenaga *ason* (朝臣) said that . . . when Buddhist ceremonies (*kanjō* 観 請) were performed at Kitano shrine, in the Aoki estate of Chikuzen province, an injured snake appeared from inside the shrine building. Everyone was surprised at this time. The god [manifested as a snake] conveyed [its thoughts] to a *miko* (巫女)[247] who said: "The foreigners have already attacked. The gods of Kashii, Hakozaki, and Kōra shrines and I have battled them. The [god of] Kashii shrine is half dead. Because of my virtue as Daijizai,[248] I have notified people by manifesting myself as a snake," and continued, saying: "If there are more prayers, I will once again depart to subjugate the foreign countries."[249]

I (*chin* 朕) [Hanazono] must lack great virtue, having ascended the

existed as well.

[246]*Hanazono tennō shinki*, vol. 1, in *Zōho shiryō taisei*, vol. 2 (Kyōto: Rinsen shoten, 1965), pp. 100–1, Shōwa 3 [1314], nineteenth day, third intercalary month. See also *Nihonshi shiryō 2 chūsei*, p. 150.

[247]A female shrine attendant.

[248]The deity of Kitano shrine, the spirit of Sugawara Michizane, also known as Tenman Daijizaiten.

[249]This claim was transmitted to Kamakura two months later. See *Kamakura nendaiki*, p. 61.

throne for no great reason. This is why such disasters appear. My despair exceeds words. I can only count on the protection of the gods and buddhas.

[Written on the reverse side (*uragaki*)]. At this shrine, one shrine official doubted [the *miko*'s words]. The *miko* again was possessed and said: "Within three days you will suffer [divine] punishment." That night [the official] suddenly died. After that, all returned to [a state of] belief (*kifuku* 帰伏).

PART THREE

In Little Need of Divine Intervention

Twice Kubilai Khan assembled a polyglot armada to conquer Japan, and twice, or so the chronicles say, mighty storms arose, smashing his ships against the rocks or scattering them out to sea.[1] From this flotsam of heroic futility was formulated the idea that these ship-wrecking storms stemmed from divine favor—or a singular lack thereof. The dramatic denouement of these invasions continued to exert a powerful pull on historical imagination. Although belief in their otherworldly annihilation has withered through the ensuing centuries, the trope of "divine winds" or kamikaze (神風) became a leitmotif of Japanese political mythology that persisted through the aerial suicide bombings of the Second World War.[2]

Relegated to legend, the Mongol invasions have generated little debate: all commentators concur that the chance passing of a typhoon spared Japan from defeat.[3] Nevertheless, Takezaki Suenaga never mentions divine succor in vanquishing the Mongols, even though his narrative is replete with prayers, and ends with praise for the Kōsa deity.

[1] Kubilai Khan (1215–94) founded the Yuan dynasty in 1271. The armies that he dispatched to subjugate Japan in 1274 were composed of Mongols, "Han" Chinese, Jurchen, and men from Koryo (Korea). Sailors from the surviving remnants of the Sung navy were added for the second invasion of 1281. See Murai Shōsuke, *Ajia no naka no chūsei nihon* (Azekura shobō, 1988), pp. 162–63.

[2] Allusions to "divine winds" repelling foreign invaders reappeared during times of international crisis from the thirteenth century onward. For an 1863 depiction of the "divine winds" crashing into a "Mongol fleet" resembling contemporary European ships, see *Shibunkaku kosho shiryō mokuroku*, no. 196 (October 1996): 116, illus. 294, Kōan Kamikaze dekisen no zu (弘安神風蒙古溺船の図). Likewise, prayers promulgated in 1853 were based upon thirteenth-century curses for the subjugation of foreigner invaders. See the *Chiba ken shiryō, chūsei hen*, comp. Chiba kenshi hensan shingikai (Chiba, 1957), Gaii kitō kiroku 17, pp. 687 and 702.

[3] For an early study in English, see Kyotsu Hori, "The Economic and Political Effects of the Mongol Wars," in *Medieval Japan* (Stanford: Stanford University Press, 1988), pp. 184–98 and also his "Mongol Invasions and the Kamakura Bakufu" Ph.D. diss., Columbia University, 1967). In Japanese, the most influential monographs include Aida Nirō's *Mōko shūrai no kenkyū*, 3d ed. (Yoshikawa kōbunkan, 1982); Amino Yoshihiko's *Nihon no rekishi 10: Mōko shūrai* (Shōgakkan, 1974); Kawazoe Shōji's *Mōko shūrai kenkyū shiron* (Yūzankaku, 1977); and Murai Shōsuke's *Ajia*.

The term *kamikaze* remains absent from Kamakura documents concerning the invasions as well, and can be only found in the diaries of thirteenth-century courtiers.

Although many aspects of the invasions strain the limits of credulity, they have nevertheless evoked little critical analysis. Even recent monographs routinely assert that the first amphibious assault of Japan in 1274 was 90,000 strong, the second, in 1281, 140,000.[4] Such figures, if true, indicate that the Mongols had performed a logistical feat that in many ways surpassed that of the Normandy Invasion in 1944. To be sure, the combined Allied strength outnumbered these estimates of the second Mongol invasion force by 16,000 men, but they only had to cross 20 miles of English Channel, whereas the two fleets of the second Mongol armada managed to navigate 116 miles of ocean from Korea and 480 from the Chinese mainland! As we shall see, modern scholarly accounts of the Mongol invasions continue to be laced with exaggerations and inaccuracies. Once the accretions of memory and myth are chipped away, many of the assumptions regarding them crumble. Analysis of surviving sources, translated here for the first time, reveals that the warriors of Japan were capable of fighting the Mongols to a standstill without any explicit divine or meteorological intervention.

Rationales for the Mongol Invasions

Who can really know whether dreams of world conquest or lust for gold propelled Kubilai Khan's desire to conquer the Japanese archipelago. Japan was rumored to possess gold in measureless quantities, which led the Venetian traveler Marco Polo to surmise that "when tidings of its riches were brought to the Great Khan [Kubilai] . . . he declared his resolve to conquer the island."[5] Surviving records suggest, however, that the Mongols were in fact preoccupied with political hegemony, for such rhetoric pervades their diplomatic missives; the accumulation of wealth seems to have been perceived as a function of this dominance that deserved little explicit attention. Indeed, an aura of absolute supremacy

---

[4]William Wayne Farris, *Heavenly Warriors* (Cambridge: Harvard Council on East Asian Studies, 1992), pp. 329–35. Ishii Susumu and Kawazoe Shōji also provide estimates of 140,000 for the second invasion. See Ishii, "The Decline of the Kamakura Bakufu," in *The Cambridge History of Japan*, vol. 3 (Cambridge: Cambridge University Press, 1990), p. 145, and in the same collection, Kawazoe, "Japan and East Asia," p. 418.

[5]*Marco Polo: The Travels*, trans. R. E. Latham (London: Penguin Books, 1958), p. 244. For trade between Japan and the Mongols, which includes a summary of recent archaeological discoveries, see Sugiyama Masaaki, *Sekai no rekishi 9, Dai mongoru no jidai* (Chūō kōronsha, 1997), pp. 9–20 and 264–68.

permeates their diplomatic discourse, which when coupled with their
military offensives, led many to conclude that they intended to bring the
whole world under their domination.[6] This notion, readily recognized as
far afield as Europe, was commonly accompanied with a sense of bravado,
for each who resisted the Mongols imagined themselves to be their might-
iest foe. For example, John of Plano Carpini believed that a Mongol
offensive was imminent in Europe because "there is no country on earth
that they fear with the exception of Christendom,"while the Zen priest
Tōgen Eian claimed that the Mongols desired to conquer Japan in order
to realize their plans of world conquest, for only when the Mongols have
added Japanese warriors to their cause, he reasoned, could they successfully
conquer China, India, and the rest of the world.[7]

Diplomatic records reveal that the Mongols' quest for regional
hegemony determined the timing of their contacts with Japan. The Mongols
dispatched a missive to Japan in 1266, which has been characterized by
modern Japanese scholars as calling for peace, not surrender.[8] By Mongol
standards, the document was remarkably courteous, with none of the
vocabulary implying direct Japanese submission to Mongol rule.[9]
Nevertheless, this "friendly" document names Kubilai the "master of the
universe" and ends with the scarcely veiled threat: "Let us engage in
cordial relations. Who desires the resort to arms?"[10]

Concern over the balance of power in East Asia may have played a
role in the timing of this dispatch. When Kubilai sent this document to
Japan, his predecessor had only recently subjugated the Korean kingdom
of Koryo after thirty years of warfare, and he himself was about to engage
in a campaign to conquer the Southern Sung.[11] Because Koryo had relatively
friendly relations with Japan, providing supplies and transportation home

---

[6]Such was the view of European commentators. See the thirteenth-century
"History of the Mongols" by John of Plano Carpini, in Christopher Dawson,
Mission to Asia (Toronto: University of Toronto Press, 1980), pp. 43–44.

[7]For the former, see Dawson, *Mission to Asia*, p. 44; for the latter, see
Kamakura ibun, vol. 14, doc. 10559, Tōgen Eian ikenjō. This has been translated as
Document 1.

[8]See Ishii, "Decline of the Kamakura Bakufu," p. 134, and Kawazoe, "Japan
and East Asia," p. 414.

[9]Close analysis of the language of the document appears in Sugiyama
Masaaki, *Mongoru teikoku no kōbō* (Kōdansha gendai shinsho, 1996), pp. 118–21.

[10]*Kamakura ibun*, vol. 13, doc. 9564, 8.1266 Mōko kokuchō an. See also
Rekishigaku kenkyūkai, ed., *Nihonshi shiryō 2 chūsei*, pp. 136–37. Translations of
this passage are based on Ishii, "Decline of the Kamakura Bakufu," p. 132.

[11]For the best summary of events in English, see Kawazoe, "Japan and East
Asia," pp. 412–16.

for castaways,[12] Kubilai attempted to draw Japan into his orbit by using this "friendship" as the basis for contact,[13] in order to prevent them from aiding the Southern Sung. In many ways, Japan and Koryo were natural allies. The Koryo structure of governance had resembled that of Japan. Koryo's military regime had first appeared in 1174 and dominated governance from 1196 onward,[14] while the Kamakura bakufu, which oversaw "warrior government" while located in eastern Japan, first appeared as a political entity in 1180 and achieved a nationwide presence after military victories in 1185 and 1221. Like Japan, Koryo possessed considerable military power: fighting alone, it managed to withstand six Mongol invasions over a span of thirty years until finally surrendering to Kubilai's predecessor, Möngke, in 1259.[15]

Koryo's military prowess must have impressed Kubilai. Newly elected Great Khan in 1260, he desired to expand his control over these lands and to preclude the possibility of any potent anti-Mongol alliance developing in the process. By using the newly conquered Koryo as an intermediary, Kubilai astutely imposed Mongolian diplomatic objectives on their officials, thereby preventing Koryo from acting with any autonomy. Thus, all dealings with Japan, whether friendly or hostile, effectively solidified Mongol control over Koryo. Kubilai could either peacefully bring Japan into the Mongol sphere of influence through persuasion or, if the Japanese proved intractable, use Koryo as a base for dispatching an invasion force against them.

Japan refused to respond to the Great Khan's overtures, which allowed

[12]For an account of Koryo hospitality for Japanese castaways, see Nam Kihaku, *Mōko shūrai to Kamakura bakufu* (Kyōto: Rinzen shoten, 1996), pp. 197–99. The definitive study of Japan's relations in East Asia remains, however, Murai, *Ajia*, particularly pp. 144–226.

[13]*Kamakura ibun*, vol. 13, doc. 9564, 8.1266 Mōko kokuchō an. For surviving Koryo diplomatic documents appealing for good relations, see vol. 13, doc. 9770, 9.1267 (Chigen 4) Kōrai kokucho an, and doc. 9845, 1.[1268] Kōrai kokucho an. Reference to another such missive arriving in the Dazaifu during the first month of 1270 appears in vol. 14, doc. 10571, 1.1270 (Bun'ei 7) Nihon koku dajōkan chō, and doc. 10588, 2.1270 (Bun'ei 7) Dazaifu shugosho chō.

[14]For the rise of the Koryo military regime, see Murai, *Ajia*, pp. 147–49.

[15]For the best summary in English, see W. E. Henthorn, *Korea: The Mongol Invasions* (Leiden: E. J. Brill, 1963), pp. 102–39. Koryo's court likewise took the lead in attempting to repel the Mongol invaders through religious ceremonies, and even had recarved the 81,137 woodblocks required to print the Buddhist Tripitaka (*Taejanggyong [Daizōkyō]* 大蔵経). As we shall see, the Japanese court would also embark on a similar pattern of religious patronage. For this, and the close resemblance of the Korean and Japanese systems of governance, see pp. 103–4, and Murai, *Ajia*, p. 148.

him to establish a powerful presence in Koryo. The Kamakura *bakufu* instructed its gokenin to be vigilant during the second month of 1268, while the court began issuing prayers for protection against the foreigners in the third month of the same year.[16] By the fifth month of 1268, Kubilai ordered the construction of a fleet of one thousand ships to chastise the Japanese.[17] This levy, along with the need to secure three months of provisions, caused festering Korean dissent to erupt into an armed insurrection some thirteen months later.[18] The rebels, led by the remnants of Koryo's military regime, requested aid from Japan and concurrently warned that the Mongols planned to invade the archipelago.[19] Members of the Japanese court considered supporting the Koryo rebels, but they became locked in a petty debate over whether or not they should be considered the legitimate government of Koryo. This hesitation allowed the Mongols to crush this uprising in 1271 and consolidate their control over the Korean penninsula.[20] During this same year, Kubilai adopted the dynastic name of Yuan.

The years 1271–73 set the stage for the later invasions of Japan. Japan continued to ignore Mongol envoys, but at the same time, the

[16]For the former document, see *Kamakura ibun*, vol. 13, doc. 9883, 2.27.1268 (Bun'ei 5) Kantō migyōsho; for references to the court's prayers, see the *Tohōki*, located most conveniently in *Fukutekihen*, maki 1, pp. 25–26, which describes rituals of destruction performed on 3.23.1268.

[17]For Korean reluctance on this endeavor, see Nam, *Mōko shūrai to Kamakura bakufu*, pp. 199-200; for Kubilai's construction of an invasion force, see Ishii, "Decline of the Kamakura Bakufu," p. 135.

[18]See Henthorn, *Korea*, pp. 158–62; for the "Rebellion of the Three Patrols," during 1269–71, see pp. 173–93. See also Murai, *Ajia*, pp. 149–50. Furthermore, Mongol accounts state that three months of provisions were transported along with the troops of their armada. See Tsunoda, *Japan*, p. 88. The crudely shaped storage jars that were uncovered in the wreckage of the Mongol fleet attest to the strain imposed by these levies. See Nagasaki ken Takashima chō kyōiku iinkai, comp., *Takashima kaitei iseki* (Takashima chō bunkazai chōsa hōkokusho, 1992–96), particularly vol. 1, pp. 58–59 and 117–18. Iron implements were also of poor quality. See Ibid., vol. 3, pp. 97–103. An English summary, and illustrations of recent Japanese archaeological finds, appears in David Nicolle, *The Mongol Warlords* (London: Firebrand Books, 1990), p. 65.

[19]Reference to this document appears in *Kamakura ibun*, vol. 14, doc. 10880, 9.1271 Tōgen Eian ganmon. The best coverage of the rebellion can be found in Murai, *Ajia*, pp. 147–88, particularly pp. 163–64. See also Document 57 herein for evidence of Koryo warnings reaching the court.

[20]See Murai, *Ajia*, pp. 162–64 and Ishii Masatoshi, "Bun'ei hachinen rainichi no kōraishi ni tsuite–sanbesshō no nihon tsūkō shiryō no shōkai," *Tōkyō daigaku shiryōhen sanjohō* 12 (1978): 4. According to Henthorn, the Mongols first established military control over Koryo in 1269. See *Korea*, pp. 200, 210–11.

Kamakura *bakufu* began warning warriors throughout the land that a Mongol attack was imminent. Kamakura, too, took the lead in organizing defense efforts against the foreign invaders by dispatching its warriors to the western island of Kyūshū.[21] Conversely, the Mongols embarked on an amphibious invasion of Koryo's southernmost island in 1273 and stamped out the final pockets of resistance to their rule. With the successful breach of a major defensive line of the Southern Sung that same year, Kubilai could now afford to dispatch an army to conquer Japan.[22]

Reconstructing the Invasions

The notion of "divine winds" twice smashing into the Mongol fleet has exerted such a strong pull on the historical imagination that other aspects of the invasions have been spared from rigorous analysis. The chronicles describing the invasions, both Mongol and Japanese, must be used with care, for both exaggerate the importance of the storms and the strength of the invading forces. For the Mongols, the typhoons provided the perfect excuse to justify a devastating defeat, for it left their military reputation untarnished, while for the priestly or courtier chroniclers of Japan, these winds "proved" the miraculous nature of their victory over an overpowering adversary. By contrast, documentary sources, letters, prayers, and edicts pertaining to the Mongol invasions provide in their limited and careful way a collage of individual experiences whose prosaic reality contrasts with the expansive tone of the chronicles.

Inspections and Rewards

Much about the invasions is knowable because numerous records survive. The Kamakura *bakufu* rewarded its warriors for their verifiable military service. By the latter half of the thirteenth century, Kamakura's administrative machinery became finely attuned to judging how well a warrior had fought in battle. Warriors, too, were acutely aware that their deeds had to be witnessed if they were to be compensated.

These precise sources provide a glimpse into the nature of defense efforts during the invasion that remain uncolored by ex post facto

[21]For the fruitless efforts of a Mongol envoy, see *Kamakura ibun*, doc. 10884, 9.25.1271 Mōko no tsukai Chao Liang-pi shojō; for the Kamakura *bakufu*'s 1271 orders, see docs. 10873–74, 9.13.1271 Kantō migyōsho. See also Murai, *Ajia*, pp. 168–69.

[22]Further proof that the invasions were used to solidify Mongol control over Korea can be found in their establishment of "The Mobile Bureau for the Subjugation of Japan," in 1280, which ultimately became the supreme administrative organ in Koryo. Although occasionally abolished, it lingered until 1365. See Henthorn, *Korea*, p. 199.

rationalizations of the outcome. Some documents record how warriors were mobilized; others reveal when and where they served on guard duty. The most illuminating documents consist of petitions for rewards, which were submitted by *gokenin* after battle, recording where they had fought, what they had done, and who had witnessed their actions.[23]

One needed tangible "proof" of battle service to receive rewards. When Takezaki Suenaga traveled to Kamakura in search of compensation, he was questioned by Adachi Yasumori regarding whether he had taken any enemy heads or lost any of his own men. When he admitted that he had not, Yasumori informed him that his military service was insufficient. Other warriors, such as Kikuchi Jirō, achieved fame by decapitating as many of the battle dead as possible.[24]

For warriors lacking the resourcefulness of Kikuchi Jirō, "proof" had to be supplied by several witnesses. Kamakura astutely recognized that the statements of close friends or relatives were unreliable. Hence many relied upon strangers to vouch for their deeds.[25] Togō Korechika, for example, did not even know the first name of one of his witnesses.[26] Witnesses recorded their statement in the form of an oath and handed this document to the warrior in question, who would append it to his petition describing his deeds.[27] Thereupon, *bakufu* administrators summoned these witnesses and questioned them. If all accounts were consistent, then the petition would be approved and dispatched to Kamakura, where rewards might be forthcoming.[28] If discrepancies existed, then these men would be questioned once again. Kamakura refused to grant rewards if inconsistencies could not be resolved.[29] These records reveal both the *bakufu*'s institutional strengths and weaknesses. Although Kamakura possessed elaborate procedures for evaluating an individual's actions in battle, it did not, however, provide any mechanisms for organizing their armies, or any detailed registers delineating how its troops were mobilized for war.[30]

---

[23]For more on these petitions, see Conlan, "State of War," pp. 14–61.

[24]The *Hachiman gudō kun* lauds Kikuchi Jirō for collecting many heads, thereby making a name for himself that would last throughout the generations. See *Hachiman gudō kun*, in *Gunsho ruijū*, vol. 1, comp. Hanawa Hokinoichi, 447–97 (Keizai zasshi shū, 1894), p. 468.

[25]See Document 20.

[26]Document 23.

[27]See Documents 21–22.

[28]Documents 25–28.

[29]See Document 29.

[30]One can surmise that *shugo* were responsible for drawing up registers for

Estimating Troop Strength

One of the most important and yet elusive aspects of reconstructing the invasions remains the size of each army. Kamakura officials apparently never recorded the composition of its units that fought against the Mongols, nor did they ever tally the total number of men that were mobilized in 1274 and 1281. By contrast, chroniclers invariably provide an estimate of an army's strength, but their accounts are notoriously prone to exaggeration, often by a factor of ten or more. For example, a twelfth-century courtier had his servants secretly observe an army, noting that a force estimated to have been as high as 10,000 consisted only of 1,080 horsemen.[31] In another case, one priest calculated that a Kamakura bakufu army that passed by Tōshōdaiji in 1333 consisted of several thousand warriors, but chroniclers exaggerated this figure to include anywhere from twenty-three to sixty thousand men.[32] The numbers that appear in such narrative sources are thus better conceived as metaphors for an army's strength than as reliable estimates.

Because duty reports and other administrative documents survive in abundance, scholars have managed to offer credible estimates of the Japanese forces. Ishii Susumu has speculated that anywhere from 3,600 to 6,000 warriors fought against the Mongols, while Kaizu Ichirō has estimated that Kamakura fielded an army that ranged from 2,300 to 5,700 men.[33] Guard duty registers provide some of the most comprehensive

those *gokenin* liable to serve from each province, but unfortunately, no such records survive that pertain to the Mongol invasions.

[31]*Gyokuyo*, 2.7.1183 (Jūei 2), in *Kokushi taikei*, vol. 2, p. 608, and for an English translation, see Farris, *Heavenly Warriors*, p. 301.

[32]A priest recorded an estimate of the army's size in a sutra that he was copying. His notations (*okugaki* 奥書) are most accessible in *Taiheiki*, ed. Okami Masao vol. 1, (Kadokawa Nihon koten bunko, 1975), note 7.7, pp. 448–49. The Jingu chōkokan version of the *Taiheiki*, which contains a Muromachi era colophon (Hasegawa Tadashi, Kami Hiroshi, et al., eds., Izumi shoin, 1994), states that 23,000 warriors were in the force that he witnessed. See maki 6, "Kantō sei jōraku no koto," p. 147. Nevertheless, this version states that this army ultimately swelled to 60,000 men. See maki 7, "Yoshinojō kassen no koto," p. 158. By contrast, the Seigen'in text of the *Taiheiki* (Washio Junkei, ed., Tōei shoin, 1936) provides estimates markedly different from those given in the Jingu chōkokan text. For estimates of this army initially constituting 37,500 men, see maki 6, "Tōgoku sei jōraku no koto," p. 134.

[33]See Ishii, "Decline of the Kamakura Bakufu," p. 139. For more detailed analysis, based upon mobilization patterns and the amount of arable land, see Kaizu Ichirō, "Kassen no senryokusū," *Nihonshi kenkyū*, no. 388 (1994): 88–97. The first to hazard estimates of troop strength was Aida, *Mōko shūrai no kenkyū*, particularly pp. 223–24.

data on the size of Kamakura's forces. A guard duty register of Izumi province warriors reveals that only nineteen *gokenin*, or "housemen" of the Kamakura bakufu and 79 low-ranking followers (*heishi* 兵士) (a total of 98 warriors) served on guard duty in 1272, with the most powerful warrior leading eighteen men, and the five least powerful *gokenin* only one man each.[34] Admittedly, Izumi was one of Japan's smaller provinces, but it nevertheless provides an important basis for comparison. Relatively few *gokenin* were mobilized from each province, and of those who were, only a handful were accompanied by more than five men.

Few records survive pertaining to the gokenin of Takezaki Suenaga's home province of Higo. Seno Sei'ichirō could only find references to fourteen "eastern" *gokenin* in all of Higo.[35] If these men were capable of enlisting followers at a similar rate to Izumi *gokenin*, then one can extrapolate that they brought only 58 men to battle. Undoubtedly this figure represents a low estimate because Seno does not record the Takezaki and the Ōyano, two local Higo *gokenin* families that appear in Takezaki Suenaga's scrolls, and because Higo *gokenin* were generally more powerful than their Izumi brethren.[36] By contrast, the relatively comprehensive records from the neighboring province of Hizen reveals that 72 out of 279 prominent local families were *gokenin*.[37] If Hizen *gokenin* mobilized according to a rate comparable to that of Izumi, then they would have led 299 warriors, while if one were to include the 279 prominent non-*gokenin* families of Hizen as well, then an army surpassing a thousand men could be mobilized from this province alone.[38] Nevertheless, because the sum of these transplanted

---

[34]Indeed, twelve of the nineteen *gokenin* mobilized three or fewer *heishi*. For more on this list, see *Takaishi shishi,* vol. 2, *shiry ōhen 1,* comp. Takaishi shi (Takaishi, 1986), doc. 60, 10.6.1272 (Bun'ei 9) Izumi no kuni gokenin ōban'yaku shihaijō an, pp. 499–500. Another transcription of this document appears in *Kamakura ibun,* vol. 15, doc. 11115.

[35]Seno Sei'ichirō, *Chinzei gokenin no kenkyū* (Yoshikawa kōbunkan, 1975), pp. 258–70.

[36]Although the record is spotty, surviving sources reveal that Kyūshū warriors mobilized anywhere from five to ten men. For a *gokenin* mobilizing five followers for an aborted invasion of Korea, see Document 18; for another leading three on horseback and seven on foot, see *Kamakura ibun,* vol. 16, doc. 12276, Chikuzen Nakamura zoku gunzei chūshinjō.

[37]*Chinzei gokenin no kenkyū*, pp. 165–208; for the figure of seventy-two *gokenin* houses, see p. 188.

[38]Assuming that Hizen could mobilize followers at an analogous rate to *gokenin*, then this province alone could have supported a force of 1160 men. This figure is, however, undoubtedly an overestimate, because non-*gokenin* were generally less powerful than their *gokenin* brethren.

eastern *gokenin*, the ruling strata of Kyūshū, and their immediate retainers can be estimated as constituting approximately 750 men, then a total force of two or three thousand Japanese defenders seems more plausible than even an army of five thousand troops.[39] Suenaga's account supports the assertion that the Japanese forces were not particularly large. Not only did Suenaga serve with nearly every prominent Japanese commander, but rank-and-file warriors such as Takuma Jirō Tokihide also appear in both the documentary record and in Suenaga's narrative, thereby suggesting a relatively small cohort of defenders. Nevertheless, the Mongol chronicles estimated Japanese forces as consisting of 102,000 men![40]

Mongol estimates of their own forces appear to be relatively conservative when compared to their extravagant claims regarding the Japanese defenders–only 15,000 Yuan soldiers and 8,000 Koreans set off for Japan in 1274[41]–but this number should elicit skepticism as well. Judging from the Mongol's inability to roam far from their boats, it seems likely that they were outnumbered by the Japanese, which was in fact asserted in the *Yuanshi* (元史).[42] Perhaps only two to three thousand fought against a similar number of Japanese defenders in 1274.

The 1281 armada was, by all accounts, significantly larger than the first. The *Yuanshi* depicted it as consisting of well over 100,000 men,[43]

[39]A figure of 747 warriors was extrapolated from the Izumi registers by assuming that the average number of followers was the same for the *gokenin* of Izumi and the nine provinces of Kyūshū. No evidence exists to suggest that non-*gokenin* formed the backbone of Japan's army in 1274 or 1281, which is why estimates of up to five thousand are too high. Nevertheless, these figures also reveal that an army drawn solely from *gokenin* possessed insufficient manpower to provide adequate defense against the Mongols.

[40]The Yuan account is most accessible in Tsunoda, *Japan*, pp. 73–105. This estimate appears on p. 81. For the original Chinese text (元史記事本末), I consulted *Li-Tai-chi-shi-pen-mo Chung-hua shu-chū-pien*, (歷代記事本末) (Pei-ching: Chung-hua-shu-chū, 1997), pp. 2056–7 and also compared this with passages transcribed in Yamada An'ei's dated but still useful compilation, the *Fukutekihen*. Ishii Susumu acknowledges the Mongol exaggeration in "Decline of the Kamakura Bakufu," p. 139.

[41]Tsunoda, *Japan*, pp. 81.

[42]Ibid., p. 82. The *Hachiman gudō kun* declares, however, that the Mongols outnumbered the Japanese by a ratio of ten to one. See *Hachiman gudō kun*, p. 466.

[43]Tsunoda, *Japan*, p. 88 for the Southern Army's numbers of 100,000. This same figure appears in the *Hachiman gudō kun*, p. 475.

while the *Kamakura nendaiki uragaki* claimed that 150,000 soldiers arrived on 3,500 ships.[44] Both accounts clearly overestimate the size of this army. It remains doubtful that even as many as ten thousand invaders attacked a reinforced Japanese contingent of several thousand men in 1281.

Tactics

Did the Mongols compensate for their insufficient troop numbers by utilizing effective tactics? One can infer from the *Hachiman gudō kun* that their forces were tightly organized.

> The Mongols left their ships, raised their flags and attacked. The general of the Japanese forces, Shōni nyūdō Kakuei's grandson, a mere lad of ten or twelve years, unleashed whistling arrows (*kaburaya* 鏑矢) [as was customary for the onset of battle, but] the Mongols all laughed. Incessantly beating their drums and gongs, they drove the Japanese horses leaping mad with fear. Their mounts uncontrollable, none thought about facing [the Mongols].[45]

The Mongols coordinated their cohesive units through gongs and drums. Their troops were not so tightly packed as to present a solid wall, thereby causing horses to shy away, but they were grouped closely enough to be able to use hooks or other weapons to pull charging Japanese warriors from their mounts. According to the *Hachiman gudō kun*, of those who galloped into the enemy forces, none returned alive, but this exaggerated portrayal of Japanese weakness served to highlight the power of the deity Hachiman's protection.[46] Takezaki Suenaga's account reveals to the contrary that some, such as Shiroishi Michiyasu, managed to pass through the Mongol forces and return unscathed.

The Japanese defenders were not as outclassed on the battlefield as the passage regarding Shōni Kakuei and his grandson implies.[47] Harrying

---

[44]*Kamakura nendaiki*, p. 54, the seventh month of 1281. By contrast, this source laconically characterizes the 1274 forces as "arriving" in Tsushima and, at the battle of Dazaifu, being "defeated." See p. 53, the tenth month, fifth day of 1274.

[45]*Hachiman gudō kun*, pp. 466–67.

[46]Ibid., p. 467.

[47]Kakuei and his grandson were laughed at by the Mongols, lampooned by their comrades, and perished defending Iki Island in 1281. For this ridicule, see *Hachiman gudō kun*, p. 470. Their deaths on Iki Island are recorded in *Fukutekihen*, maki 4, p. 19. Ōtomo Yoriyasu, the other Chinzei commissioner (*bugyōnin*), was also mocked for his aversion to fighting in the *Hachiman gudō kun*, but surviving records attest to his administrative skill.

the enemy from afar proved to be far more effective a stratagem than engaging in a frontal assault. For example, one Japanese warrior named Yamada sensibly preferred picking off scattered soldiers. After selecting his most powerful archers to fire "distant arrows" at the Mongols, Yamada and his men unleashed their arrows (after praying "Hail the Hachiman Bodhisattva," *Namu Hachiman bōsatsu*) and killed three Mongols, thereby causing the Japanese to laugh while the Mongols, who had previously enjoyed the spectacle of Shōni Kakuei's grandson and his humming arrows, silently collected their dead and departed.[48]

Both Japanese and Mongol accounts refer to the prowess of Japanese archers. Shōni Kagesuke, for example, was lauded by the Mongols as a warrior "adept in horsemanship and archery," because he shot the Mongol commander Liu Fu-hsiang in the face and captured his horse.[49] From this episode alone, one can infer that the skirmishing skills of the Mongols and the Japanese were roughly comparable.

The Mongols appear to have preferred skirmishing to hand-to-hand combat, a sentiment reflected in contemporary European accounts of their tactics as well.[50] Such comments suggest that the Mongol infantry formations were not as cohesive as has been commonly assumed. In spite of their close coordination of units, one can find little evidence that they fought *en masse*. Indeed, whether or not the Mongols can be accurately characterized as being capable of massing their forces and engaging in "group tactics" deserves further research.

Surviving sources suggest that military parity existed between the Mongol invaders and the Japanese. Although the Mongols enjoyed naval superiority, they lacked sufficient forces to occupy northern Kyūshū and accordingly avoided close confrontations with the Japanese defenders. For example, according to Takezaki Suenaga's account, the Mongols set up camp in Akasaka (赤坂), an area of poor terrain, but could not hold off a Japanese attack and so were forced to retreat. The Mongol sources also

---

[48]*Hachiman gudō kun*, pp. 467–68. The copy of this text dating from the *bunmei* era (1469–87) states that two Mongols were shot to death. See *Fukutekihen*, maki 2, pp. 16–17. "Distant arrows" were fired at a distance of approximately 50 to 100 yards, which marked the effective limit of a bow's range.

[49]*Hachiman gudō kun*, pp. 468–69, and Tsunoda, *Japan*, p. 82. References also appear in Kagesuke's genealogical record. See *Fukutekihen*, maki 2, pp. 30–31 and maki 4, p. 19.

[50]See the thirteenth-century "History of the Mongols" by John of Plano Carpini, in Dawson, *Mission to Asia*, p. 37, which states: "The Tartars do not like to fight hand to hand but they wound and kill men and horses with arrows; they only come to close quarters when men and horses have been weakened by arrows."

suggest that their 1274 retreat from Japanese waters was premeditated.[51] After Liu Fu-hsiang was seriously wounded, he withdrew his forces and returned to the ships. The *Yuanshi* claims that thereupon, "a great storm arose and many warships were dashed against the rocks and destroyed."[52] These storms certainly provided a convenient excuse for commanders to explain their defeat at the hands of the Japanese.[53] Continental sources emphasize the severity of the 1274 storm more than the Japanese sources do. The *Hachiman gudō kun*, otherwise devoted to finding a miracle at every possible opportunity, fails to mention any storms at all, which led the meteorologist Arakawa Hidetoshi to postulate that no typhoons struck the first Mongol fleet.[54] Supporting evidence appears in the *Kanchūki* (勘仲記), a diary by the Japanese courtier Kadenokōji Kanenaka.[55] On 11.6.1274 he described meteorological conditions as merely a "reverse wind."

> Someone said that several tens of thousands of invaders' (*kyōzoku* 凶賊) boats came sailing in on the high seas. Nevertheless, suddenly, a reverse (easterly) wind blew them back to their native lands. A few of the [enemy] boats were beached. The retainers (*rōjū* 郎従) of Ōtomo shikibu taifu[56] captured fifty of the invaders (*kyōzoku*), bound them, and are escorting [them] to the capital. The reverse wind must have arisen [as a result of] the protection of the gods. Most wonderful! We

---

[51]Tsunoda, *Japan*, p. 82.

[52]Ibid.

[53]In another passage of the *Yuanshi* pertaining to the second invasion of 1281, a certain Fan Wen-hu "made false representations . . . that he had reached Japan and was about to attack . . . when a storm struck and destroyed the ships." Ibid., p. 89.

[54]Arakawa Hidetoshi, "Bun'ei no eki no owari o tsugeta no wa taifu de wa nai," *Nihon rekishi*, no. 120 (June 1958): 41–45. See also Amino, *Nihon no rekishi 10*, pp. 161–64, and *Hachiman gudō kun*, p. 470. No one has doubted the existence of a typhoon that slammed into the second Mongol armada in 1281.

[55]The *Kanchūki* (勘仲記), a diary of the courtier Kadenokōji Kanenaka (1243–1308), originally spanned the years of 1274 until 1300, but only fragments of the original survive at the Tōyō bunko. Kanenaka, who had been appointed to minor court post in 1259, became chamberlain (*kurōdo*) in 1284, Lesser Controller of the Right (*ushōben* 右少弁) in 1287, Lesser Controller of the Left in 1288, and finally, Provisional Major Counselor (*gon dainagon* 大納言) in 1293. Kanenaka also served as a scribe for the Fujiwara regent. Hence, his diary represents one of the most valuable records chronicling both the Mongol invasions and internal political developments during the late thirteenth century. Although published in the *Shiryo taisei* (史料大成), the 1274 portion of the text, which contains significant references to the first invasions, has not yet been transcribed.

[56]Ōtomo Yoriyasu.

should praise [the gods] without ceasing. This great protection can only have happened because of the many prayers and offerings to the various shrines . . . throughout the realm.[57]

Northeasterly winds provided the Mongol fleet with an unusual opportunity to sail back to the continent. In 1274, perhaps both the Japanese and Mongols perceived this wind to have been a godsend. Oddly, neither side believed that the 1274 encounter had been decisive. The Mongols attributed their initial failure simply to insufficient manpower, while the Japanese, uncowed by the Mongols, initiated preparations for an invasion of Korea in order to belatedly aid anti-Mongol forces.[58]

The Japanese defenders realized that their success stemmed from their entrenched fortifications. Although the Mongols burned the coastal city of Hakata (博多), they were unable to attack the fortified hills surrounding the Dazaifu (太宰府).[59] Slightly less than a year and a half after the first invasion had been repulsed, Kamakura commenced construction of stone walls on coastal beaches.[60] These fortifications decisively influenced the course of the second invasion.

During the fifth month of 1281, Yuan forces once again departed for Japan. Quickly overwhelming Tsushima (対馬) and Iki (壱岐) Islands, their northern fleet sailed to Hakata. Here, the surprised Mongols discovered that they could not disembark because all suitable beaches were hemmed in by walls.[61] Although some defenders, such as Kawano Michiari, fought in front of the walls in order to prove their bravery, most preferred the relative safety of entrenched positions.[62] Thwarted in their initial objective,

---

[57]This passage was not transcribed with the rest of the *Kanchūki*. For an explanation, and a transcription of the text, see Ryō Susumu's *Mōko shūrai* (Chibundō, 1966), p. 101. For a published version of the remainder of this diary, see the *Kanchūki*, in *Shiryō taisei*, vols. 26–28 (Naigai kabushiki kaisha, 1935–36).

[58]See Documents 16–18 and Aida, *Mōko shūrai no kenkyū*, pp. 128–47. This invasion of Koryo was aborted in the planning stages.

[59]Reference to the 1274 fortifications appears in *Hachiman gudō kun*, pp. 469–70.

[60]The first reference to the walls appears in the Fukae monjo on 3.10.1276 (Document 41). See *Chūkai, Genkō bōrui hennen shiryō*, pp. 147–48. See also *Fukutekihen*, maki 3, pp. 27 and 52. For a fine study of recent archaeological excavations of the wall, see Yanagida, "Genkōbōrui to chūsei no kaigan sen," pp. 180–94.

[61]*Hachiman gudō kun*, pp. 474–75, and *Fukutekihen*, maki 4, p. 14. Yanagida Yoshitaka explains the importance of walled fortifications in his "Genkō bōrui," p. 194.

[62]*Yosōki*, in *Gunsho ruijū*, vol, 17, kassen bu 2 bukebu 1 (Naigai shoseki

the Yuan landed at the Shiga island, but this position too proved untenable. Harried by defenders attacking in small boats, the northern armada retreated to distant Iki Island during the middle of the sixth month in order to wait for reinforcements coming from the south. The second flotilla, composed of ships from the recently conquered Sung navy, arrived in the seventh month. The combined forces launched an invasion of Takashima Island in Hizen province, just off the main coast of Kyūshū, but could advance no further. Continually harried by the Japanese, the Mongols again were forced to withdraw from Takashima.

The second invasion proved less successful than the first, for the Mongols only managed to occupy a few outlying islands after a campaign of six weeks. Hakata, which had been burned in 1274, remained unscathed. Inland Kyūshū might as well have been on the moon. Fighting was confined to the outlying islands or the sea itself on terms increasingly unfavorable for the invaders. A few intrepid warriors, such as Kawano Michiari, boarded the Yuan ships during the night and killed their occupants with longswords and *naginata* (長刀),[63] slipping away on their skiffs in the cover of darkness before others realized anything was amiss.[64] Yuan losses mounted, and their supplies were inexorably depleted. According to lore, Kawano Michiari managed to capture a Mongol commander, while another warrior took twenty-one heads.[65] Takezaki Suenaga, depicted in his scrolls as meeting

---

kabushiki kaisha, 1930), p. 255. The Kawano, who are depicted in Scene 11, had been on the losing side in the 1221 Jōkyū war, so they, like Suenaga, perceived the Mongol invasions as an opportunity to advance their standing. See Jeffrey Mass, *Development of Kamakura Rule* (Stanford: Stanford University Press, 1979), pp. 20–21 for a brief history of the family. More translated documents pertaining to the Kawano can be found in Mass, *The Kamakura Bakufu* (Stanford: Stanford University Press, 1976), doc. 172, p. 182; and Mass, *Development of Kamakura Rule*, doc. 32, pp. 183–84.

[63]A *naginata* is depicted in Scene 3, where one warrior has impaled a Mongol head on a curved blade that is attached to a long wooden shaft.

[64]For the impressive deeds of Kawano Michiari, see the *Yosōki*, pp. 255–56, and *Hachiman gudō kun*, pp. 474–75. Michiari was severely wounded during the second invasion when fighting from ship to ship but survived. Takezaki Suenaga's scrolls also imply that Michiari fought valiantly. Further proof of Michiari's valor can be found in the Ōyama zumi shrine of modern-day Ehime prefecture, where the Mongol bows and helmets that he collected remain to this day. Kawano Michiari received lands that were, in all probability, rewards for his action against the Mongols. See *Kamakura ibun*, vol. 20, doc. 15612, 6.25.1285 (Kōan 8) Shōgun ke mandokoro kudashibumi. A good summary of the Kawano's role in the Mongol invasions can be found in *Zennōji monjo*, comp. Kageura Tsutomu (*Iyo shiryō shūsei 2*) (Matsuyama, 1965), pp. 73–82.

[65]See *Yosōki*, pp. 255–56, and *Hachiman gudō kun*, pp. 475–76. For textual comparison, see *Fukutekihen*, maki 4, pp. 15–16.

Michiari, likewise behaved with similar élan.[66] The sudden onset of a typhoon merely provided the coup de grace for a defeat that had been long in the making.[67]

Aftermath

Kamakura's need to mobilize an army and build an extensive wall exacerbated tensions within Japanese society. Those dissatisfied with the status quo believed that the crisis provided an unprecedented opportunity for advancement. By serving generals and provincial constables (*shugo* 守護), these men could ignore the commands of their family chieftains (*sōryō* 惣領), who were responsible for mobilizing their families and members of collateral lineages for war.[68] Takezaki Suenaga, for example, disobeyed the commands of his relatives in order to receive lands and rewards from ranking *bakufu* officials such as Adachi Yasumori. Likewise, Shōni Kagesuke also fought with unusual bravery, while his *sōryō* brother, who had been appointed *shugo*, preferred wielding the brush to the sword. *Sōryō* generally resented the creeping autonomy of some family members, which they perceived to stem from encroaching *bakufu* authority.

The 1281 invasions also generated increasing anti-foreign sentiment. Although Kamakura never codified regulations regarding the treatment of prisoners, attitudes hardened between 1274 and 1281.[69] While some prisoners were initially taken,[70] Mongols captured in 1281 were mostly killed. The *Yuanshi* states that "twenty to thirty thousand" (two to three

[66]Suenaga had an audience with Kawano Michiari after Michiari was wounded in a naval encounter. This was first revealed by Ikeuchi Hiroshi, *Genkō no shinkenkyū* (Tokyo: Tōyō bunko, 1931). See also *Zennōji monjo*, p. 78.

[67]Excavations at Takashima island have revealed that only the wood surrounding the Mongol anchors has survived. This indicates that the ships were so light that they did not sink deeply into the mud, thus providing powerful evidence that the Mongol fleet was close to exhausting its provisions. See *Takashima kaitei iseki*, vol. 3, pp. 131–33. For a contrary example of a heavily-laden merchant ship, dating from the early fourteenth-century, that was discovered virtually intact off the coast of Korea, see Sugiyama, *Dai mongoru no jidai*, pp. 9–20 and Amino et al., eds., *Yomigaeru chūsei I Higashi ajia no kokusai toshi Hakata*, pp. 23-30 and 120-122.

[68]See Jeffrey Mass, *Lordship and Inheritance in Early Medieval Japan* (Stanford: Stanford University Press, 1989), for the definitive survey of the *sōryō*. The parameters of *sōryō* authority varied according to time and region, and were often contested by relatives attempting to assert their own autonomy.

[69]See Document 36.

[70]See the diary of Kadenokōji Kanenaka translated in the previous "Tactics" passage.

thousand?) were slaughtered by the Japanese while only a few recruits were spared.[71] Terrified captives resorted to a variety of desperate stratagems. For example, three men claimed to be a Mongol general to their captor, Kawano Michiari. Michiari, unable to establish the truth, simply cut down all three.[72]

The defenders' desire for vengeance had been inflamed by the brutal occupation of the outlying islands. The Mongols murdered most men and cruelly pierced the center of the palms of captured women and tied them to the sides of the ships.[73] From this point on, little quarter was taken. Suenaga and his cohorts coolly killed most sailors and soldiers captured on the high seas.

Kubilai Khan had succeeded all too well in drawing Koryo into the Yuan sphere of influence. Koreans were portrayed as being indistinguishable from Mongols in Japanese accounts of the second invasion, and its people were treated accordingly.[74] Koryo sailors were killed indiscriminately along with Mongols, although castaways from the Southern Sung were spared.[75] This disparity in treatment can also be attributed to the fact that apparently the combined Mongol and Koryo fleet managed to find safe harbor, for few of their ships were sunk, while the ex-Sung navy bore the brunt of the storm's fury.[76]

This difference in treatment also suggests that the Japanese desired to punish those that they perceived as aggressors rather than to attack all foreigners per se. Pejorative epithets reflect this animosity quite well. The Japanese defenders mocked Mongol myths of descent from blue wolves, and instead declared that the Central Asian invaders were born from dogs.[77] These insults came to include Koreans, who became also known as "the dogs of Japan" in fourteenth-century chronicles.[78] Nevertheless,

---

[71]Tsunoda, *Japan*, p. 90.

[72]*Yosōki*, p. 256.

[73]Tsunoda, *Japan*, p. 81.

[74]Murai, *Ajia*, pp. 169–75 and Nam, *Mōko shūrai to Kamakura bakufu*, p. 201.

[75]For leniency toward the Sung sailors, see Tsunoda, *Japan*, p. 90 and Nam, *Mōko shūrai to Kamakura bakufu*, p. 201.

[76]Sung artifacts constitute the lion's share of those excavated at Takashima. See *Takashima kaitei iseki*, vol. 1, pp. 117.

[77]For the Mongol mythology, see Paul Khan, *The Secret History of the Mongols* (Boston: Cheng & Tsui Company, 1998), p. 3. Being called a dog was not necessarily an insult. According to the *Secret History*, Chingis Khan referred to his four greatest generals as his "four dogs." See pp. 101–2. For the Japanese use of the term to describe the Mongols, see *Hachiman gudō kun*, pp. 477.

[78]*Taiheiki*, maki 40, "Kōraijin raichō no koto" (Izumi shoin, 1994), p. 1185. The text refers to the three seventh-century kingdoms of Silla, Paekche, and

these attitudes were neither strong enough, nor widespread enough, to significantly impact a thriving trade that continued between Japan and the rest of the Asian continent throughout much of the Yuan era.[79]

Nowhere in Takezaki Suenaga's account can one uncover evidence of a "national" consciousness, whereby "Japan" existed as a transcendent entity worthy of defense. Although Takezaki Suenaga explained in his audience with the high-ranking *bakufu* official Adachi Yasumori that normal "rules" of precedent did not apply when fighting foreign invaders, he stated so in order to convince Yasumori to grant him rewards that otherwise did not appear to be forthcoming. Rather than fighting for the defense of Japan, personal and familial goals–the desire to be first to charge, to have an audience with his lord, and to receive ample rewards–propelled him to risk his life in battle. Even his grim determination to behead as many enemy as possible stemmed more from the need to have proof of his "valor" than to extract revenge from foreign invaders.[80] Nevertheless, the memory of the Mongol invasions caused Koreans and Mongols to be perceived as "enemies" and ultimately provided fertile ground for the courtly notion of Japan as a divinely favored land to spread throughout the archipelago.

Society, Religion, and War

Little evidence exists that the belief in Japan as the "land of the gods" had spread beyond a small coterie of courtiers and priests throughout the thirteenth century. Takezaki Suenaga referred to the protection of the gods, but he was merely explaining how divine succor allowed him to be granted rewards rather than how these deities spared Japan from foreign invasion. From the final passage of his Mongol scrolls, one can infer that Suenaga came to believe that the deity of Kōsa shrine had spoken directly to him in a dream, thereby causing him to set off for Kamakura and,

Koguryo. Conversely, Koryo supporters of the Mongols referred to the Japanese as "ugly island barbarians." See the thirteenth-century sources transcribed into Japanese by Nam in his *Mōko shūrai to Kamakura bakufu*, pp. 230–31.

[79]For an excellent summary of Yuan-Japan trade during the thirteenth and fourteenth centuries, see Sugiyama, *Sekai no rekishi 9*, pp. 264–68. Further evidence of liberal Yuan trading attitudes appears in Nam, *Mōko shūrai to Kamakura bakufu*, pp. 188–92. Nam suggests, however, that some evidence exists of increasing regulation during the final years of Kubilai's reign. Trade was restricted further in the fourteenth century, thereby leading to an increase in "armed merchants," or *wakō* (倭寇).

[80]As the wars of the fourteenth century would reveal, the warriors of Japan had no qualms about inflicting such indignities on their own countrymen. Compare Suenaga's actions to those of Nomoto Tomoyuki in the fourteenth century, recounted by Conlan in "State of War," pp. 14–56.

ultimately, to receive his rewards. Rather than perceiving Japan as the land of the gods in a purely nationalistic sense, Suenaga simply attributed the outcome of battle and his worldly success to the designs of divine will. In the inherent uncertainty of war, all desperately searched for patterns of divinely inspired order. Some warriors who attempted to curry otherworldly favor and success prayed to the gods before unleashing their arrows, while others prayed in order to muster enough courage to face the Mongol armada in small boats.[81] During the thirteenth century, even routine administrative matters were based on what might be characterized as "religious" beliefs. Witnesses' statements were recorded through oaths (kishōmon 起請文), which possessed special meaning as the ultimate instrument for pledging one's word. They were not lightly disregarded. When the helmet-less Suenaga attempted to "borrow" the helmet of another warrior's retainer in the midst of battle, this man evaded Suenaga's request with various excuses. Suenaga was finally silenced when the resourceful retainer replied that he had written an oath preventing him from giving the helmet to another.

"Otherworldly" forces were perceived as being the wellspring of causality. The courtier Kadenokōji Kanenaka attributed the typhoon that smashed the second Mongol fleet to divine intervention. On the fourteenth day of the seventh intercalary month in 1281, Kanenaka wrote as follows:

A report arrived from Dazaifu. On this past first day [of the seventh month] a typhoon sank most of the foreign pirates' ships. Several thousands were killed or captured. Not one [enemy] boat remains at Iki or Tsushima. Most of the foreign invaders who came [to Japan] lost their lives or were captured. This event reveals unprecedented divine [support]. A source of great rejoicing in the realm–what could exceed this? This is no random event (tadanaru koto ni arazaru nari). Even though we live in the final age (matsudai 末代) [of the Buddhist law], the gods' support has not ceased. One must more fervently worship the gods and buddhas.[82]

The Mongols also apparently attributed their defeat to the potent prayers

---

[81]For prayers to Hachiman for firing arrows, or praise for collecting heads, see Hachiman gudō kun, pp. 467–69. Kawano Michiari prayed to "all of the great and small" gods of Japan, including the Hachiman deity of the Mishima shrine, which was closely tied to the Kawano family. Yosōki, p. 255. See also Hachiman gudō kun, pp. 475, and Fukutekihen, maki 4, p. 26.

[82]Kanchūki, vol. 1, (Naigai shoseki kabushiki kaisha, 1936), p. 140. This passage is also found in Nihonshi shiryō 2 chūsei, pp. 149–50.

of the Japanese court. The *Yuanshi* describes how shortly after the Japanese ruler visited the Hachiman shrine, and had a rescript read at Ise shrine imploring that the country be saved in exchange for his own life, the Mongol soldiers "saw a great serpent appearing on the surface of the water, and the water smelled of sulphur"–unambiguous signs of impending doom.[83]

Because of this belief in otherworldly causality, offering prayers for the destruction of foreigners was perceived as a military act.[84] Although courtiers and warriors alike prayed for success in war, Kyōto, and not Kamakura, took the lead in mobilizing the gods. The court ignored the initial Mongol missives of 1266, but began enacting esoteric rituals of destruction against foreigners (*ikoku chōbuku* 異国調伏) during the third month of 1268, shortly after establishing the precedent for such rituals to be performed on a national scale.[85] By contrast, Kamakura monopolized diplomatic intercourse but engaged in only desultory attempts to secure otherworldly intervention before the first invasion.[86] After the 1281 invasion, the court (and the retired sovereign Kameyama in particular) took the most active role in cursing the Mongols.[87] The Kamakura *bakufu* belatedly

---

[83]Tsunoda, *Japan*, pp. 87–88.

[84]For references to a deity, the Amano daimyōjin, setting off to join a military encampment in order to fight with the other gods of Japan against the Mongols on 4.5.1281 (Kōan 4), see *Kamakura ibun*, vol. 23, doc. 18134, 3.28.1293 (Shō-ō 6) Dajōkan chō. The topic of divine participation in war is addressed with more detail in Conlan, "Sacred War" in "State of War," pp. 170–202.

[85]The *Tohōki* describes rituals of destruction performed on 3.23.1268. See *Fukutekihen*, maki 1, pp. 25–26. One can find references to a need to establish the precedent for such prayers of destruction in *Kamakura ibun*, vol. 13, doc. 9889, 3.15.[1268 (Bun'ei 5)] Sōshun shojō, and vol. 14, docs. 10600 and 10601, 3.15.[1270 (Bun'ei 7)] Sōshun shojō, and doc. 10602, Ikoku o-inori senrei chūshinjō. A comparison of the documents reveals that they were written at the same time. Because the *Tohōki* reveals that prayers were promulgated during 1268, all of the above documents should be dated to that same year of 1268. Finally, for more references to such cursing by the court, see *Fukutekihen*, pp. 23, 33, 43, and 51, and the *Hachiman gudō kun*, pp. 476–78.

[86]For reference to Kamakura bestowing a sword to Itsukushima shrine for prayers to subjugate the Mongols, see *Kamakura ibun*, vol. 15, doc. 11766, 12.2.1274 (Bun'ei 11) Fujiwara Chikasada kakikudashi, which has been translated as Document 58.

[87]*Fukutekihen*, maki 4, pp. 64–78, which even includes references (on p. 78) to a *garan* built at Gokurakuji, in southwestern Kamakura, for the purpose of "protecting the country [with Buddhist] law." By contrast, see p. 70, where one can infer that retired sovereign's prayers possessed more prestige than those of the Kamakura shōgun's. The *Hachiman gudō kun* also refers to the court's prayers as being performed throughout Japan.

promulgated prayers in eight of Japan's sixty-six provinces in 1283[88] and did not apparently start issuing nationwide prayers throughout Japan until 1290.[89]

Contrary to common assumptions, warriors did not begrudge the preponderance of rewards granted to religious institutions, for they themselves believed that victory and defeat were subject to the will of the gods. Although the historian Kyotsu Hori dismisses the petitions of shrines and temples as fabrications designed to extract better rewards,[90] few contemporaries mustered such cynicism. On the contrary, the policy of favoring temples was initially promulgated by the Kamakura official Adachi Yasumori in 1284 and was reasserted by the *bakufu* during the years 1301 and 1312.[91] Takezaki Suenaga supported this policy of restoring shrines, for as his precepts revealed, he devoted considerable attention to rebuilding the Kaitō and providing for the upkeep of the Kōsa shrine. This policy of favoring religious institutions by both Kamakura and the Kyōto court did not lead to any changes in warrior attitudes regarding religion per se. Disputes that arose between warriors, temples, and shrines tended to focus on the propriety of particular land transfers.[92] The necessity of restoring temples and shrines was never questioned.

In fact, only the slightest stirring of skepticism can be discerned from, ironically, members of religious institutions. The sovereign,

---

[88]See *Kamakura ibun*, vol. 18, doc. 13815, 12.28.1279 (Kōan 2) Suruga no kami bōhōsho an, and vol. 20, 12.28.1283 (Kōan 6), Kantō migyōsho, for prayers pertaining to Musashi, Izu, Suruga, Wakasa, Settsu, Harima, Mimasaka, and Bitchū provinces. The document attributed to 1279 appears in fact to have been written in 1283. See *Nihonshi shiryō 2 chūsei*, p. 151. See also *Fukutekihen*, maki 5, pp. 9–11, 25, 29, 41–54, 58–67 for prayers by Go Fukakusa and Fushimi.

[89]*Kamakura ibun*, vol. 22, doc. 17277, 2.23.1290 (Shō-ō 3) Utsunomiya Michifusa jungyōjō. For evidence of a more systematic incorporation of all Ichinomiya shrines, see *Kamakura ibun*, vol. 23, doc. 17564, 3.6.1291 (Shō-ō 4) Shimazu Tadamune shigyōjō, and doc. 18075, 12.21.1292 (Shō-ō 5) Shimazu Tadamune shigy ōjō. See also *Fukutekihen*, maki 5, pp. 49–53 and Documents 60–63 herein.

[90]Hori, "Economic and Political Effects," pp. 186–87.

[91]*Chūsei hōsei shiryōshū*, vol. 1 (Iwanami shoten, 1955), pp. 257–58, amendment 544 of 6.25.1284 (Kōan 7); for its revocation in 1286, after his death, see p. 277, amendment 602 of intercalary 12.9.1286 (Kōan 9). For references to Kamakura orders for the shrines of Kyūshū to be rebuilt and their lands to be restored once again, see p. 302, amendment 681 of 2.24.1299, and p. 346, for the document of 12.2.1312 (Shōwa gannen). Kaizu Ichirō has devoted considerable attention to these issues in his *Chūsei no henkaku to tokusei* (Yoshikawa kōbunkan, 1994) and *Kamikaze to akutō no seiki* (Kōdansha, 1995).

[92]For one typical dispute, see *Kamakura ibun*, vol. 32, docs. 25015–6, 10.12.1313 (Shōwa 2) Chinzei gechijō an.

Hanazono, referred to a shrine attendant who doubted the veracity of another's prophecy, but these sparks of disbelief were snuffed out by the attendant's sudden death.[93] Such skepticism was not, however, directed toward the notion of otherwordly agency per se, but rather the veracity of particular claims of otherwordly influence. For example, upon hearing the priest Eison's claims of having generated the 1281 storms, Nichiren acidly remarked that "little more than an autumn wind and a tiny amount of water" destroyed the Mongol fleet.[94] To most, however, the importance of otherworldly agency remained unquestioned and indeed apparently rose in the aftermath of the Mongol invasions.[95]

The thirteenth-century Japanese did not perceive superior tactics or cunning strategies as the ultimate "cause" of victory. Other sources suggest that the Japanese provided stiff resistance to the Mongols. Nevertheless, even those who fought with considerable skill attributed their successes to the gods. Suenaga certainly believed so: not only do his prayers constitute a major theme in his narrative, but his account ends with praise for the deity of the Kōsa shrine. Hence, although one can argue that military skill and not the storms proved decisive in the encounter, the very same facts led Takezaki Suenaga and his contemporaries to conclude that their victory had been caused by divine intervention. And herein lies, perhaps, the distinction between the modern and the medieval mind-sets.

---

[93]See Document 65.

[94]*Kamakura ibun*, vol. 19, doc. 14491, 10.22.[1281 (Kōan 4)] Nichiren shojō. See also Kawazoe Shōji, *Nichiren to sono jidai* (Sankibō busshorin, 1999), p. 219. I am indebted to Jacqueline Stone for bringing this to my attention.

[95]For example, the *Hachiman gudōkun* was written sometime between 1308 and 1318, when rewards to temples and shrines for their services were most common. See Sakurai Tokutarō et al., eds., *Jisha engi* (Iwanami shoten, 1975), pp. 492–93. For an informative document concerning this, see *Kamakura ibun*, vol. 22, doc. 17073, 7.22.1289 (Shō-ō 2) Ikoku kōbuku kitō kuyōhō chūshinjō an.

Appendices

Appendices

APPENDIX ONE

The Precepts (okibumi) of Takezaki Suenaga

Precept 1. *Suenaga's 1293 precept (okibumi 置文). Takezaki Suenaga wrote the following regulations for Kaitō shrine, which effectively allowed him to consolidate his local lordship through control of religious ceremonies.[1] Two copies survive of this document. One now belongs to Tōfukuji, while the other is in the possession of the Akioka family. The latter appears to have been originally stored at the Kaitō shrine, and is translated herein.[2]*

The shrine in Kaitō district: A copy of established regulations[3]

[1.] Paddies for shrine ceremonies inside the one *chō* of land in Shimokowara-chō.[4]

Three *tan* and two *jō* of paddies [shall be reserved] for the spring ceremonies to the south.

Three *tan* and two *jō* of paddies [shall be reserved] for the congregation on the fifth day of the fifth month [near] Mizuguchi.

Three *tan* and two *jō* of paddies [shall be reserved] for the congregation on the ninth day of the ninth month; one *jō* is in the middle [of Shimokowara]. The three *tan* are in one place in Nofuku village (*sato* 里). To the south of that same village (*sato*) is one *jō*.

Three *tan* and two *jō* of paddies [shall be reserved] for ceremonies.

Three *jō* of paddies [which are located] to the north of the partial dwelling (*ichibu yashiki* 一分屋敷) [shall be reserved] for the Tsurugi shrine festival (*gozensai* 御前祭). One *jō* is inside Oharachō.

One *tan* of paddies [shall be reserved] for the Wakamiya festival. [They are located to] the north of Dōzono.

One *tan* and four *jō* of paddies [shall be reserved for] lamp oil. [They are located in] Nofuku village (*sato*).

[2.] Concerning the portion [of revenue reserved for] the highest-ranking [male] shrine attendant (*hauri* 祝) Fujii Suenari: He shall live in his current

---

[1]*Kamakura ibun*, vol. 23, doc. 18098, 1.23.1293 (Shō-ō 6) Takezaki Suenaga *okibumi*.

[2]For more on these documents, see *Takezakijō*, p. 147–66.

[3]*Sadamete oki jōjō no koto utsushi tatematsuru.*

[4]One *chō* equals 2.94 acres. Ten *tan* equal one *chō*. One *jō* equals one fifth of a *tan*.

279

residence. He shall receive rice fields consisting of eight *tan* inside the southern space (*tsubo* 坪) of Iwashita.[5]

[3.] The portion [reserved for] the *senmei* (宣命) and the *miko* (命帰): one *tan* inside Takaura [is for the] Kōsa [*miko*]; inside the same area (*tsubo*) one *tan* [is for the] Aso *miko*; and one *tan* at Gyakuno tani [is for the] Tsujiwaka (*miko*).[6]

[4.] The two *tan* and two *jō* of paddies [reserved] for the ceremonies of New Year's day are [located in] Kitaura.[7]

[5.] Lands for the repair of the [Kaitō] shrine [shall consist of] two *tan* at Kamimae, in Iwashita. Every year, one *koku* (石) of rice from these lands shall be given to the shrine.[8] An able manager (*kumon* 公文) should [be responsible for] ceremonies. When rice shall be lent for planting (*suiko* 出挙) [the loan will be assessed at] fifty percent [interest].[9] This [rate] should be [levied] impartially. [Borrowers without] collateral (*genshitsu* 現質) shall not [receive loans]. Even a descendant of Suenaga cannot use his authority [to borrow rice]. Without collateral, nothing can be loaned. Nevertheless, [Suenaga's] special representative shall determine the number of people [needed] during the times of spring planting and autumn harvest. If the amount of rice (*suiko*) reaches two hundred *koku*, then concentrate on repairing the shrine and then build Jingūji (神宮寺) temple inside the shrine compound [including] a hall of worship, dining hall, and a records hall. Clothes for the *miko* shall be provided and they shall wear [them and] makeup on days of worship. Furthermore, it is decided that shrine attendants [of the] first and second [rank], *miko*, and *hassha*[10] shall each

---

[5]Fujii Suenari received lands at Iwashita, a central location of the Kaitō, one hundred meters south east the Hirabaro region where Takezaki Suenaga would later retire, and one hundred meters to the west of the temple of Tōfukuji. See *Takezakijō*, p. 160–63. Apparently, the Fujii lived in the Hirabaro region of the Kaitō, which is where Suenaga would eventually retire. The Kaitō shrine is located at the far west of the Kaitō lands, where the paddies are the largest. Suenaga's original residence was in this same area.

[6]The *senmei* is a shrine attendant who chants prayers, while a *miko* is a female shrine attendant.

[7]The following is on a separate sheet of paper. Suenaga signed the back of both of these pages.

[8]One *koku* constituted approximately 4.5 bushels of rice.

[9]He specifies a rate of five *hi*, or five out of ten stalks of rice.

[10]The meaning of *hassha* (発者) is unclear. It presumably designates a shrine attendant.

receive one *koku* of rice at year's end. In addition, [Suenaga's] representative (*tsukai* 使) and the *kumon* [of Kaitō shrine] should each provide ten *koku* of rice exempt [from other taxes to the shrine] each year. If [any of these officials] performs a crime, even if he is a *kumon* or [Suenaga's] representative (*tsukai*), they will be punished [and removed from office]. An honest person shall be appointed [in their place].

[6.] During times when paddies [reserved for] ceremonies suffer from poor harvests, the amount in arrears shall be investigated [*sic*] and the rice for seedlings (*suikomai* 出挙米) shall be levied on the person [in charge of these fields] (*tōnin* 頭人). [Thereupon] the ceremonies shall be performed.

[7.] Among those people who have been designated as [official] prayer [specialists] there shall be no gambling, theft, disobeying the [Buddhist] law while engaged in one's duties, negligence, or slander (*akkō* 悪口). Any who do so will be dismissed and a person with ability, capable of diligently performing [ceremonial] duties, [will be appointed to replace them].

The above regulations are established as such. Hence, shrine officials (*hauri*, *seimei*, and *miko*) must perform services on the first seven days of the new year, the twice yearly [services for] enlightenment (*higan* 彼岸), the spring and winter ceremonies [during the] the fifth day of the fifth month and the ninth day of the ninth month and [services during] the first day of each month. In addition, they must pray for nobles (*kuge* 公家) [at the court], and warriors (*buke* 武家) [in Kamakura]. Next they should pray for Suenaga and perform service (*chūsetsu* 忠節) for him and his descendants in this world and the next. Thus.

The sixth year of Shō-ō [1293], twenty-third day, first month

Jitō Sahyōe no jō Fujiwara Suenaga (monogram)

Precept 2. *This document, written in 1314, superseded Suenaga's 1293 precept.*[11]
*A comparison of these two documents reveals that Suenaga's rules were modified
during the intervening years. Notice how the obligations of commoners increased
over time as did the amount of revenue for shrine officials. Suenaga also provided
greater detail about the particular sutras to be chanted at his shrine, which
reflects his greater concern for religious affairs. Kaitō shrine lands are, however,
delineated more clearly in the 1293 document.*

Regulations concerning Kaitō shrine.

[1.] [Revenue from] two *tan* and two *jō* of paddies [which are located in]
Kitaura [shall be reserved for] New Year's ceremonies.

[2.] [Revenue from] three *jō* of paddies [which are located] to the north of
the *ichibu* dwellings [shall be reserved for the] Tsurugi shrine ceremonies
(*gozen*).

[3.] [Revenue from] one *tan* of paddies [which are located] to the north of
Dōzono [shall be reserved for the] Wakamiya [shrine] ceremonies.

[4.] Concerning the portion [of revenue belonging to] the highest-ranking
[male] shrine attendant, Fujii Suenari: He shall live in his current residence.
He shall receive rice fields consisting of eight *tan* inside the space (*tsubo*)
of Iwashita and five *tan* to the south.

[5.] The *senmei* shall receive four *jō* at Nofuku and also four *jō* inside the
space (*tsubo*) [of Iwashita]. The Sō [shrine] female attendant (*miko*) shall
receive one *tan* inside Takaura. The Kaitō [shrine] *miko* shall receive one
tan within the same area (*tsubo*). The Aso [shrine] *miko* shall receive one
tan at Gyakuno tani. The Tsujiwaka *miko* shall receive a dwelling (*yashiki*)
and one *tan* at Mizoguchi from the seven *jō* of newly cultivated [lands].
[These] second [rank] shrine attendants [shall receive these] grants.

[6.] Lands for the repair of the [Kaitō] shrine [shall consist of] two *tan* at
Kamimae, in Iwashita. Every year, one *koku* of rice from these lands shall
be given to the shrine. [Suenaga's] representative (*ontsukai* 御使), the
shrine official (*hauri*), and treasurer (*okura no kumon* 御蔵公文) shall lend

---

[11]*Kamakura ibun*, vol. 23, doc. 18097, 1.16.1314 (Shōwa 3) Takezaki Suenaga
okibumi. Suenaga's 1314 precept can also be found in *Chūsei seiji shakai shisō jō*, ed.
Ishii Susumu et al., pp. 372–75; also see pp. 531–32. Close examination of the
original revels that this document, like precent 1, constitutes a copy (*utsushi* 写).

rice for planting (*suiko*) at 50 percent [interest].[12] This [rate] should be
[levied] impartially. [Borrowers without] collateral (*genshitsu*) shall not
[receive loans], with the exception of commoners (*hyakushō*) who need the
rice for cultivation. They need only sign an agreement (*rensho no jō* 連書之
状) and receive [loans of rice]. [Suenaga's] retainers (*miuchi no hitobito* 御内
人々) shall receive four *tan* of land per *koku* of rice [still in arrears] by the
twelfth month. Lower-ranking followings (*shimobe* 下部) shall take over
this land, taking with them the pawned collateral, and [cultivate the land],
paying the specified (*bungen* 分限) amount [of taxes].

[7.] Buddha [statues], sutras, and religious implements shall not be pawned
[from Kaitō shrine and used as collateral for loans]. As for weapons (*bugu*
武具), they shall be pawned after consultation with the *jitō* [Suenaga or his
heir]. The weapons of the powerful family (*kenmon* 権門) shall not be
pawned.[13] In addition, even Suenaga's sons and grandsons cannot borrow
[rice] without collateral (*genshitsu*). An oath to this effect has been signed
by [Suenaga], his special representative, the shrine official, and the
treasurer.[14]

[8.] [Suenaga's] special representative shall determine the number of
people [needed] during the spring planting and autumn harvest. This is
to ensure that the gods [of the shrine] be provided for. If the amount of
rice (*suiko*) reaches three hundred *koku*, then concentrate on repairing the
shrine and then build Jingūji (神宮寺) temple inside the shrine compound.
Priests from Tōfukuji (塔福寺) shall perform prayers there. Their stipend
shall consist of three *koku* each year. [They shall] perform services during
the first seven days of the new year, as well as the ceremonies of the four
seasons, and the twice yearly [services for] enlightenment (*higan* 彼岸).
During the first day and the eighteenth day of every month, all (*ichiza* 一
座) of the Ninnō hannya sutra and one scroll of the Kanzeon sutra shall
be chanted.[15]

---

[12]The *okura no kumon* was the person in charge of the shrine's storehouse.
This office does not appear in the earlier document. Nevertheless, Suenaga's
interest rates of 5 *hi*, or five out of ten stalks of rice, remains unchanged.

[13]Although Kuroda Toshio has commonly used the term *kenmon* to refer to
major shrines and institutions, in this case the term seems to refer to powerful
members of Suenaga's clan (*ichimon*).

[14]The identity for this figures is unknown, except that the shrine official
was Fujii Suenari.

[15]Suenaga refers to the "Benevolent Kings Protecting Their Countries" Sutra
(or Prajñāpāramitā sūtra), a tantric text devoted to the protection of the state
while the other sutra is probably an abbreviation for the *Kanzeon bōsatsu nyoiman*

[9.] Funds for the candles of Jingūji, five hundred *mon*, [shall be] levied in a like manner. These candles shall be lit [and maintained] by the priests who serve the shrine (*kuzō* 供僧).

[10.] Funds for [Kaitō] shrine, five hundred *mon*, shall be administered by the shrine attendant (*hauri*) who is also responsible for lighting them.

[11.] [Proper] attire should be provided for *miko*. On ceremonial days they are to wear [these] clothes and makeup.

[12.] The designated ten people–shrine attendants of the first and second rank along with *miko* and a *hassha*–shall all receive ten *koku* of rice at year's end. One *koku* shall be given to each person.

[13.] Seeds harvested from the one *chō* and five *tan* of paddies [designated for] shrine ceremonies shall be given [to the shrine as well].

[14.] The commoners (*hyakushō*) of Kaitō shall each give two *tō* of rice to each [of the ten shrine attendants].[16]

[15.] [Suenaga's] representative (*ontsukai*) and the *kumon* [of Kaitō shrine] shall each provide ten *koku* of rice [to the shrine] per year. If, however, the *kumon* is a *miuchi* who has received rewards [from Suenaga], then he only need pay five *koku*.

[16.] The shrine official (*hauri*), treasurer (*okura no kumon*), and [Suenaga's] representative (*ontsukai*) shall not abuse their power even in the slightest way. If they [nevertheless do so], then they will be dismissed and an honest person be appointed [to their office].

[17.] The ten people of [Kaitō] shrine shall meet once a month and clean shrine precincts. If they are negligent, then they will be dismissed and a person with ability [will be appointed to replace them].

[18.] Among the shrine officials (*shashi* 社司) there must be no gambling, theft, disobeying the [Buddhist] law while engaged in one's duties, negligence, or slander (*akkō*). Any who do so will be dismissed and a person with ability, capable of diligently performing [ceremonial] duties will be appointed to replace them].

arani kyō, an esoteric text dedicated to one of the six Kannon (Cintāmanih), who was reputed to provide for wealth in this life and the next.

[16]One *to* (斗) equals one-tenth of a *koku*, or approximately eighteen liters.

The above regulations are established as such. Hence, shrine officials (*shashira*) must perform ceremonial services on the first seven days of the new year and the twice yearly [services for] enlightenment (*higan*), the spring and winter ceremonies [during the] the fifth day of the fifth month and the ninth day of the ninth month and [services during] the first day of each month. In addition, they must pray for nobles (*kuge*) [at the court] and warriors (*buke*) [in Kamakura]. Next they should pray for Suenaga and perform service (*chūsetsu*) for him and his descendants in this world and the next. Thus.

The sixth year of Shō-ō [1293], twenty-third day, first month

Jitō Sahyōe no jō Fujiwara Suenaga (monogram)

This prescript (*okibumi*), promulgated in the sixth year of Shō-ō [1293], has been rewritten in [this, the] third year of Shōwa [1314]. I have signed this with my later [style of] monogram. In order to prevent any doubts from arising, I have personally written this statement.

The third year of Shōwa [1314], seventeenth day, first month

Hōki (はうき[法喜]) (monogram)

Commendation 1. *Takezaki Suenaga commended the following to pay for the upkeep of his clan temple, Tōfukuji, and the nearby Kōsa shrine. Such grants of proprietary revenue by provincials only became possible in the fourteenth century as the system of partible land rights based on status began to disintegrate. This document also reveals that the Kaitō jitō, presumably Suenaga's heir, directly controlled 5 chō (14.7 acres) of land.*[17]

Another commendation of the proprietor's (*ryōke* 領家) revenue (*nengu* 年貢) for the repair of Tōfukuji and the honorable [Kōsa] shrine.

A levy of three *shō* of rice per *tan* (*tanbetsumai* 段別米) shall be collected, without fail, during every tenth month [based on the revenue of] all paddies, and [from all] relatives, retainers (*wakatō* 若党) and commoners (*hyakushō*).[18] [Nevertheless], eight *chō*, eight *tan* and two *jō* of paddies–three

[17]See *Takezakijō*, p. 147–52. This document, a later copy (*utsushi*) survives among the records of Tōfukuji, but is not reproduced in the *Kamakura ibun*.

[18]As we have seen, one *tan* equals .294 acres. One *shō* (升) equals approximately

chō of Tōfukuji's exempt paddies, eight *tan* two *jō* of exempt temple and [Kaitō] shrine lands, and five *chō* of lands directly controlled by the *jitō* (*yōsakubun* 用作分)–are excluded [from this commendation].[19]

The shrine's highest-ranking attendant (*hauri*), the *jitō's* representative, [and] the treasurer (*okura kumon*) shall together convert their money (*yōtō*) into rice and loan the profits from the seed rice (*suiko*) at a rate of fifty percent.[20] Furthermore, from this [rice], every year three *koku* of rice shall be given to Tōfukuji for repairs. Concerning [the shipping of] both [revenue] for the repair of the honorable [Kōsa] shrine and the proprietor's revenue, a total of seven *koku* shall be granted yearly to the boatmen (*kajitori* 梶取) according to precedent. This [amount] shall be collected by the jitō [or his representatives] (*jitō kata* 地頭方).[21]

Save for the [aforementioned] eight *chō*, eight *tan* and two *jō* [of exempt lands], [my] sons and grandsons must not be remiss in [paying these] thirty *mon* (文) of *tanbetsu* funds even if [their landholdings] are separately conveyed.[22] If, however, [some of my progeny] are remiss [in paying their dues] then those in charge (*satanin* 沙汰人) [of administering this estate][23] shall confiscate these lands and paddies [in arrears]. How could those who have received benevolence be remiss? They will suffer forfeiture of [my] largess (*on* 恩). All shall worship the three treasures of the gods and buddhas[24] and pay the *ryōke's* taxes for now and all times. In order to pray for the salvation of [my] parents and honored teachers, and for my descendants' prosperity this commendation is thus.

The *jitō's* representative, the ranking shrine attendant (*hauri*), and the

---

1.8 liters, or one-tenth of a *to*. As we shall see, one *shō* was also assessed a value of 10 *mon* (文) of cash.

[19] One *chō* equals 2.94 acres. Ten *tan* equal one *chō*. One *jō* equals one fifth of a *tan*.

[20] This is levied at the same rate as appears in Suenaga's precepts. Of the three officials, only the identity of the *hauri*, Fujii Suenari, is known.

[21] The Kaitō lands were located on the coast, and so its revenue could be shipped directly. From these expenses, can infer that this revenue was transported in kind rather than in cash.

[22] The thirty *mon* that Suenaga mentions can be equated with three *shō* (a total of 5.4 liters) of rice.

[23] The deputy *jitō*, the *hauri*, and the *okura kumon*.

[24] The three treasures refers to the Buddha, Buddhist scriptures, and the priesthood. Although this represents a Buddhist term, Suenaga specifically refers to the gods and buddhas in this passage.

storehouse manager (*okura kumon*) shall be relieved of their position if they abscond (*yokuryū* 抑留) with even the slightest amount of revenue, and their posts shall be bestowed on an honest person. [My] sons and grandsons must strictly abide by these provisions and disobey them in no way whatsoever. Thus.

The third year of Shōwa [1314], seventeenth day, first month

Jitō Shami Hōki [法喜] (monogram)

Commendation 2. *The following document represents the only surviving record written by Suenaga himself.*[25] *This second commendation is noteworthy for several reasons. The first is that it reveals the increasing power the ranking shrine attendant (hauri), who is now referred to as the head (daigūji 大宮司) of the Kaitō shrine. Secondly, it shows that Suenaga now lived in retirement in Hirabaro, the remote, easternmost region of the Kaitō. Finally, one can ascertain that Suenaga found it increasingly difficult to extract revenue from the lower Kugu region, which was located over a day's march to the northwest of the Kaitō.*[26] *Of Suenaga nothing else is known, although a fourteenth-century marker thought to be his grave can be found in the peaceful hills of Hirabaro.*

[A commendation] concerning the endowment (*sata*) of funds for the repair [of the Kaitō shrine, which constitute] one hundred and sixty-two *kanmon* and the sixty-seven *koku* of rice. [Revenue from] the lower Kugu [region] shall be supplanted (*sakushiro* さくしろ)[27] [with funds drawn from] one *chō* of Inoshiri lands, which I state are hereby conveyed in perpetuity. [These lands include] seven *tan* and three *jō* of paddies located [next to] the Hirabaro dwelling and four *tan* and slightly less that one *jō* of [prime paddies and fields] located in front of the Wanarisaka dwelling, including two *tan* and one *jō* from the [paddy] culverts (*minakuchi* 水口) [of Wanarisaka].[28] Various levies are henceforth prohibited, and [the assessed] taxes shall be collected yearly as public [paddy] land, and stored in the shrine storehouse. Both the shrine attendant, the deputy *jitō*, [and] the

---

[25]Unlike the first commendation, this second document appears in *Kamakura ibun*. See vol. 37, doc. 28691, 3.4.1324 (Genkō 4) Shami Hōki Takezaki Suenaga kishinjō. This document is analyzed in *Takezakijō*, pp. 163–66.

[26]See *Takezakijō*, p. 147–66.

[27]The meaning of the term remains unknown. This document was written phonetically in *kana*. Wherever possible, important terms have been translated into characters.

[28]The Kaitō plains, located furthest west in Suenaga's lands, and site of the shrine, the best paddies, and the *jitō*'s main residence.

representative (*daikan* 代官) shall [loan] the seed rice (*suiko*) at a rate of fifty percent and use [these profits] for shrine repairs. My sons and grandsons must never disobey [the purport of] this commendation even in the slightest.

The fourth year of Genkō [1324], fourth day, third month

Shami Hōki [法喜]
(monogram)

Appendix Two
A Table of Hours

Rat	11 P.M.	1 A.M.
Ox	1 A.M.	3 A.M.
Tiger	3 A.M.	5 A.M.
Rabbit	5 A.M.	7 A.M.
Dragon	7 A.M.	9 A.M.
Serpent	9 A.M.	11 A.M.
Horse	11 A.M.	1 P.M.
Sheep	1 P.M.	3 P.M.
Monkey	3 P.M.	5 P.M.
Cock	5 P.M.	7 P.M.
Dog	7 P.M.	9 P.M.
Boar	9 P.M.	11 P.M.

Appendices

APPENDIX THREE
Chronological Index of Translated Documents

Appendix Three

Bibliography

(Unless otherwise noted, the city of publication is Tōkyō)

Azuma kagami (吾妻鏡). Edited by Kuroita Katsumi. 4 vols. In *Kokushi taikei* (国史大系), 1932–33.

Bungo no kuni Ōno no shō shiryō (豊後国大野荘史料). Compiled by Watanabe Sumio. Yoshikawa kōbunkan, 1979.

Chiba ken shiryō, chūsei hen (千葉県史料中世編). Compiled by Chiba kenshi hensan shingikai. Chiba, 1957.

Chūkai, Genkō bōrui hennen shiryō—Ikokuhen keigo ban'yaku shiryō no kenkyū (注解元寇防塁編年史料). Compiled by Kawazoe Shōji. Fukuoka: Fukuoka kyōiku iinkai, 1971.

Chūsei hōsei shiryōshū (中世法制史料集), vol. 1. Compiled by Satō Shin'ichi and Ikeuchi Yoshitsuke. Iwanami shoten, 1955.

Dai Nihon komonjo iewake 13 Aso monjo (大日本古文書家わけ十三阿蘇文書). Compiled by Tōkyō teikoku daigaku shiryō hensanjo. 3 vols. Shiryō hensanjo, 1932–34.

Emaki (絵巻). Compiled by the Kyōto National Museum. March 1987.

Emaki–Mōko shūrai ekotoba, Eshi no sōshi, Kitano Tenjin engi (絵巻—蒙古襲来絵詞、絵師草紙、北野天神縁起). Compiled by Sannomaru Shōzōkan. October 1994.

Fukutekihen (伏敵編). Compiled by Yamada An'ei. Yoshikawa kōbunkan, 1891.

Gunsho keizubushū (群書系図部集). Fukyū ban. Compiled by Hanawa Hokinoichi. 7 vols. Zoku gunsho ruijū kanseikai, 1985.

Gyokuyo (玉葉) (Kujō Kanezane). Edited by Kuroita Katsumi. 3 vols. In *Kokushi taikei* (国史大系), 1906–7.

Hachiman gudō kun (八幡愚童訓). In *Gunsho ruijū* (群書類従), vol. 1. Compiled by Hanawa Hokinoichi, 447–97. Keizai zasshi shū, 1894.

Hachiman gudō kun (八幡愚童訓). Edited by Hagiwara Tatsuo. In *Jisha engi* (寺社縁起). Compiled by Sakurai Tokutarō et al., 169–273. Iwanami shoten, 1975.

Hanazono tennō shinki (花園天皇宸記). In *Shiryō taisei* (史料大成). 2 vols. Kyōto: Rinsen shoten, 1965.

Hennen Ōtomo shiryō (編年大友史料). Compiled by Takita Manabu. 2 vols. Fuzanbō, 1942–46.

Jisha engi (寺社縁起). Compiled by Sakurai Tokutarō et al. Iwanami shoten, 1975.

Kamakura ibun (鎌倉遺文). Compiled by Takeuchi Rizō. 51 vols. Tōkyōdō shuppan, 1971–97.

Kamakura ibun munengō monjo mokuroku (鎌倉遺文無年号文書目録). Compiled by Seno Sei'ichirō. Yoshikawa kōbunkan, 1993.

Kamakura nendaiki, Buke nendaiki, Kamakura dai nikki (鎌倉年代記、武家年代記、鎌倉大日記). In *Zōho zoku shiryō taisei 51* (増補続史料大成). Compiled by Takeuchi Rizō. Kyōto: Rinsen shoten, 1979.

Kawano ke monjo (河野家文書). Compiled by Kageura Tsutomu *(Iyo shiryō shūsei 3* 伊予史料集成*)*. Matsuyama: Iyo shiryō shūsei iinkai, 1967.

Kanchūki (勘仲記) (Kadenokōji Kanenaka). 3 vols. In *Shiryō taisei* (史料大成). Naigai shoseki kabushiki kaisha, 1935–36.

Komonjo yōgo jiten (古文書用語辞典). Compiled by Arai Eiji et al. Kashiwa shobō, 1983.

Kokushi daijiten (国史大辞典). 15 vols. Yoshikawa kōbunkan, 1979–97.

Li-Tai-chi-shi-pen-mo Chung-hua shu-chū-pien (歴代記事本末). Pei-ching: Chung hua shu chū, 1997.

Mikkyō jiten (密教辞典). Compiled by Sawa Takeshi. Kyōto: Hōzōkan, 1975.

Mōko shūrai ekotoba (蒙古襲来絵詞). In *Nihon no emaki 13* (日本の絵巻). Edited by Komatsu Shigemi. Chūō kōronsha, 1988.

Mōko shūrai ekotoba (蒙古襲来絵詞). In *Shinshū Nihon emakimono zenshū 10* (新集日本絵巻物全集). Kadokawa shoten, 1975.

Muchū mondō (夢中問答) (Musō Kokushi). Edited by Satō Taishun. Iwanami shoten, 1934.

Nanbokuchō ibun, Kyūshū hen (南北朝遺文九州編). Compiled by Seno Sei'ichirō. 7 vols. Tōkyōdō shuppan, 1985–92.

Nichiren bunshū (日連文集). Edited by Kabutoki Shōkō. Iwanami bunkō, 1968.

Nihonshi shiryō 2 chūsei (日本史史料 2 中世). Edited by Rekishigaku kenkyūkai. Iwanami shoten, 1998.

Sata Mirensho (沙汰未練書). In *Zoku gunsho ruijū* (続群書類従), vol. 25. Compiled by Hanawa Hokinoichi, 1–14. Zoku gunsho ruijū kanseikai, 1975.

Shibunkaku kosho shiryō mokuroku (思文閣古書資料目録) (Kyōto), no. 196. (October 1996).

Shinpan Emakimono ni yoru Nihon jōmin seikatsu ebiki (新版絵巻物による日本常民生活絵引). Compiled by Shibuzawa Keizō. 5 vols. Heibonsha, 1994.

Sonpi bunmyaku (尊卑文脉) (Tōin Kinsada). 5 vols. In *Shintei zōho kokushi taikei*. Yoshikawa kōbunkan, 1964.

Taiheiki (大平記). Edited by Okami Masao. 2 vols. Kadokawa Nihon koten bunko, 1975, 1982.

Taiheiki (Jingū chōkokan hon 神宮微古館本). Edited by Hasegawa Tadashi et al. Osaka: Izumi shoin, 1994.

Taiheiki (Seigen'in hon 西源院本). Edited by Washio Junkei. Tōei shoin, 1936.

Takaishi shishi 2, shiryō hen 1 (高石市史 2 史料編 1). Compiled by Takaishi shi. Takaishi, 1986.

Takashima kaitei iseki (鷹島海底遺跡). Compiled by Nagasaki ken Takashima chō kyōiku iinkai. 3 vols. Takashima chō, 1992–96.

Takezakijō –Jōseki chōsa to Takezaki Suenaga (竹崎城–城跡調査と竹崎季長). Compiled by Kumamoto ken kyōiku iinkai bunkaka. Kumamoto, 1975.

Yosōki (予章記). In *Gunsho ruijū* (群書類従), vol. 17. Compiled by Hanawa Hokinoichi, 235–72. Naigai shoseki kabushiki kaisha, 1930.

Yūsoku kojitsu daijiten (有識故実大辞典). Compiled by Suzuki Keizō. Yoshikawa kōbunkan, 1995.

Zennōji monjo (善応寺文書). Compiled by Kageura Tsutomu *(Iyo shiryō shūsei 2* 伊予史料集成). Matsuyama: Iyo shiryō shūsei iinkai, 1965.

Zōtei Kamakura bakufu shugo seido no kenkyū (増訂鎌倉幕府守護制度の研究). Compiled by Satō Shin'ichi. Tōkyō daigaku shuppan, 1971.

Secondary Works in Japanese

Aida Nirō. *Mōko shūrai no kenkyū* (蒙古襲来の研究). 3d ed. Yoshikawa kōbunkan, 1982.

Amino Yoshihiko. *Nihon no rekishi 10: Mōko shūrai* (日本の歴史 1 0 蒙古襲来). Shōgakkan, 1974.

Arakawa Hidetoshi. "Bun'ei no eki no owari o tsugeta no wa taifū de wa nai" (文永の役の終を告げたのは台風ではない). *Nihon rekishi* (日本歴史), no. 120. (June 1958): 41–45.

Fujimoto Masayuki. *Yoroi o matō hitobito* (鎧をまとう人びと). Yoshikawa kōbunkan, 2000.

Horimoto Kazushige. "Mōko shūrai ekotoba no genjō seiritsu katei ni tsuite–Aoyanagi Tanenobu hon no kentō to shōkai (「蒙古襲来絵詞」の現状成立過程について一青柳種信本の検討と紹介)." *Fukuokashi haku-butsukan kenkyū kiyō* 8 (福岡市博物館研究紀要) (Fukuoka, 1998): 15–57.

Ikeuchi Hiroshi. *Genkō no shinkenkyū* (元寇の新研究). 2 vols. Tōyō bunko, 1931.

Irumada Nobuo. *Nihon no rekishi 7 Musha no yo ni* (日本の歴史 7 武者の世に). Shūeisha, 1991.

Ishii Masatoshi. "Bun'ei hachinen rainichi no kōraishi ni tsuite—sanbesshō no nihon tsūkō shiryō no shōkai (文永八年来日の高麗使について一三別抄の日本通交史料の紹介一)." *Tōkyō daigaku shiryōhen sanjohō* 12 (東京大学史料編纂所報) (1978): 1–7.

Ishii Susumu. "Takezaki Suenaga ekotoba (竹崎季長絵詞)." In *Chūsei seiji shakai shisō jō* (中世政治社会思想上), ed. Ishii Susumu et al., 416–28; 559–63. Iwanami shoten, 1972.

——. "Takezaki Suenaga ekotoba no seiritsu (竹崎季長絵詞の成立)." *Nihon rekishi* (日本歴史), no. 273 (1971): 12–32.

Kaizu Ichirō. *Kamikaze to akutō no seiki* (神風と悪党の世紀). Kōdansha, 1995.

——. *Chūsei no henkaku to tokusei* (中世の変革と徳政). Yoshikawa kōbunkan, 1994.

——. "Kassen no senryokusū (合戦の戦力数)." *Nihonshi kenkyū* (日本史研究) no. 388 (1994): 88–97.

Kawazoe Shōji. *Hōjō Tokimune* (北条時宗). Yoshikawa kōbunkan, 2001.

——. *Nichiren to sono jidai* (日蓮とその時代). Sankibō busshorin, 1999.

——. *Mōko shūrai kenkyū shiron* (蒙古襲来研究史論). Yūzankaku, 1977.

——. *Gyobutsuhon Mōko shūrai ekotoba (fukusei) honbun, sakuin, kaisetsu, kenkyū mokuroku* (御物本蒙古襲来絵詞（複製）本文索引解説研究目録). (Fukuoka kyōiku iinkai, 1975).

Kuroda Toshio. *Nihon no rekishi 8: Mōko shūrai* (日本の歴史8蒙古襲来). Chūō kōronsha, 1974.

Matsumoto Aya. "Mōko shūrai ekotoba no seiritsu to denrai ni tsuite–sono saikō (「蒙古襲来絵詞」の成立と伝来について一その再考)." *Sanno-maru Shōzōkan nenpō kiyō* 1 (三の丸尚蔵館年報紀要) (1996): 61–76.

——. "Mōko shūrai ekotoba ni tsuite no ichikōsatsu–arata na mondaiten o kuwaete (『蒙古襲来絵詞』についての一考察一新たな問題点を加えて)." *Emaki–Mōko shūrai ekotoba, Eshi no sōshi, Kitano Tenjin engi* (絵巻一蒙古襲来絵詞、絵師草紙、北野天神縁起). Sanno-maru Shōzōkan, 1994.

——. "Mōko shūrai ekotoba (蒙古襲来絵詞)." *Emaki–Mōko shūrai ekotoba, Eshi no sōshi, Kitano Tenjin engi* (絵巻一蒙古襲来絵詞、絵師草紙、北野天神縁起). Sanno-maru Shōzōkan, 1994.

Miya Tsugio. *Kassen no emaki* (合戦絵巻). Kadokawa shoten, 1977.

Miyajima Shinichi. *Shōzōga* (肖像画). Yoshikawa kōbunkan, 1994.

Murai Shōsuke. "Jūsan yon seiki no Nihon (十三一四世紀の日本)." In *Iwanami kōza Nihon tsūshi 8 chūsei 2* (岩波講座日本通史第8巻中世2), ed. Asao Naohiro et al., 3–68. Iwanami shoten, 1994.

——. *Ajia no naka no chūsei nihon* (アジアのなかの中世日本). Azekura shobō, 1988.

—. "Takezaki Suenaga ekotoba (竹崎季長絵詞)." In *Shūkan Asahi hyakka Nihon no rekishi 9 chūsei I Mōko shūrai* (週刊朝日百科日本の歴史 9 中世 1 蒙古襲来), ed. Murai Shōsuke, 4.276–77. Asahi Shinbun, June 8, 1986.

Nam Kihaku. *Mōko shūrai to Kamakura bakufu* (蒙古襲来と鎌倉幕府). Kyōto: Rinsen shoten, 1996.

Ryō Susumu. *Mōko shūrai* (蒙古襲来). Chibundō, 1966.

Satō Testutarō. *Mōko shūrai to Takezaki Suenaga* (蒙古襲来と竹崎季長). Fukuoka: Tōkashobō, 1994.

Seno Sei'ichirō. *Chinzei gokenin no kenkyū* (鎮西御家人の研究). Yoshikawa kōbunkan, 1975.

Sugiyama Masaaki. *Sekai no rekishi 9, Dai mongoru no jidai* (世界の歴史 9 大モンゴルの時代). Chūō kōronsha, 1997.

—. *Mongoru teikoku no kōbō* (モンゴル帝国の興亡). 2 vols. Kōdansha gendai shinsho, 1996.

Sujaku Shinjō. "Mōko shūrai ekotoba denzon katei no fukugen ni tsuite (『蒙古襲来絵詞』伝存過程の復原について)." *Hakata kenkyūkaishi* 7 (博多研究会誌) (Hakata, 1999): 87–110.

—. "Mōko shūrai ekotoba kenkyū no genjō to kadai (『蒙古襲来絵詞』研究の現状と課題)." *Hōgōdachi* 5 (法哈達) (Hakata, 1997): 7–18.

Tanaka Minoru. "Kamakura jidai ni okeru Iyo no kuni no jitō gokenin ni tsuite (鎌倉時代における伊予国の地頭御家人について)." In *Shōensei to buke shakai* (荘園制と武家社会), ed. Takeuchi Rizō hakasei kanreki kinenkai, 245–92. Yoshikawa kōbunkan, 1969.

Urushihara Tōru. *Chūsei gunchūjō to sono sekai* (中世軍忠状とその世界). Yoshikawa kōbunkan, 1998.

Yamaguchi Osamu. *Mōko shūrai–Genkō no shijitsu no kaimei* (蒙古襲来 元寇の史実の解明). Kofusha sensho, 1988.

Yanagida Yoshitaka. "Genkō bōrui to chūsei no kaigan sen (元寇防塁と中世の海岸線)," In *Yomigaeru chūsei I Higashi ajia no kokusai toshi Hakata* (よみがえる中世 1 東アジアの国際都市博多), ed. Amino Yoshihiko et al., 180–94. Heibonsha, 1988.

Yonekura Michio. *Minamoto Yoritomo zō chinmoku no shōzōga* (源頼朝像沈黙の肖像画). Heibonsha, 1995.

Works in English

Asakawa, Kan'ichi. *The Documents of Iriki* (入来文書). The Japan Society for the Promotion of Science, 1955.

Conlan, Thomas Donald. "State of War: The Violent Order of Fourteenth Century Japan." Ph.D. diss., Stanford University, 1998.

Dawson, Christopher. *Mission to Asia* Toronto: University of Toronto Press, 1980.

Farris, William Wayne. *Heavenly Warriors: The Evolution of Japan's Military, 500–1300*. Cambridge: Harvard Council on East Asian Studies, 1992.

Henthorn, William E. *Korea: The Mongol Invasions*. Leiden: E. J. Brill, 1963.

Hori, Kyotsu. "The Economic and Political Effects of the Mongol Wars." In *Medieval Japan: Essays in Institutional History*, ed. John W. Hall and Jeffrey P. Mass, 184-98. Stanford: Stanford University Press, 1988.

——. "The Mongol Invasions and the Kamakura Bakufu." Ph.D. diss., Columbia University, 1967.

Ishii, Susumu. "The Decline of the Kamakura Bakufu." In *The Cambridge History of Japan*, vol. 3, ed. Kozo Yamamura, 396–446. Cambridge: Cambridge University Press, 1990.

Kahn, Paul. *The Secret History of the Mongols: The Origin of Chingis Khan*. Boston: Cheng & Tsui Company, 1998.

Kawazoe, Shōji. "Japan and East Asia." In *The Cambridge History of Japan*, vol. 3, ed. Kozo Yamamura, 128–74. Cambridge: Cambridge University Press, 1990.

Mass, Jeffrey P. "The Kamakura Bakufu." In *The Cambridge History of Japan*, vol. 3, ed. Kozo Yamamura, 46–88. Cambridge: Cambridge University Press, 1990.

——. *Lordship and Inheritance in Early Medieval Japan: A Study of the Kamakura Soryō System*. Stanford: Stanford Univesity Press, 1989.

——. *The Development of Kamakura Rule*. Stanford: Stanford University Press, 1979.

——. *The Kamakura Bakufu*. Stanford: Stanford University Press, 1976.

Murdoch, James. *A History of Japan*. Kobe: The Japan Chronicle, 1910.

Nicolle, David. *The Mongol Warlords*. London: Firebrand Books, 1990.

Ohta, Aya. "The Mongol Invasion." In *Twelve Centuries of Japanese Art from the Imperial Collections*, ed. Lynne Shaner, 90–93. Washington D.C.: Smithsonian Institution, 1997.

Polo, Marco. *The Travels*. Translated by R. E. Latham. London: Penguin Books, 1958.

Steenstrup, Carl. "*Sata mirensho:* A Fourteenth-Century Law Primer." *Monumenta Nipponica* 35 (1980): 405–35.

Tsunoda, Ryusaku. *Japan in the Chinese Dynastic Histories*. Pasadena: P. D. and Ione Perkins, 1951.

Tyler, Royall. *The Miracles of the Kasuga Deity*. New York: Columbia University Press, 1990.

Index

Selected Names and Regional Institutions
of the Kamakura *bakufu*

Index

298

Index

Index

301

CORNELL EAST ASIA SERIES

55 Jingyuan Zhang, *Psychoanalysis in China: Literary Transformations, 1919-1949*

56 Jane Kate Leonard & John R. Watt, eds., *To Achieve Security and Wealth: The Qing Imperial State and the Economy, 1644-1911*

57 Andrew F. Jones, *Like a Knife: Ideology and Genre in Contemporary Chinese Popular Music*

58 Peter J. Katzenstein & Nobuo Okawara, *Japan's National Security: Structures, Norms and Policy Responses in a Changing World*

59 Carsten Holz, *The Role of Central Banking in China's Economic Reforms*

60 Chifumi Shimazaki, *Warrior Ghost Plays from the Japanese Noh Theater: Parallel Translations with Running Commentary*

61 Emily Groszos Ooms, *Women and Millenarian Protest in Meiji Japan: Deguchi Nao and Ōmotokyō*

62 Carolyn Anne Morley, *Transformation, Miracles, and Mischief: The Mountain Priest Plays of Kyōgen*

63 David R. McCann & Hyunjae Yee Sallee, tr., *Selected Poems of Kim Namjo*, afterword by Kim Yunsik

64 HUA Qingzhao, *From Yalta to Panmunjom: Truman's Diplomacy and the Four Powers, 1945-1953*

65 Margaret Benton Fukasawa, *Kitahara Hakushū: His Life and Poetry*

66 Kam Louie, ed., *Strange Tales from Strange Lands: Stories by Zheng Wanlong*, with introduction

67 Wang Wen-hsing, *Backed Against the Sea*, tr. Edward Gunn

68 Brother Anthony of Taizé & Young-Moo Kim, trs., *The Sound of My Waves: Selected Poems by Ko Un*

69 Brian Myers, *Han Sŏrya and North Korean Literature: The Failure of Socialist Realism in the DPRK*

70 Thomas P. Lyons & Victor Nee, eds., *The Economic Transformation of South China: Reform and Development in the Post-Mao Era*

71 David G. Goodman, tr., *After Apocalypse: Four Japanese Plays of Hiroshima and Nagasaki*, with introduction

72 Thomas P. Lyons, *Poverty and Growth in a South China County: Anxi, Fujian, 1949-1992*

73 Hwang Suk-Young, *The Shadow of Arms*, tr. Chun Kyung-Ja, foreword by Paik Nak-chung

74 Martyn Atkins, *Informal Empire in Crisis: British Diplomacy and the Chinese Customs Succession, 1927-1929*

75 Bishop D. McKendree, ed., *Barbed Wire and Rice: Poems and Songs from Japanese Prisoner-of-War Camps*

76 Chifumi Shimazaki, *Restless Spirits from Japanese Noh Plays of the Fourth Group: Parallel Translations with Running Commentary*

77 Brother Anthony of Taizé & Young-Moo Kim, trs., *Back to Heaven: Selected Poems of Ch'ŏn Sang Pyŏng*

To order, please contact the Cornell University East Asia Program, 140 Uris Hall, Ithaca, NY 14853-7601, USA; phone 607-255-6222, fax 607-255-1388, ceas@cornell.edu, www.einaudi.cornell.edu/eastasia/CEASbooks

NOTE
The scrolls reproduced herein unfold in Japanese order, from right ot left. This is the end of the book.

SB/8-03/.6M pb